ANTONIO GRAMSCI

ANTONIO GRAMSCI

A Biography

Andrew Pearmain

I.B. TAURIS
LONDON • NEW YORK • OXFORD • NEW DELHI • SYDNEY

I.B. TAURIS
Bloomsbury Publishing Plc
50 Bedford Square, London, WC1B 3DP, UK
1385 Broadway, New York, NY 10018, USA

BLOOMSBURY, I.B. TAURIS and the I.B. Tauris logo are trademarks
of Bloomsbury Publishing Plc

First published in Great Britain 2020

For legal purposes the Acknowledgements on p. vii constitute
an extension of this copyright page.

Series design by Adriana Brioso
Cover image: Antonio Gramsci, 1934. (© Laski Diffusion/Getty Images)

A catalogue record for this book is available from the British Library.

A catalogue record for this book is available from the Library of Congress.

ISBN: HB: 978-1-8386-0160-7
        PB: 978-1-8386-0161-4
        ePDF: 978-0-7556-0007-6
        eBook: 978-0-7556-0008-3

Typeset by Integra Software Services Pvt. Ltd.
Printed and bound in Great Britain

To find out more about our authors and books visit www.bloomsbury.com
and sign up for our newsletters.

CONTENTS

ACKNOWLEDGEMENTS

I am immensely grateful to Matt Worley for commissioning this book, and for his key role in the new communist historiography. Derek Boothman helped with the latest Italian studies of Gramsci and kindly shared his own research into the pre-prison letters. Geoffrey Nowell-Smith provided invaluable insight into the making of Selections from Prison Notebooks, the main source for the dissemination of Gramsci's genius in English. Sally Davison has encouraged my own attempts at a latter-day Gramscism, primarily by publishing *The Politics of New Labour: A Gramscian Analysis* (2011). David Purdy, Mike Prior and Pat Devine gave freely of their time and understanding, and hospitality, in helping bring Gramsci's philosophy and politics back into focus; one day we really will get 'out of the ghetto' of 'Feelbad Britain'. Finally, I dedicate this book to the memory of Stuart Hall, who first sparked my fascination with Gramsci at the 1976 Communist University of London, and rekindled it in an interview thirty years later.

Chapter 1

THE END

On 21 April 1937 Antonio Gramsci's prison sentence formally expired, but he was not well enough to leave the Quisisana Clinic in Rome, where he had been confined since August 1935, nine difficult years after his arrest on Mussolini's orders in 1926. 'Nino', as he was known to his close friends and relatives, had planned to return to Sardinia on release to live near his birth-family. A room had been rented for him in Santu Lussurgiu, where he had attended secondary school, near the family home in Ghilarza. But his very final wish, stated to his closest friend the economist Piero Sraffa on a visit from England, was to join his wife Julia and their sons Delio and Giuliano in Soviet Russia. Before any of these plans could be finalized or implemented, Gramsci suffered a cerebral haemorrhage on the evening of 25 April, lay unconscious throughout the next day and died early the next morning, on 27 April 1937, aged 46 and 4 months. The only relatives in attendance were Gramsci's sister-in-law Tatiana Schucht, more usually called Tanya, and his brother Carlo, who arrived at the clinic after Antonio had died. Together they oversaw funeral arrangements.

On 12 May, Tanya wrote from Rome to Sraffa at King's College, Cambridge, with a detailed account of Nino's final hours, and a request for advice on what to do with his effects, in particular the treasured notebooks he had kept during his imprisonment.[1] She had smuggled them out of the clinic, hidden among Nino's clothes and other personal possessions, with the help of a sympathetic nursing assistant who distracted the guards. They were then stored in the vaults of the Banca Commerciale, whose Director Raffaele Mattioli remembered Nino fondly from his time as a journalist and MP. Gramsci had asked that everything be sent to his wife Julia in Moscow, but Tanya clearly thought this might prove politically and practically complicated, and asked Sraffa what he thought she should do. Depositing them in the bank vaults was most probably his idea.

The cremation had already taken place, and she went on after a difficult journey across Rome in a sudden thunderstorm. It was difficult to get permission to proceed with the funeral from the police, who put all kinds of legalistic and bureaucratic obstacles in the way, but they finally relented. Before they left Quisisana, Tanya arranged for a photograph of the corpse and for a death mask, intending to have it cast in bronze, along with the right hand.[2] She also had some photos that had been taken when Nino received his conditional liberty at his previous clinic in 1935.

They were, she wrote to Sraffa, 'quite precious, not least for the look of satisfaction – even the hint of a smile – on his face.' In the days before he died, she added, Nino hadn't felt any worse than usual, but rather seemed a lot more serene than he had been. She arrived at the clinic as usual at around 5.30 pm on 25 April. As they always did, they talked about that day's news. When she took out her books for a French literature lesson she had later that evening, Nino objected and insisted that they carry on talking. In any case, he scolded her with a laugh, 'You shouldn't have taken a job that demanded specialised knowledge and would exhaust you! How would you be able to continue looking after me?'

Even so, they looked up some words together in the Larousse. Then they talked until dinner time, when he ate the usual minestrone, fruit compote and a piece of sponge cake. He left the room to go to the toilet but was brought back on a chair carried by several orderlies. He had collapsed there, lost control of his whole left side but managed to crawl to the door and cry for help. When he was back in bed, Nino asked for a tonic to drink, but the doctor refused until it was clear what was wrong. They brought him a hot water bottle for his feet; he said it was too hot, but that the left foot didn't feel very much at all. At about 9 pm the Clinic Director Professor Puccinelli finally arrived and conducted an examination. He ordered that the patient be bled, and be kept absolutely still. Nino struggled to get comfortable, grasping the bars of the bed with his right hand, and almost toppling out. Over the next hour he vomited several times. He tried to blow his nose, which was blocked up with food, and continued breathing with some difficulty. Another doctor examined him and advised that his condition was extremely serious. At this point, the nursing sisters brought in a priest. Tanya objected strongly and insisted that they leave. After some argument, during which the priest questioned her authority, they left. Throughout the next day, 26 April, Nino lay still and barely conscious. Very early the next morning, the vomiting began again, and Nino's breathing became terribly laboured. Tanya kept watch over him, wetting his lips, reminding him to breathe when he seemed to have stopped. Then he took a last deep breath and fell back into silence. She called the doctor, who confirmed that it was all over. It was 4.10 am on 27 April. At 5.15 am the nurses carried the body to the mortuary. Later that morning Carlo came. Together he and Tanya arranged for the photographer and the man who would make the death mask to come and do their work. It wasn't easy; they had to make all kinds of written declarations about who they were and what they were doing. Later in the afternoon Carlo asked to see his brother one more time, but was refused, supposedly on orders from the government.

Carlo and Tanya were the only people present at the cremation, apart from a large escort of police guards. The ashes were deposited in a zinc box laid inside a wooden one, and stored at the Verano Cemetery, where they could stay for up to ten years without payment. The news of Gramsci's death was broadcast by the Italian state radio and published in the newspapers, in a tone Tanya found deeply upsetting: 'It's obscene; I don't know how to go about protesting,' she wrote to Sraffa. Most of the newspapers published a curt statement supplied to them by the Fascist wire service: 'The former deputy Gramsci died at the Quisisana clinic in Rome where he had been a patient for a long time.'[3] But some of the coverage portrayed Gramsci as a political criminal and communist subversive, with one article calling him 'the maddest, most fanatical of all'.

*

At the time of his death in 1937, Antonio Gramsci had effectively been abandoned by everybody he knew, apart from Tanya Schucht, Carlo Gramsci and Piero Sraffa. He had not seen his parents since before his arrest in 1926, and was only informed of his mother's death several years after she died in 1932. The only other siblings to visit him in prison were his brothers Gennaro and Mario; each visited him just once in eleven years, for separate purposes of their own. They were now both in military service but for opposing sides on different continents: Gennaro with the Republicans in Spain, and Mario in the Italian army in Africa. Antonio had seen neither of his two surviving sisters, whom he had been close to in childhood, since October 1924. He had not seen his wife Julia and older son Delio since August 1926, when they returned to Moscow after spending six largely unhappy months with him in Rome. When they left Italy, Julia was pregnant with Giuliano, whom Gramsci never met. His relationships with his in-laws, the large and dispersed Schucht family, had always been complicated and often strained. When he was arrested, Gramsci had been the secretary of the tiny, embattled *Partito Communista d'Italia (PCd'I)* for little more than two years, its effective leader after the arrest or exile of almost all its other higher officials following the Fascist takeover of Italy in 1922. Through the later 1920s and 1930s, as the party adjusted to the changing circumstances of Fascist hegemony in Italy and its own illegality, and just as important, Stalinist hegemony in the Communist International, Gramsci was by turns lionized, ostracized and finally largely forgotten by the outside world. He died in almost total personal and political obscurity, just as he had been born and brought up, on the periphery of life and history.

Chapter 2

THE BEGINNING

Antonio Gramsci was born on 22 January 1891 in the town of Ales, near the Sardinian capital Cagliari. He was the fourth of seven children: Gennaro, Grazietta, Emma, Antonio, Mario, Teresina and Carlo, all named by their devout parents after the most prominent local saints. At six days old, Antonio was baptized at Ales Cathedral by the Vicar General, attended by his father Francesco and a representative of his godfather, a local worthy called Francesco Puxeddu who would play no further part in his life. Antonio was given the baptismal names Francesco after his father and godfather and Sebastiano after the Vicar General. Antonio's mother, *née* Giuseppina Marcias and generally known as Peppina, couldn't suckle him at first because of a bout of mastitis, so for the first couple of weeks he was nursed by a neighbouring family friend Signora Melis alongside her own newborn son.

Antonio's father Francesco had been born in 1860 in Gaeta on the Italian coast halfway between Rome and Naples. His family were of Greek-Albanian origins, which is where the unusual surname came from. Throughout his life and to his considerable annoyance, Antonio would have to pronounce and spell it out to people, and contend with multiple variations. His paternal grandfather Gennaro had been a police colonel in the ill-fated Kingdom of the Two Sicilies, an odd collection of territories which was widely considered at the time the most reactionary, inefficient, inegalitarian state system in Europe. The kingdom was violently overthrown and absorbed into the newly unified Italian state by the *Risorgimento* of 1861, the year after Francesco was born. Colonel Gennaro Gramsci survived the siege of Gaeta by General Caldini's army, having sent his wife and infant son to safety through enemy lines, as family legend would have it. He quickly transferred his allegiances to the triumphant Piedmontese, and retained his rank of colonel in the new state's *carabinieri*. His older children did well. Three sons became high-ranking civil servants and an artillery officer, and his daughter married into wealth and nobility.

The youngest of Gennaro's five children, Francesco had been studying to be a lawyer when his father died unexpectedly in 1881. The sudden change in family circumstances required Francesco to find immediate, less prestigious work in the civil service. He was sent to run the Land Registry in the Sardinian town of Ghilarza, serving his time on the far-flung margins of the new country, with the reasonable expectation that he would soon return to the mainland. Sardinia was widely regarded as an absolute hole by outsiders, while most of the indigenous population hated these arrogant *stranieri* sent to rule over them and extract their labour, produce and taxes on behalf of the far-away 'continentals'.[1] In a semi-feudal agricultural economy where common lands had only recently been enclosed, and foreign, generally absentee landlords still owned vast estates, disputes over land were an obvious focus for these social tensions. The 'blow-in' bureaucrat Francesco, tasked with adjudicating and recording these bitter but often petty territorial quarrels, was generally in favour of the most powerful party (usually fellow mainlanders), and surely resentful of this posting he'd been forced to take; it would have been doubly resented by the islanders.

Within a year of his arrival in Ghilarza, Francesco fell in with the dissolute local gentry 'and (according to Davidson) became part of the joking, card-playing petty bourgeois *circolo* of the village ... doing favours for favours in an elaborate *clientele* system'.[2] These *signori* considered themselves a definite cut above the labouring and smallholding masses. Francesco's son Antonio would later characterize the social stratum from which his father's companions were drawn as 'pensioners of economic history' or more harshly 'the scum of society ... monkey people', subsisting on dwindling legacies and sinecures and making no productive contribution of their own to economy and society, 'Italians who now live only for their petty personal interests, men born only to enjoy drinking'.[3] Antonio's early intellectual hero Gaetano Salvemini offered a similarly damning verdict of 'these country idlers ... flaccid, inert and good-for-nothing'; this social group would go on to provide the bulk of the burgeoning officer class of the Italian army and subsequently of the Fascist state bureaucracy.[4]

Francesco Gramsci certainly looked and played the part, 'corpulent, given to grandiose schemes of little practicality, to vanity and boasting ... a typical authoritarian type (whose) values Antonio rejected completely'.[5] Antonio's father, who outlived him by just two weeks, would – within the constraints of discretion and taboo which characterized the Gramsci family atmosphere – serve in his son's notes and letters and recollections as the personification of profound weaknesses in Italian society. Once established in Ghilarza, Francesco looked around for romantic attachment. He married Giuseppina 'Peppina' Marcias in 1883, against strong disapproval from his family of her island background and, as the daughter of a local tax collector, ostensibly of lower social standing than theirs. Like her husband-to-be, Peppina bore a double stigma within Sardinia's highly stratified class hierarchy. Her tax collector father might have been one of 'that most hated of all officials' for the locals, but 'for a mainlander (like Francesco), marrying a Sard bordered on miscegenation'.[6] This sense of social indeterminacy, of being between castes and classes and territories and never quite belonging in any, would haunt the Sardinian Gramscis. On top of a family atmosphere 'lacking in compassion, (where) affection was undemonstrative, dry and formal', the Gramscis' separateness superimposed an air of subterfuge and reserve bordering on shame with which they would respond to adversity, and leave a residue of closely recalled slights and grievances.[7] Antonio would carry plenty of these resentments into his adult life, alongside a persistent sense of social vertigo. He was himself not always clear on his precariously middle-class background. Well into adulthood, his comrade and fellow Sardinian Palmiro Togliatti was telling people that Gramsci came from peasant stock.

Perhaps Francesco understood better than his family on the mainland that Peppina was actually something of a catch and would prove, within the restrictive gender roles of a time when the father ruled with a clenched fist and a harsh word or glance, to be an exceptional woman, wife and mother. Not only did she bring with her a substantial dowry of inherited land and rental income and an extensive, supportive and comparatively prosperous local family, which helped to mask her socially superior husband's indolence, she also had the benefit of three years' elementary schooling and advanced literacy skills. In a village where only an estimated 200 out of a population of over 2200 could read and write, it was even more unusual for a girl. She read voraciously from the Italian classics, and could recite from memory whole passages of Dante and the rather racier Boccaccio. She also dressed in 'European' rather than traditional clothes and, despite never travelling further than forty kilometres from Ghilarza in her whole life, had considerable knowledge and understanding of the outside world. Antonio gained much of his extensive early grasp of geography, which he would later compare favourably with his own city-dwelling sons, from maps and atlases under his mother's tutelage.

Unusually for a *straniero*, Francesco settled in rural Sardinia for the rest of his life. His choice not to move on to a more promising post elsewhere, or even to be nearer his own mainland family, may be further tribute to 'Signora' (as she was known respectfully among her neighbours) Peppina's strength and dependability, as much as inertia and lack of ambition on his part. Their first child Gennaro was born in Ghilarza in 1884, and named after his paternal grandfather the *carabiniero* colonel. The family then moved to the larger cathedral town of Ales where their next three children were born in quick succession, including Antonio. At this stage the family was relatively well-off, with Francesco in secure, prestigious state employment and Giuseppina set to inherit considerable holdings of land back in Ghilarza. Their friends and acquaintances in Ales included the court bailiff, notaries and other administrative notables. By 1892, there was a female domestic, and Antonio also had a nursemaid. He was born into a privileged social group by Sardinian standards.

The Gramsci children were healthy and robust, including baby Antonio, fine and fair, with curly blonde hair and light-coloured eyes, according to a family friend. For his first three or four years, he was happy and thriving. There then occurred a period of illness and debility which he himself would struggle to make sense of for the rest of his life, and which left him with a hunchback, stunted growth and always fragile health. The family story was that he fell or, in a rather darker version, was dropped by his nursemaid down a steep flight of stairs. Her alleged motivation was similarly convoluted. She had become pregnant by the local doctor, who then fled the village in fear of a *vendetta*. Antonio's 'accident' and the subsequent swelling on his chest and back offered her the opportunity, with the family's blessing, to go and see the doctor a long, bumpy ox-cart ride away. On the way back, Antonio began to haemorrhage from his mouth and anus. The bleeding went on for three days, and he was seriously ill for three months. At one point, he recalled in a letter years later, his condition was severe enough for him to be given up for dead by the doctors, and to warrant the construction of a little coffin and a shroud.[8] His maternal aunt Grazia Delogu insisted that he was only saved by her anointing his feet with holy oil and praying to the Virgin. She would also pray, Antonio would later recall, to 'a very pious lady called Donna Bisodia, so pious that a place had been found for her in the Lords Prayer, when it was actually the Latin phrase *dona nobis hodie* ("give us this day")'.[9] His mother kept the coffin and the shroud until he was well into adulthood and settled on the mainland.

Again, Francesco Gramsci did not emerge favourably from the episode. The local family doctor had advised taking Antonio to the mainland for more specialized (and costly) treatment, but his father resisted. When it was clear that the illness had left Antonio with signs of stunted growth, a hunchback and a smaller swelling on his chest, Francesco visited 'specialists' in the local towns of Orestano and Caserta and obtained a harness with which Antonio was to be suspended from the kitchen ceiling. A neighbour recalled 'a kind of corset with rings on it. Nino would put this on, then they would hook him up to the ceiling and leave him there hanging in mid-air'.[10] His mother would also 'stretch him out and massage him with tincture of iodine, but it was no good', and quite possibly made the swelling worse. Antonio's supposed accident, illness and deformity had been poorly managed by the unfortunate pregnant nursemaid, and she made a convenient scapegoat for the family. But the underlying cause was more probably a childhood infection, of which there were many in impoverished, under-developed, late-nineteenth-century Sardinia. In Gramsci's later adult life, long after chronic disability and illness had set in, a properly expert doctor would diagnose Pott's disease, a tuberculosis of the upper spine which commonly causes a hunchback, and suggest that he may have had it since infancy. Whatever the cause, Antonio never grew taller than 1.5 metres or five feet, and carried a hunchback and smaller chest swelling for the rest of his life.

From the age of three to seven, Antonio attended a kindergarten run by nuns near the town of Nuoro, where the family had moved when his father took another Registrar's post in Sorgono. At the time it was one of only eleven kindergartens on the whole island, which offered some further measure of the growing Gramsci family's relative prosperity and privilege. Antonio went there with his sisters, and grew especially close to Teresina, who was four years younger than him and had a similar studious temperament. Education was highly valued in the Gramsci household, especially by mother Peppina, whose literacy was a valued aid as well as a notable marker of her superiority over her neighbours back in Ghilarza. Antonio later recalled how other women would come to her to compose letters to their migrant or, saddest of all, imprisoned husbands. She taught all of her children to read from an early age.

In 1897 – by which time Antonio's disability was established and permanent – further and more far-reaching disaster befell the Gramsci family and brought an abrupt end to the relative tranquillity and prosperity of his childhood. Francesco was dismissed from his post in Sorgono, and then the following year arrested and imprisoned. He had chosen the losing side in a closely and bitterly fought electoral battle for the local parliamentary constituency of Isili between two local 'big men' and their personal followings, which is what the Sardinian politics of the time mainly consisted of. The winner, the established MP and Italian government Cabinet Minister Coccu Ortu and the spiteful, violent clique behind him set about distributing favours to the victors and punishing the losers. This latter group, around the defeated candidate Enrico Carbone Boy, included Francesco Gramsci. While he was away at his older brother's funeral, Cocco Ortu's supporters in Sogorno instigated an investigation into the Registry Office accounts. Predictably, this revealed some small irregularities, and Francesco was suspended without pay. He sank into a dark impassive mood, and Peppina set about dealing with the consequences. She moved the family back to Ghilarza, to stay with her sister Grazia Delogu, and summoned her oldest son Gennaro back from school to start paid work at the local Land Registry where Francesco's career had begun. On 9 August 1898 Francesco was arrested and accused of embezzlement, extortion and falsification of documents, and held in Oristano prison awaiting trial for over two more years. He was eventually sentenced on 27 October 1900 to five years, eight months and twenty-two days' imprisonment, the minimum possible because the judge had found misdemeanours of only 'slight damage and small value'.[11] He was to serve his sentence near his own mainland hometown of Gaeta, one of quite a few local worthies to suffer the vengeance of the victorious *coccisti*.

At the time of Francesco's arrest, Signora Peppina Gramsci was aged 37 with seven children between one and fourteen, including sickly, disabled Nino, and no other source of income beyond her own dwindling legacy. In the extant photographs from this period, she looks understandably weary, careworn and preoccupied. She refused to seek help from Francesco's family, 'to (according to Fiori) avoid the humiliation of asking for assistance from these relations she scarcely knew', and who had shown little warmth towards her, but also to hide her husband's imprisonment just a few kilometres away from them in Gaeta.[12] She would even take delivery of Francesco's letters from prison to his family and other relatives, then re-post them from her own home, with the precious postmark from Ghilarza. And of course, ever the reluctant traveller, in all this time she never visited her husband in prison. Meanwhile, all their own children except Gennaro were told that their father had gone on a long visit to his family back in Gaeta.

Peppina sold her own small inheritance of land and took in a lodger, a veterinary surgeon called Vittorio Nessi. She charged for sewing and sold clothes she made herself, assisted domestically by her daughters and, insofar as they could, financially by her sons. She always made sure the family ate relatively well, and even more untypically gave and received birthday presents, residual tokens (like the commitment to literacy and education) of their middle-class cultural values. The family just about scraped by, and enabled Nino to attend the first years of primary school in Ghilarza from the age of seven and a half. He was the brightest and most studious of the Gramsci children and did well at school, despite starting a year late.

He was always top of the class, partly because he spoke far better Italian than most of his classmates. But he also revealed a surprising practical streak, constructing in his own time a shower from a big metal can attached to the wall, an array of toy boats and carts, and even (with his older siblings' amused assistance) rudimentary weight-lifting equipment of sticks and stones to try to build his puny body.

His relatives later recalled a rather reserved character, always very kind and affectionate but conscious of his deformity and frailty, which meant he preferred solitary reading or rambles to rough and tumble with other children. He spent more time with the similarly bookish Teresina, his younger sister, or Mario the brother nearest in age and the family joker. His favourite books were *Robinson Crusoe* and *Treasure Island*, which he was given by the wife of the local tax collector Signor Mazzacurati before he was transferred elsewhere. Antonio later wrote, 'I never left the house without some grains of wheat in my pocket and a few matches wrapped in oilcloth, just in case I should be cast away on a desert island.'[13] On long walks around the surrounding countryside, he captured animals, some of which he kept as pets, including a beautiful hawk which he fed on mice and grass snakes. He was a keen observer of wildlife, with detailed recollections in his later letters from prison of the antics of foxes and hedgehogs.

But his later childhood was anything but carefree. Very early on, he and his siblings saw through their father's supposed years-long visit to the mainland, from overheard adult conversations, other children's teasing and name-calling or scraps of neighbourhood gossip. After all, not only older son Gennaro but 'everybody in the village knew that Francesco Gramsci was in jail, and yet Peppina maintained the ridiculous subterfuge.'[14] Antonio would later recall how every little lie or doubt would bother him, even if they were meant to prevent upset, and make him turn in on himself; 'By the age of ten I had become a real trial to my mother because of my fanatical desire for frankness and absolute truth, and the terrible rows and scandals this caused.'[15] His childhood was 'a sewer of bitterness' which would mark his temperament and dealings with other people for life, despite his mother's best efforts to hold the family together and maintain a veneer of respectability. Even in adulthood, he protected her from knowing that he had known the truth about his father's disgrace and imprisonment all along, because 'it would poison the rest of her life.'[16] As it was, he retained vivid memories of her creeping out of the house at night in a black shawl to go to church on her own, to pray and weep for hours on end, and return for another day of hard toil and worry.

Antonio never made much of it, and contemporaries' recollections tended to downplay it for their own reasons, but there is little doubt that he also routinely suffered other children's taunts and worse at his disability, his uncertain social status as a child of the fallen middle class, his father's imprisonment and his mother's 'stuck up' ways, and the withdrawn, solitary temperament that inevitably flowed from these misfortunes. The abnormality of his hunchback, in a place where it was widely believed both that such deformity was caused by the devil and that touching a hump would bring good luck, would have been enough to draw unwelcome attention. But this was also a deeply conformist and largely uniform society and culture, overwhelmingly peasant, superstitious, pre-modern and ill-educated, where in the countryside 'hotels were unknown because people there had not yet imagined that a person could stay away amid the perils of the night without family contact.'[17] For all their shared material impoverishment, the Gramsci family were well aware that they were different from their neighbours, neither peasant nor fully Sard, and inclined amongst themselves to 'make fun of various village personalities and their rural foibles.'[18] This would have made Antonio even more aware of his added personal differences, socially separate and vulnerable to mockery and bullying.

He later recalled:

> When I was a child the village boys never came near except to make fun of me. I was almost always alone. Sometimes they might find me near them and set upon me, and not only with insults. One day they started throwing stones at me more viciously than usual, with the malice peculiar to children and the downtrodden. I lost my temper and threw stones back, so fiercely that they fled. From that day they let me be.[19]

There may well have been an element of fear in the bullying, which on this occasion worked to his advantage; the hunchback who snarls back is a common type in the popular literature of deformity and monstrosity. But the psychic cost to a young child would nonetheless have been immense, notwithstanding Gramsci's final punchline that when he reported the incident back to his mother she kissed him proudly and affectionately. When he concludes that this alone made the stoning worthwhile, the further question arises of how often and readily he received such love at home. It also casts in a rather different light his fond recollections of losing himself in storybooks, of solitary rambles around the hills and fields and orchards of Ghilarza; of catching and training animals and birds as pets and teasing them; of the gentle companionship and quiet solicitude of his mother and sisters; of pranks and skits with his spirited younger brother Mario; of copying and colouring of pictures from the newspapers; and of quiet absorption in little construction projects (sometimes accompanied by the pharmacist's son Luciano, surely also set apart by his father's professional status). We see rather the enforced self-reliance of the manifold, manifest misfit, 'the desperately lonely child' whom an untypically candid neighbour 'never saw laugh with joy … or joining in with other children's games', and who self-harmed to the extent of 'hitting himself with a rock till he drew blood', effectively mimicking the treatment he was routinely receiving from other children.[20] It's also easy to see the source of a lifelong identification with victims of arbitrary cruelty, recalled by Gramsci himself in other luridly detailed accounts of witnessing a severely disabled son kept chained in a pigsty by the mother on a nearby hill farm, or a landlady's senile mother repeatedly abused physically and verbally by her daughter.

Chapter 3

SCHOOLDAYS IN SARDINIA

Turn–of-the-century Sardinia was a place of grinding poverty and squalor on the outer edge of the European landmass and civilization, a dangerous and fearful place where death by starvation was frequent; in extreme hardship people lived on grass and weeds, and up to a third of communal income was taken in tax by the national government on the mainland.[1] Most of its working population scratched a bare living from the land or, failing that, the seams of ore in the earth beneath it. The traditional island economy, such as it was, was based on agricultural exports of wine, olive oil, dairy produce and cattle. They went mainly to France, whose southern coast is as near to Sardinia as Italy, with the French island of Corsica in between, and which over previous centuries had supplied some of the island's bewildering line of occupying powers. In ancient times Sardinia had been successively Carthaginian, Roman and Byzantine, and exploited primarily for grain grown by slaves on huge prairies in the west and south of the island, before attaining a measure of independence in 900 AD. From 1400 it had been ruled from Aragon, then absorbed into the Spanish empire for two centuries. From 1700 it was briefly Austrian, then Savoyard under the Kingdom of the Two Sicilies. To keep the locals in their place, commerce was deliberately reserved for foreigners like the Genovese and Pisans. In 1861 Sardinia was incorporated into the newly unified Italy, but in reality government from the mainland or 'continent' was not that different from what had gone before. The island was treated as a source of raw materials to be extracted and taken elsewhere for industrial processing and commercial exploitation, whether that be its agricultural produce, the metal and minerals in its mountains, or the value of its people's manual labour.

In the late 1880s a succession of bank crashes shattered the Sardinian economy, and forced many small farmers to turn to loan sharks. This led to a wave of bankruptcies and foreclosures. To make matters worse, the Italian government introduced heavy tariffs on trade with France to protect the big northern industrial interests around Turin and Milan, abruptly closing off Sardinia's principal line of foreign trade. As a consequence, through the 1890s Sardinia saw steep rises in unemployment and underemployment; emigration mainly to mainland Italy, France and the United States; the revival of banditry and feuding in the countryside; and intensified exploitation of the mines on the south-west coast which provided the only plentiful work. These were mostly absentee French or Belgian-owned, and labour conditions were appalling, not very different from those of Roman mining slaves. The miners worked without rest days or sick pay, hacking at the ore by pick and shovel in treacherous narrow tunnels deep underground.

Industrial disease and early or accidental deaths were rife among the roughly 15,000 miners at work in 1900. A 1906 Parliamentary Commission of Inquiry was told that over the twenty years from 1884 to 1905, 35 per cent of the mineworkers died of tuberculosis, while in 1905 alone there were 2,219 industrial accidents. The miners were housed in barracks away from their families and almost wholly reliant on credit at the company stores, whose prices were substantially higher than elsewhere. As production increased, wages were cut. This was the most ruthlessly exploitative and extractive form of capitalism imaginable, unrestrained by any concerns for humanity or environment. It was almost as bad as the French and Belgian colonies in Africa, with similar undercurrents of racism in the attitudes of northern 'white' employers towards their southern employees, whose lungs and spittle at least (according to a doctor's evidence to the 1906 Parliamentary Commission) were always black.

The island's politics were merely the private followings of those able to provide the largest handouts, while new ways and ideas came mostly from individuals from the mainland who found themselves in Sardinia by chance, prone to their own forms of personal careerism and ideological opportunism. Public affairs were dominated by the kind of *signori* and their fawning cliques and clients that had firstly embraced and then brought shame on Francesco Gramsci and his family. As for the peasant and labouring masses, according to a contemporary account, their natural reaction to (their generally) resigned suffering was the occasional riot, rather than any kind of disciplined, patient struggle.[2] Attempts at union organization and agitation were viciously suppressed but, without any political resolution of basic grievances, just as steadfastly resumed.

Tensions came to a head in 1906, the same year as the Parliamentary Commission, initially among the more advanced, unionized workers in the docks, shops and bakeries of Cagliari, who went on strike for shorter hours and higher pay, with some considerable immediate successes. On 12 May a labour demonstration turned violent, with government offices and company stores stormed and set on fire. As trouble spread across the island, thousands of troops were sent in by the government, and dozens of people were killed or injured. By early June the authorities had regained control, albeit with extreme brutality and many more deaths, and imprisoned hundreds of socialist, peasant and union activists. The political response was an upsurge in *Sardismo*, Sardinian nationalism, which saw the distant Italian state as 'a monstrous machine for repressing strikes and imposing armies of tax-collectors, prefects and police inspectors in cahoots with the mining companies'.[3]

Life had not got much easier for the Gramsci family after Francesco's early release from prison in January 1904. He was ostracized by the village community at first and for a full year struggled to find work or, perhaps predictably, to re-establish cordial relationships with his wife and children. He eventually took on a post as secretary of the cattle breeders cooperative, then as an advisor to the magistrates where he could make some use of his legal training. As his public position slowly improved, he returned to the local Land Registry as a part-time document writer. This paid him a small stipend for the rest of his life, but by then 'he had frittered away all the money that his wife had brought into the marriage', and he remained something of a stranger to his family.[4]

Antonio had completed elementary school by the time of his father's release, consistently top of the class in each year. But with Francesco initially out of work and making further demands on the straitened family finances, his father insisted that Antonio leave school and take full-time work at the Land Registry in Ghilarza under his older brother Gennaro. It was back-breaking work for just nine lire a month, enough for two daily loaves of bread, ten hours every day plus Sunday mornings, 'carrying around register books that weighed more than I did. I cried secretly at night because my whole body ached from it', he later recalled.[5] When Gennaro was sent to Turin for his national service, adolescent Antonio was for at least a year the main male wage earner in the family. Many years later he wrote to his wife: 'For a long time I believed absolutely that it was totally impossible that I should ever be loved …. When I was ten I began to feel like this about my own parents. I was physically feeble, and forced to sacrifice so much I was convinced I was a burden, an intruder in my own family.' Above all, he resented being prevented by his father from studying, while the butcher's boy, the pharmacist's boy (the earlier playmate, Luciano), the draper's boy were able to. Francesco the absent father had returned the domestic tyrant. This would have a profound effect on Antonio's temperament, already watchful and detached, as well as his politics: 'I got used to hiding my feelings behind a hard mask or an ironic smile.'[6] In the very first extant piece of his writing, an essay from his final year of school in 1911, he declared, 'When men realise their strength and responsibility and value, they will no longer suffer another man to impose his will on them and claim the right to control their actions and thoughts.'[7] This was as much a personal as political aspiration.

In the meantime he tried to keep up his own private studies, with what little spare time and stamina he had left, including the beginnings of Latin. After two years dragging registers about, Antonio was able to return to school, aged fourteen in 1905, with financial, material and moral support from his mother and sisters. He undertook the last three years of secondary school in the town of Santu Lissurgiu, eighteen kilometres from Ghilarza, and lodged there with a peasant family during term time for five lire a month. His living quarters were meagre, and his landlady unfriendly. He found her cruelty to her own frail, senile mother deeply upsetting. He regularly had to write home begging for money to pay for rent, school fees and equipment and provisions, and complaining at the deaf ear turned to him by his family. He often sold the food he was sent in order to pay for books, to his mother's frequent consternation and his own physical detriment. But he made friends among the children of the town's better-off families, frequently visited their homes and presumably enjoyed their hospitality, while well aware of the social and cultural gulf between them. As he wrote to his mother, 'My school friends play the piano rather than the rustic mandolin.'[8] Antonio's main academic interests at this stage were maths and science. He would remember the school at Santu Lissurgiu as 'a very down-at-heel place … where three so-called teachers made short work of teaching all five classes'. The school had great difficulty attracting qualified staff, and when they did turn up from the mainland, 'often took one look at the place and scarpered'.[9] While he was there, the natural sciences and French were taught by a teacher with a degree in engineering. Antonio's final school year did not begin until January because of teacher shortages. Not surprisingly, his initial interests in maths and science dwindled. In the summer of 1908 Antonio took his final secondary-level exams, and initially did poorly. After resits in September he was awarded the certificate, but not before having to cajole his father into sending the required fees and completed paperwork: 'Hurry up then; if you don't, it's goodbye to everything!'[10]

This was the setting for Antonio Gramsci's early intellectual and political formation, an impoverished island childhood in a large, disrupted, effectively lone-parent family, and an interrupted, partial and barely adequate schooling. Certain incidents, usually involving some form of humiliation or unwarranted correction, would continue to rankle for the rest of his life, such as being asked without warning to recite the eighty-four basic articles of the Italian constitution during a test, which he recounted in a prison letter and even, in the third person of 'a poor boy', in a 1915 newspaper article.[11] His childhood privations and struggles bred in him a detachment and self-reliance and a fierce work ethic that would see him through life but always keep him at a certain distance from other people, along with a sense of physical detachment common amongst those who felt themselves superfluous or unwanted as children. It also gave him a temperamental predisposition towards the objectivity and historicism of Marxism, as well as a profound and intimate understanding of the material, psychological and cultural effects of poverty and inequality. But Gramsci's socialist politics were slow to emerge and cohere, not least because he was just as interested – as he always would be – in culture and history. His older brother Gennaro had got involved in the turn-of-the-century upsurge of trade union militancy in Cagliari and Turin, and brought radical ideas, newspapers and literature back to the family, above all to an especially receptive, inquisitive Antonio. When Gennaro was away doing his national service, he would send his younger brother the socialist newspaper *Avanti!*, to their deeply conservative father's great annoyance. Antonio had to intercept the postman before settling down to some avid private reading. But for the moment his own politics were little more than a heavily rhetorical and emotional *Sardismo*, derived as much from his own adolescent resentments and upsets as any broader political understanding. A school essay famously concluded with a ringing call to 'throw the mainlanders into the sea!'[12] He absorbed whatever Sard literature and folklore he could get hold of, especially the poems of Sebastiano Satta about the ordeals of the emergent proletariat toiling in the mines.[13]

In 1908, aged 17, Antonio enrolled at the Dettori Liceo in Cagliari. Gennaro was by now working in the Sardinian capitol, initially in the Land Registry as he had in Ghilarza. Then he took a job, for better money and prospects, as a cashier at an ice factory. Antonio lodged for the first school year with his older brother, but they really didn't get on, not least because both had to live on Gennaro's humble salary of 100 lire a month, plus whatever their family cared to send them, and would avoid each other as much as they could. Nonetheless, Antonio was drawn towards the same youthful radical circles and discussions his brother was involved in. Cagliari was a large lively city, especially compared to the small towns and villages where he had lived up till then. It had three daily newspapers; several periodicals; two good theatres; and numerous cinemas, cabarets, restaurants, clubs and societies.

Antonio's new city life was exciting and eye-opening but also challenging, not least because of his material poverty. A classmate recalled 'never seeing him in an overcoat. He always wore the same clothes, a pair of short narrow trousers and a jacket too small for him. On cold days he might have a woollen scarf under his jacket but that was all. He had no books of his own, so we lent him some, or the teacher did.'[14] He frequently had to write home for money, including back pay owed him by the Ghilarza Land Registry where his father still worked. If Francesco didn't sort it out, Antonio threatened, he would write directly to the Registrar 'and then we'll see what's what'.[15] Likewise, his academic performance was initially patchy, partly because he struggled with the administrative requirements – 'I was suspended for three days, just when the exam was being held, for not supplying the school leaving certificate I'd asked you (his father) to send me' – and partly because of the inadequacies of his previous schooling – 'I didn't come from Santu Lissurgiu very well prepared, especially in Latin, Greek and mathematics.' For his second year in Cagliari, he took his own attic room, which a fellow lodger recalled smelling of cheese, with books and papers everywhere. Gramsci complained in another letter home that the walls were damp and crumbling with only one little window that opened on to a kind of shaft that was more like a toilet than a courtyard, but he was much happier than he had been with Gennaro. 'One evening we were invited to his room', recalled his housemate, 'There was music and singing, and lots of people we didn't know, mostly from the country. And Gramsci was in the middle of it, performing Sardinian folk-dances accompanied by a harmonium.'[16] His marks were also much improved, and he appeared absorbed in his studies, partly because he simply couldn't afford to go out much. He was embarrassed by his own scruffiness; he wrote to his father, 'I look really terrible in this worn, shiny old jacket … I didn't go to school today because I had to get my shoes resoled.'[17]

In 1910 Antonio published his first article in *L'Unione Sarda*, a local radical daily newspaper owned and edited by one of Gramsci's more sympathetic teachers under the patronage and subsidy of the MP Cocco Ortu who had been instrumental in Francesco Gramsci's disgrace and imprisonment. As if in ironic consolation, Antonio was appointed its correspondent from Aidomaggiore, a small town near Ghilarza, and given his first precious press card. The article itself was a fairly innocuous twenty-five lines about a local election, whose only notable feature was a certain scepticism towards the recent extension of the vote to the peasantry. Its perspective was very much in line with the Sardinian nationalists' distaste for parliamentary democracy which Gramsci would retain as an element of his politics, even when he himself became an MP, with its cliques and intrigues in the service of mainly northern corporate interests. Antonio began reading more widely in the journals and periodicals of Italy's burgeoning intellectual culture, with particular interest in its leading lights Salvemini, Croce, Prezzolini and Cecchi, whose writings he collected and filed away. For the first time and for now merely out of intellectual curiosity, he studied odd pieces by Marx. A recurring theme of the time, to which he would himself return throughout his life, was the Italian 'Southern Question' and within that the situation of the islands. Gramsci's political awareness was somewhat deepened by a school trip 'to study the mines at Montevecchio, since we're studying mineralogy', he wrote to his father as an aside in one of his frequent begging letters.[18] This was his first personal encounter with the industrial proletariat, and coincided with a growing interest in the ideology of syndicalism, the notion widespread in the early twentieth century that proletarian revolution would come about through workplace self-organization and industrial action, in stark contrast to the parliamentary reformism and passive, fatalistic Marxism of the mainstream Socialist Party led by Filippo Turati.

Meanwhile, Gennaro Gramsci was elected to the Executive Committee of the local *Camera del Lavoro*, labour exchange, and subsequently made its treasurer. He also became secretary of the local branch of the Socialist Party. In an atmosphere of heightened industrial and political tension across Sardinia, his background was investigated by the police. When Francesco and Peppina Gramsci heard about this back in Ghilarza, they became very anxious and angry, and Francesco threatened to come to Cagliari to sort it out. Antonio wrote to them not to be so silly: the police were simply investigating a hitherto unknown name among the trade union leadership, especially since Gennaro as treasurer held the union funds which the police had powers to sequester in the event of a strike. There was really nothing to bother about, Antonio reassured his parents, and urged them to 'try to laugh in the faces of the carabinieri, as I've been doing for some time now. Poor things, one ought to feel sorry for them. They're so obsessed with socialists and anarchists they don't have time to go after robbers and ruffians ...'[19] He clearly wasn't entirely miserable and took some part in city and student life. In the same letter home he told his mother how, during a trip to the theatre, 'people pointed at me up in the gods because I remarked on a policeman character's whiskers, and told him he should shave it off if he didn't want people commenting on it. Because of my splendid mane, which even the slightest breeze ruffles, they thought I was a girl, and were then amazed that a female should make such a commotion in the theatre. They could only see the back of my head with my fingers to my mouth blowing a raspberry!'

Still money was tight, and the cause of recurring friction with Gennaro, who at one point threatened to send his little brother back to Ghilarza. Antonio's daily diet consisted of not much more than coffee in the morning, then a single meal as late as possible. For eight months he ate only once a day, and ended his third year at the *liceo* in a state of severe malnutrition. He fainted on several occasions. On top of his disability, this caused him to submit an official request for exemption from gymnastics, an application which itself cost sixty cents. During school holidays Antonio worked as a cashier, like his older brother, and as a private tutor to pay towards his living and studying expenses. He finished school in the summer of 1911, aged 20, and spent six weeks in the coastal village of Oristano tutoring his kindly maternal uncle Serafino's son Delio, partly with a view to restoring his own health and strength with this comfortably off and relatively congenial branch of the family. He was now making plans to go to university in Turin, and applying for one of thirty-nine Carlo Alberto College scholarships of 70 lire a month for poor students from Sardinia. With Francesco's meagre salary, Mario at home unemployed waiting to join the army, Carlo still at school and Gennaro having already contributed much towards Antonio's education, there was no other way the family could afford it.

Chapter 4

UNIVERSITY IN TURIN

Before he could gain admission to Turin University, Antonio had to first get good enough final *liceo* marks, then undergo a gruelling series of oral and written exams in Turin. He spent the final month of the summer holiday, after returning from his uncle's in Oristano, desperately trying to make up for the inadequacies of his schooling. He heard at the beginning of September 1911 that his marks were good enough for him to take the entry exams, and that he was one of the two candidates for the Cagliari scholarship. During the examination period from mid-October onwards in Turin he would receive an allowance of 3 lire a day, plus his travel costs from Cagliari. These would all be paid in arrears. First he had to get there, with 55 lire in his pocket, after spending 45 of the 100 lire they gave him at home on the third-class fare.

The great industrial metropolis of Turin was one of Europe's prime manufacturing centres, clustered around the giant vehicle-makers Fiat, Spa and Lancia and their ancillary companies and suppliers, 'a modern city (where) capitalist activity throbs with the crashing din of massive workshops which concentrate tens of thousands of proletarians into a few thousand square metres', driven on by 'a bold and unscrupulous capitalist bourgeoisie', as Gramsci would write some years later.[1] This was, as G.A. Williams observed, 'a classic industrial monolith of a city', the centre of 'a sector of European bourgeois civilization driving into revolutionary technical change, monopoly capitalism, imperial expansion and state integration', and consequently 'a stronghold of socialist militancy, working class solidarity and ambitious proletarian spirit'.[2] Gramsci himself would report hopefully to the Communist International how a combination of historical factors – the emigration during Italian unification of the 'intellectual petty and middle bourgeoisie from Turin (the capitol of the Kingdom of Piedmont) to Rome, to provide the new bourgeois state with the administrative personnel it needed to function', and the explosive growth of the automobile industry – had made Turin the 'industrial centre of Italy ... the Petrograd of the Italian proletarian revolution'.[3]

For the young student the huge bustling city came as a massive culture shock, not least because it was busily and noisily celebrating the fiftieth anniversary of Italian unification, which also had the effect of pushing up the prices of accommodation and subsistence. In his first letter home he wrote of the risk of being run down by innumerable cars and trams, as well as the customary appeal for funds. The room found for him by a family friend from Ghilarza cost 3 lire a day, his entire allowance, but fortunately the College secretary managed to find him another place for half the cost, albeit without heating and poorly furnished. The exams began on 18 October; he passed the first, an essay on Italian history, but wrote home that he was disheartened that only five of the seventy candidates failed, 'which means that everyone is very well prepared' (in fact the examination board later reported that the results were generally poor).[4] But he did well in the other exams, in History, Latin, Greek and Philosophy, despite several fainting fits, and finished with the oral on 27 October.

To his own pleasant surprise, he came ninth out of seventy, with an average mark of 7.51. Second on the list was another Sardinian, Palmiro Togliatti, the son of a school bursar. What brought these 'two rather over-sensitive, unsociable youths' together, as Togliatti later recalled, was not just their shared Sardinian background but also 'our common state of dire poverty, all too obvious from our clothes'.[5] Both of their families had suffered from their fathers' recent calamities, imprisonment in the Gramscis' case and premature death in the Togliattis'. Antonio and Palmiro's lives and political careers would run in close parallel from then on, with several periods of intense collaboration. But they were never especially close friends, with a clear mismatch between their personalities and temperaments. As we shall see, there were also to be periods of serious political and personal estrangement.

With the onset of the northern winter, which was especially severe in this city at the foot of the mountains, Gramsci was lonely, frequently cold and ill, and effectively penniless. For his first month in Turin he was caught in a bureaucratic tangle, unable to enrol at the university and claim his scholarship because he couldn't pay the first instalment of his fees – mistakenly requested in full by the university – and his father had again not yet forwarded his *liceo* certificates. He also got into trouble for travelling from Cagliari third class instead of second (and keeping the precious difference), which meant he couldn't produce the ticket as receipt and had to claim that it had been retained at the station. Francesco finally got around to paying the university 75 lire on 10 November, and six days later Antonio enrolled on the Modern Philology course in the Faculty of Letters. He received his first monthly grant of 70 lire straightaway, but found that after rent and other basic expenses there was little left for food: 'I buy a plate of macaroni for 60 cents and a paper-thin steak for about the same … I stuff down six or seven rolls and leave as hungry as I went in.'[6] He had still not found cheap, adequate accommodation to replace his damp and crumbling room, and spent as much time as he could at the university or the national library. He complained bitterly to his family about

> having to cross the city shivering with cold, then come back to a cold room and sit shivering for hours … The worst thing is that worrying about the cold prevents me from studying because I either walk to and fro to warm my feet a little, or have to stay huddled in bed … I hope that all of you have a happy Christmas, undisturbed by the danger of being turned out of your house or having to stamp around trying to keep your feet warm.

They responded to his self-pity with as much money as they could scrape together, usually 15 or 20 lire at a time. He survived but only just. Through the spring of 1912, he later recalled, 'things got so bad I barely spoke for several months. When I had to, I jumbled up my words. To make matters worse, I was living right on the banks of the River Dora, and the freezing fogs used to turn me to ice.'[7]

Nonetheless, he began to make friends, especially among the teachers in the Faculty of Letters whom he encountered in the library or around the university, and who could not have helped but notice his neediness. He would also have been a couple of years older than his fellow students, hence nearer to his teachers' age but still receptive to their concerned paternalism. Matteo Bartoli had a specialist interest in Sardinian dialect, which he thought shed light on the development of vernacular Latin, and seized on this rare example at the university of a native Sardinian speaker. Their academic collaboration, which included Antonio writing home for Sardinian translations of Italian words amongst his begging letters, grew into a warm friendship and shared interest in glottology, comparative historical linguistics. Similarly, he made friends with Umberto Cosmo, a notable teacher of Italian literature who had previously taught at the *liceo* in Cagliari before Gramsci went there. Cosmo lent him books and money, and later remembered him as one of his very best students (they would meet again in 1922 in very different circumstances, when Gramsci was a communist official and Cosmo a civil servant).

With Cosmo, despite marked political differences, Antonio found a certain common ground in the movement of moral and intellectual reform which in Italy stemmed from 'the high priest of Italian liberalism' Benedetto Croce, loosely associated with the continent-wide impulses of modernity and secularism, and whose first premise was that modern man can and should live without the consolation of religion.[8] This essentially Nietzschean, fiercely secular perspective was widespread among progressive European intellectuals at the time, and was later described by Togliatti as 'the supreme law of utter sincerity to one's own nature.'[9] Gramsci's early affinity with Croce would flavour all of his philosophical musings, and provide the basis for his later critique of positivism and 'scientism' and for his own 'absolute historicism', but his Marxian materialism would clearly distance him from Croce's (and Nietzsche's) idealism. For the moment, when he still hadn't defined his own position clearly, there was plenty to share and discuss and agree with Cosmo and the other Croceans at the university, who also suggested other fruitful sources like Machiavelli, De Sanctis and Hegel. It seems that these academics and writers provided Gramsci with his only real intellectual and social company for at least his first six months in Turin. If he was drawn to academic authority, he was also unafraid to challenge it, sometimes in surprising ways. During a lecture on Latin literature, the professor made some lewd remarks when commenting on sexually ambiguous phrases in the love poetry of Catullus – a perennial schoolboy favourite – even though there were novice nuns present. Despite the authoritarian ethos of the university, and of this particular teacher, Gramsci publicly took him to task. After a dead silence, the professor continued but stuck to the official course notes and refrained from any further suggestive comments of his own.[10]

Gramsci was slower to make friends among his fellow students, but he did get to know Angelo Tasca, the son of a Turin worker and already heavily involved in his late teens in socialist politics. Tasca had formed a group of red cyclists that went out almost every Sunday morning to spread the word among the peasants, who usually didn't want to know (there is no evidence of Gramsci going along for the ride, or for that matter ever riding a bicycle, though many years later he did consider the sight of one rattling around Ghilarza, a sign of the village's modernization). In April 1912 Tasca gave Gramsci a French copy of *War and Peace,* presciently inscribed 'For a fellow combatant of tomorrow', with the clear aim of cultivating a potential new recruit to the Young Socialists. He also sent him a couple of holiday postcards with friendly greetings. Later that year Gramsci briefly lived with Tasca while he sought better lodgings of his own, but he was troubled by what he saw as Tasca's avarice and wastefulness – buying books he never opened – and his open contempt towards his proletarian father, which he considered indicative of a lack of moral and intellectual seriousness.

Gramsci attended a debate on jurisprudence in which his fellow Sardinian scholarship student Palmiro Togliatti took part. Afterwards, they renewed their acquaintance, 'the beginning (Togliatti later recalled grandiloquently) of that long debate with Gramsci which we were to return to so many times, in so many forms, with much more experience and under different circumstances, on the eternal subject of human history, the matrix of all that men know or will ever know'.[11] But for the moment, according to Togliatti, Gramsci's politics remained strongly Sardinian nationalist, driven partly by the ignorance and prejudice he found among northerners – including most socialists and proletarians – towards the south and his own native island. He had amassed a substantial library of books on Sardinia, and (for Davidson) 'tended to romanticise the island, posing not without justice as the campus expert'.[12]

By the early summer of 1912 Gramsci was preparing for his first university exams, malnourished, mentally exhausted and persistently ill with constant headaches. As it turned out, he couldn't do the exams and had to postpone them till the autumn, and went home to Sardinia for the summer to recuperate. He did some private tutoring, but managed to take a seaside holiday at Bosa Marina. He returned to Turin in early autumn somewhat recovered, and got high enough marks for his Geography, Greek and Latin grammar and glottology exams to be exempted from that year's academic fees. For all his poverty and malnutrition and illness, he was doing very well at university, and raising high hopes amongst his teachers, especially his Linguistics teacher Bartoli, who Gramsci later wrote 'was quite convinced that I was the archangel destined to smite down the (positivist) neo-grammaticists once and for all'.[13] Bartoli was so impressed that he asked Gramsci to transcribe his glottology course in the following academic year for the other students, and encouraged his first academic articles. The research Bartoli commissioned from Gramsci into Sardinian dialect was published just a year later, in 1914, in an authoritative etymological study of romance languages by Bartoli's own thesis supervisor Wilhelm Meyer-Luebke. Gramsci also took courses in literature and law, taught by renowned teachers Arturo Farinelli, Luigi Einaudi and others; he was, it seemed, all set for a glittering academic career.

But the winter of 1912/13 brought further ill-health, including bronchitis over the whole Christmas period when he remained in Turin. This exacerbated his social isolation and loneliness, and made study a struggle. The only purchases he would not forego out of his meagre scholarship and family remittances were books and cigarettes. He preferred to attend interesting lectures outside his own faculty to going out to shows or cafes, though he took enough interest in art to write a rather overwrought article in defence of the new artistic movement of Futurism – 'the best that contemporary poetry can offer history … the last-but-one firework of a highly talented fanatic (F. T. Marinetti)' – against its bourgeois critics for the university newspaper in May 1913.[14] He communicated intermittently with home, so that for once his family complained about his lack of contact, rather than the other way round. In July 1913 he again deferred his exams before returning for the summer to Sardinia. The island was then undergoing another period of political and industrial turmoil over its terms of trade with the mainland and the rest of Europe. Gramsci added his name to a letter of support to the *Sardist* newspaper *La Voce,* which was published on 9 October 1913, the young man's first public political statement. At around the same time he joined the Sardinian Anti-Protectionist League, which included most of the island's prominent socialists and trade unionists, and argued for free trade and an end to the prohibitive tariffs favouring the industrial north.

For the first time a general election was to be held on the basis of near-universal (male) suffrage. This exposed class tensions in Sardinian society previously obscured by the politics of paternalistic cliques and amorphous, oppositional *Sardismo,* and brought forward the island's first clearly Socialist political representation. This provoked in reaction a ferocious anti-Socialist campaign of propaganda and intimidation by the local establishment and their political allies and newspapers. Nonetheless, three Socialist MPs were elected from Sardinia, with the support of the newly enfranchised peasants, as well as the organized proletariat of the mining districts. Gramsci wrote to his Socialist friend Angelo Tasca in Turin, making clear his own growing commitment to Socialist politics and abandonment of simple Sardinian chauvinism, as well as his admiration of 'the force of character and moral rectitude' of the Socialists he had met (in marked contrast, it must be said, to his own personal view of Tasca at the time).[15]

In the autumn of 1913, back in Turin, Antonio's health took another turn for the worse as he was preparing for his deferred exams. He wrote to his father in a panic of illness and nervous exhaustion that he didn't feel he was able to sit the exams because while 'I've been studying and working as hard as I can, I've done nothing except get spells of dizziness and agonising headaches again, on top of a form of cerebral anaemia which makes me lose my memory and leaves me feeling I'm going insane'.[16] His landlady called out the doctor, who administered morphine as a sedative. Gramsci thought he might be able to defer the exams again till the spring with a medical certificate, while retaining his grant and paying his tuition fees. In the meantime he begged his father to send more money for rent and subsistence, which Francesco did in late November. The College executive council considered his case on 19 February 1914, supported by his friend and mentor Bartoli and a medical certificate for 'a grave form of neurosis'. His scholarship was temporarily suspended till he'd passed the exams in Modern History, Moral Philosophy and Greek Culture, which he did with good but not as previously outstanding marks. His grant was restored in mid-April. The added effort continued to take a toll on his health, as he wrote to his sister Grazietta, 'I've had my headache every single day for at least three years now, and always at least one spell of dizziness or vertigo.'[17]

He had however finally found settled satisfactory lodgings, with the widowed mother of a fellow student, Camillo Berra, in the same block of flats as Angelo Tasca. It was a fair-sized, light and airy, comfortable attic room, where he would live for the next nine years, the rest of his time in Turin. With the exams over and done with, in the summer of 1914 he began to see more of his few friends, especially Tasca and Togliatti and another recently enrolled young socialist student, Umberto Terracini. They were all at this stage ardent Crocean anti-positivists, and fervent admirers of the youthful revolutionary editor of the socialist daily newspaper *Avanti!*, a certain Benito Mussolini. It's unclear precisely when Gramsci joined the *Partito Socialista Italiano*, though Togliatti later insisted it was before he himself joined in 1914, and Davidson suggests Gramsci applied in June or July 1913.[18] In fact, Gramsci seems to have applied for party membership much earlier in 1913, prompted by the successful three-month strike of Turin automobile workers and with Tasca's sponsorship, but had to wait till the end of the year because of administrative delays in processing a huge wave of new recruits. His transition from Sardism to socialism was facilitated by his experiences and observations of class struggle in Sardinia and now in the industrial north, as well as his reading and discussion with other socialist students.

One of his first political engagements was a campaign to offer the great southern intellectual Gaetano Salvemini the Socialist Party nomination for a safe Turin parliamentary constituency. The aim was a truly national unity between the popular masses of southern peasants and northern workers. At this stage the initiative represented a highly innovative political approach. The young Socialists won the debate in the local party, though Salvemini would – with thanks for their consideration – feel obliged to turn down the nomination because he had recently left the party in protest at its domination by northern industrial interests. With political involvement, Gramsci's social circle widened and enlivened:

> Groups of us would often leave party meetings, cluster round whoever was leader of the moment and roam through the streets of the silent city, where only a few night people stopped to gawp at us. We used to forget ourselves completely, still overflowing with impassioned feelings, and the talk would be scattered with outrageous suggestions, great gales of laughter and wild gallops into the realms of the impossible ...[19]

Meanwhile, the outbreak of war was creating profound tensions within the international socialist and workers' movements, though in Italy the crisis of socialism was to take on distinctive local forms. In 1912 Mussolini had become Secretary of the Socialist Party as well as editor of *Avanti!*, taking advantage of the parliamentary reformist leadership's vacillations over the Giolitti government's invasion of Libya, which had proved deeply unpopular with the proletariat. Once in charge, Mussolini mounted a fierce attack on bourgeois democracy and proposed the expulsion of those socialists who wished to participate in it: 'As for those comrades who claim they want to enter the democratic fortress only to conquer it, we reply: when they are inside the fortress its doors will close behind them. We do not wish the proletariat to become prisoners with them!'[20] Mussolini's new, avowedly revolutionary Marxist approach was highly successful. Under '*Il Duce* – as *socialists* were beginning to call him before 1914' (Williams' italics), the party doubled its membership, expanded and broadened *Avanti!* readership from a circulation of 20,000 to 100,000, and recruited large numbers of previously unattached but disenchanted young people, including Gramsci and much of his circle in Turin. A measure of Mussolini's popularity here was that after Salvemini turned down the parliamentary nomination, his young socialist supporters immediately offered it to *Il Duce*.[21] Sensing a rather different kind of glory, he also turned it down. Initially Mussolini opposed Italian participation in the European war, but with the prospect of Austrian invasion and the inevitable upsurge of mass patriotism in response, he abruptly switched his position to what he called 'active operative neutrality' in defence of Italian national interests and territory, effectively a temporary truce with capitalism. Italy should not attack anybody, but should prepare to defend itself against foreign invasion.

Among Turin's young socialists, Gramsci supported Mussolini's new line, and was prompted by Togliatti to write to the local socialist newspaper *Il Grido del Popolo* in response to an earlier letter from Tasca condemning it.[22] In fact it soon became clear that Mussolini's newly adopted bellicosity – expressed in his customary bombast, 'I cry a fearful, fascinating word, war!' – was also deeply unpopular with the socialist masses. He was expelled from the party, and immediately set up his own newspaper *Il Popolo d'Italia,* loudly interventionist and effectively the foundation of the Fascist Party. Gramsci's dalliance with active operative neutrality and implied interventionism did not last long, but would repeatedly be cited against him in the years ahead; Williams argues that his political reputation 'never really recovered from the effect of the article'.[23] He returned to university for the new academic year 1914/15 somewhat chastened by this first experience of mass politics. For the next two years, according to a letter he wrote in 1916 to his sister Grazietta, he proceeded 'to live outside this world, in something of a dream … an entirely self-centred existence for my solitary suffering'.[24]

Gramsci's letter in defence of Mussolini had, beneath its topical controversy, actually prefigured a number of the mature formulations of the prison notebooks: an appeal to consider 'peculiar national characteristics' that would develop into the necessarily 'national-popular' nature of successful revolutionary struggle, for example, or the notion of a 'potential state in the process of formation' that would 'take over public affairs' and direct the social and cultural process of hegemony; perhaps above all an appeal to the political agency of human will. But these finer points, obvious to Gramsci perhaps but not to many others, had predictably been lost in the furore. On the other hand, and quite unknowingly, Gramsci's defence of Mussolini as 'someone who knows how to display energy and a clear vision of where he is going' (an all too accurate summary of Mussolini's reputation at the time) and the 'somewhat disorganised declarations (of his) realistic concretism' also prefigures his later critique of the opportunism and 'Caesarism' of the Fascist state, a strong man seeking power through the dictatorship not of the socialist proletariat but of the reactionary bourgeoisie, and ultimately of course the dictatorship of Mussolini himself.

With the return of winter, Gramsci's health again worsened. He was only able to sit one of his three deferred exams in November 1914, and his scholarship was again suspended. But he continued to go to the university, and at Bartoli's suggestion attended a course given by Annibale Pastore, the professor of Theoretical Philosophy, in critical interpretations of Marxism, and also took private lessons from Pastore. The course's central theme was 'the incubation of the material conditions for revolution in the womb of existing society' as the impulse of historical change, and as such a significant adaptation of the Hegelian dialectic. According to Pastore's later recollection, 'Gramsci grasped the originality of this notion at once, and saw it as a new and critical insight into the meaning of crisis and revolution … he wanted to find out how thinking can lead to action, how ideas become practical forces.'[25] Pastore may have overstated his own influence on the young socialist student – not the only one of Gramsci's teachers and friends to do so in hindsight – but Gramsci was clearly making significant adjustments to his political and philosophical outlook, heartened by this new assertion of political agency as a practical force in history, which would provide a central and recurring theme in his own philosophy of praxis.

Finally in April 1915 he sat the last exam he would ever sit at the university, leaving his degree course unfinished with really not very much longer to go, and effectively dropping out. His scholarship had not been restored. He had survived the winter on loans and donations from his friends, bits of money from home and the proceeds of private tutoring, including that of three rich schoolboys whom he dismissed as imbeciles and whose school homework he used to do *in toto*. His tutors were clearly disappointed to see him go, having seen his best academic endeavours as the beginnings of a promising teaching career, and would continue for many years afterwards to express their regret at his departure. His own perspective at the time must have been somewhat more mixed. An article in *Avanti!* published in July 1916 referred to 'universities (as) suppurating sores which produce prattlers and misfits', and called for a new education system which would create 'a new generation of producers who will give the country fewer sonnets and novels and more machines and factory chimneys'.[26] On the other hand, as late as 1918 this disaffected university dropout was considering returning to finish his degree, with a thesis to be supervised by Bartoli that would bring Gramsci's new Marxist perspective to bear on the history of language. Fully eight years later, in 1926, the British *Sunday Worker* described him in a report before his trial as a 'former MP, professor and well-known etymologist'.[27]

But his lack of a degree made no material difference to the course of his life, and while acknowledging that he had disappointed his teachers he would never express any personal regret at dropping out of university. If anything, he would declare wholehearted contempt for the 'weak and colourless intellectualism' or more concisely 'bloodless erudition' of which academic life has always largely consisted, especially when it saw itself as 'superior to even the best-skilled workman', and expressed clear relief at having escaped a career in it.[28] He would be several years into his prison sentence before he declared his plan for a programme of study *für ewig,* for posterity, which would include elements of his degree subject – literature and linguistics most prominently – but that was largely designed to keep his mind alive and resist the torpor of prison routine.[29] This is not to say that his time at Turin University from 1911 until 1915 – the length of a normal degree course, albeit with repeated deferrals and intervals in Gramsci's case – was wasted or worthless. This was a major academic institution with an international reputation for advanced study and research, including his own chosen field of comparative linguistics, at which he had excelled. His studies had given him a solid and rounded methodological grounding, and valuable contacts and networks which would bear substantial fruit in future collaborations and projects. But it had required intense intellectual effort and serious personal hardship, not to mention cultural adaptation to life in a major mainland metropolis. He clearly wanted and needed a break. The global political turmoil caused by what would become known as the First World War offered far more immediate and exciting opportunities and rewards.

In another more placid time and setting, he may well have returned to the university and completed the very final stages of his degree. He continued to present himself, in a controversy in the pages of *Avanti!* over the viability of the 'universal' language Esperanto (he considered it an unhistorical, faintly preposterous construct), as a student preparing a thesis on the history of language. But the pace of change was clearly quickening, and drawing many thousands of bright and committed young people into political action. Gramsci had begun to campaign actively against nationalism on campus, and to write anti-nationalist articles for *Il Grido del Popolo,* the local Socialist newspaper. With his credibility partially restored among the Turin proletariat after the brief dalliance with Mussolini, he began to give lectures to socialist organizations on topical themes and Marxist theory, for which there was a massive popular audience in Italy, if not always full understanding or textual accuracy. Participants remembered his quiet, steady, calm way of speaking, and his emphasis on the content rather than the delivery of his lectures, which made a refreshing change from the rhetorical flourishes and gestures of many other speakers of the time.

In November 1915, Gramsci joined the staff of *Il Grido del Popolo* as a writer and sub-editor. By 1916 he was also writing a regular column for the Turin section of *Avanti!,* called '*Sotto la Mole*' after *La Mole Antoniellana,* the city's most prominent building which towered over his lodgings and newspaper office on Corso Siccardi. He had been offered a much better paid job as the head of a school in the Alpine resort town of Sauze d'Oulx, eighty kilometres west of Turin, but turned it down for what he thought would be a much more politically and culturally rewarding post. He was now a full-time working journalist, under the *Avanti!* editor and left-wing Socialist leader Giacinto Menotti Serrati. Gramsci's choice of career seems to have been questioned by his family, as much for the strain they feared on his always limited physical and mental resources as for any overtly political reasons. In the absence of any clear news from him, they had only gossip and rumours relayed by other Sardinians in Turin. In response he requested their practical help, and wrote to his sister Grazietta 'I could have one of you come to Turin and I would be better all round'. In the same letter, he said he would write to his brother Mario for further (unspecified) help. But apart from the occasional visit by one or other of his brothers the family would stay in Sardinia, and in his own infrequent communications of this period he would continue to complain about their neglect and his own material hardships.[30]

Chapter 5

THE WORKING JOURNALIST

Antonio Gramsci wrote in a letter from prison that in his roughly ten years as a journalist he had churned out enough copy to fill up fifteen to twenty volumes of four hundred pages apiece. His output amounted to well over a thousand articles, often unsigned, initialled or under a pseudonym (most commonly 'Alpha Gamma'). Even now, every few years, some are newly attributed. He was actually approached in 1918 by his academic mentor Umberto Cosmo with a proposal to compile a collection of the short editorial pieces from the war years. In 1921 his friend and colleague Piero Gobetti compiled an anthology of Gramsci's articles from *L'Ordine Nuovo*, which for unknown reasons was never published. Later on, when he was a nationally known communist official and soon-to-be MP, an independent publisher made a similar proposal. After the Second World War, they formed a substantial, sometimes perplexing, portion of the rush of posthumous *PCI*-sanctioned 'Gramsciana'.

But from the sheer volume and variety of his journalism, and his own and others' accounts of his daily life, it's clear that for a number of years from 1916 onwards it was his primary occupation, and the practical and reputational basis for his other political engagements. In so far as he ever had a conventional job, to be declared in a curriculum vitae or a passport, it would be journalism; more specifically what we would now call reviews, features and commentary, rather than the daily grind of news. This was not unusual for political activists, at the time or since, especially those on the revolutionary left with no other source of steady income, but it was never just a job. As he wrote in one of the few surviving letters of the period, while commissioning an article from another prominent Socialist, and in the process disputing Giacinto Serrati's (possibly playful) description of him (Gramsci) as a 'purist', 'I am a revolutionary, a *historicist*', with an entirely practical approach open to others' correction and persuasion.[1] Gramsci regarded his journalism as a contribution to the grand project of socialist revolution.

Even as Secretary of the *PCd'I* in the final years of freedom and legality before his own arrest, Gramsci was writing prolifically, sometimes whole issues of its periodicals on his own as the party struggled against Fascist harassment and falling membership to maintain its public profile. A substantial section of the prison notebooks is devoted to technical matters of journalistic practice, editorial policy and publishing strategy, with the twin aim (for Forgacs) 'to understand how the bourgeois press is organised and to plan the organisation of a Communist press ... in effect a scale model accurate down to such details as visual layout, the subdivision of a publication into sections, and the training of journalists', clearly infused with his own experience as a working journalist.[2] He would also bring a journalist's keen eye to what was topical, relevant and significant in anything he read or encountered, and in his writing always relate the story with a firm sense of narrative pace and structure. Many of his private letters from prison, especially those which recount incidents or journeys or interesting characters, read more like articles than personal communications.

At the same time, he was at pains to distinguish himself from the kind of jobbing journalist who would sell his pen to the highest bidder, regardless of political or professional principles, and write whatever suited his editor or proprietor. The Italian press had been notoriously beholden to elite interests in the economy and society, not least because the publication of mass newspapers and periodicals required substantial capital investment. This, like other features of bourgeois hegemony, came under severe strain in the final years of liberal democracy under the Giolitti government during and after the war. In a period of spectacularly heightened political interest, tension and activity, forms of committed, fastidious journalism with an explicit political agenda of their own in an independent press were now entirely possible and even commercially successful, not least because of the strength of the organized industrial proletariat and the reach of Socialist, Cooperative, trade union and radical movements. The sheer range and concentration of printed material – from several daily newspapers in each region and even the larger cities of Italy, to a vast array of reviews and journals on every conceivable subject – is astonishing, though as Gramsci later pointed out the country lacked an authoritative national 'paper of record' comparable to the British *Times*.

As the First World War spluttered to an end, and proletarian revolution spread across the world in its wake, Gramsci's journalistic writings were openly and proudly partisan and directive; even, or perhaps especially, those which dealt with culture. They also had a style all their own, tightly argued and devoid of bombast, unafraid to draw on complex themes from philosophy, history or literature, to challenge his readers, and always looking for the broader picture behind any specific event or personality. For a glimpse of what Gramsci the jobbing journalist was trying hard *not* to be (and a wryly apposite sketch of many of our own era's politically engaged journalists), here's the beginning of an April 1917 theatre review:

Witty people are a very important part of modern social life, and they are very popular. They replace seriousness and profundity with a quip that makes people laugh. The ideal of their spiritual life is the elegant drawing room, its fatuous and brilliant conversation, its measured applause and the veiled smile of its *habitués* ... a lot of words, amiable skepticism, and a light sprinkle of melancholy sentimentalism. The wit has become even more important through the latest incarnation of drawing room life, namely the offices of the bourgeois newspapers. Here the wit has enlarged the circle of his audience and has made everything a source of humour – politics, war, pain, life and death – thereby winning much applause and earning a pile of money.[3]

At the same time, we should be careful not to glamourize Gramsci's newspaper career. There were times when his journalistic instincts led him to actions or judgements which in hindsight came to seem politically questionable, such as an attempt to meet and interview the proto-fascist ideologue and poet Gabriele D'Annunzio – retrospectively justified as an attempt to drive a wedge between D'Annunzio and Mussolini – or in the same year (1921) the submission of an article to Mussolini's avowedly Fascist newspaper *Il Popolo d'Italia*. Fortunately for Gramsci's reputation – he had quite enough to contend with in the persistent accusations of 'interventionism', 'idealism' and 'voluntarism' – the meeting with D'Annunzio did not come off, and the article was rejected.

The offices of *Il Grido del Popolo* and the Turin section of *Avanti!* (which contributed regular columns to the Milan-based newspaper) were on the top floor of the *Casa del Popolo* building on Corso Siccardi, whose lower floors were occupied by the Cooperative Alliance and the local trade unions. The whole ground floor was taken up by a large and very popular cafe. When Gramsci started work on *Il Grido*, it was being edited by Maria Giudice, a formidable primary schoolteacher and mother of eight children, ferociously intransigent in her politics and populist in her propaganda, with an insistence on simple writing and clear messages which did not require high levels of literacy or political sophistication. She seems to have applied the same pitch to her newspaper as her classroom. The *Avanti!* office in Turin was run by Ottavio Pastore. Gramsci received a weekly wage from *Avanti!* of just fifty lire, less than he'd received as a scholarship student, and worked for nothing on *Il Grido*. This required him to continue giving private lessons in order to make ends meet. What little free time he had was spent with fellow Sardinians or Young Socialists. He made lasting friendships with Attilio Carena and his sister Pia, who worked for the newspaper as a shorthand note-taker and typist, with some suggestion (by Fiori, but never documented) of a romantic attachment between her and Gramsci.[4]

The tone of Gramsci's early journalism was strident, under the evident influence of his editor Giudice, and sometimes laboured and facetious, as he sought political perspective and theoretical orientation on a rapidly changing global situation where news was always partial and often unreliable. Developments in Russia, for example, were fully reported in Italy months late and often inaccurately, and while there was enormous popular interest there was very little real appreciation of their political detail and historical implications, or of the distinctions between the various groups and shades of anti-Tsarist agitators. When a delegation from Kerensky's provisional (and thoroughly liberal-bourgeois) government addressed a huge crowd in front of the Casa del Popolo in Turin in August 1917, they were greeted warmly with a chant of 'Viva Lenin!'[5]

The October Revolution was initially understood in Italy more as an outbreak of anarchist insurrection – or even, in one conservative newspaper, as a rampage by a drunken mob – than a deliberate, purposeful strategy ruthlessly pursued by Lenin and the Bolsheviks. Not without reason perhaps, because that's what it looked like from afar, especially under conditions of wartime censorship. Even close up the picture was muddled in the October Revolution's very early days following the collapse of Kerensky's provisional government, when Trotsky famously observed that 'power fell into the streets'.[6] It was hard for active participants and present observers, let alone far distant bystanders, to make sense of the headlong rush of historical events, in which (as Trotsky's confidante John Reed recalled) all established 'government had absolutely broken down'.[7] There was at this early stage more than a hint of anarchism to the world's first proletarian revolution. Gramsci wrote an article for *Avanti!* on 24 December 1917 entitled 'The Revolution Against *Capital*', Karl Marx's *magnum opus*. The article aired much of Gramsci's own lingering idealism as well as his attempts to elucidate what was happening in Russia. Marx's *Capital*, he wrote,

> in Russia belonged more to the bourgeoisie than the proletariat … and purported to show how events should follow a predetermined course, how in Russia a bourgeoisie had to develop and a capitalist era had to create a Western-style civilisation before the proletariat could even think in terms of its own revolt, its own class demands, its own revolution … But events have surpassed ideologies, the Bolsheviks reject Karl Marx. Their achievements show that the canons of historical materialism are not so rigid as might have been thought … These people are not 'Marxists', they have not used the works of the Master to compile a rigid doctrine of unchallengeable dogma. They live Marxist thought, as the continuation of German and Italian idealism, which in Marx was contaminated by positivist and naturalist encrustations.[8]

The immediate rhetorical target of 'The Revolution Against *Capital*' was actually the stuffy, cautious and formulaic Marxism of the Second International and its dominant element the German Social Democrat Party guided by the 'revisionism' of Eduard Bernstein et al., as well as Gramsci's more customary positivist intellectual *bête noires*. Bernstein insisted that the construction of socialism had to follow a predetermined course through fully fledged bourgeois democracy and an industrial economy (which of course has remained the strategic perspective, such as it is, of social democracy), and in the short term sanctioned an accommodation with capitalism and parliamentary democracy, within which the everyday socialism of the industrial proletariat would gradually mature and spread. This strategy of compromise and gradualism would take Friedrich Ebert and the other 'scientific' Marxists of the SPD into government in the post-war Weimar Republic, and involve their police forces' vicious suppression, in collaboration with the proto-Nazi *Freikorps*, of Germany's own proletarian revolution in November 1918. In Italy, 'reformist' or 'gradualist' Marxism remained the strongest single element within the Socialist Party until the splits of the early 1920s and the onset of Fascism, not least because it was so securely embedded in the system of patronage and subsidy operated by the state and the political institutions.

So, perhaps confusingly, by attacking Marx and *Das Capital*, Gramsci was setting his sights on the mechanistic determinism of social democracy's mainstream devotees of what they thought of as 'Marxism' (as well as, perhaps inadvertently, identifying the early social basis of Russian Bolshevism amongst the radical bourgeois intelligentsia rather than the popular masses). But understanding this line of argument required an understanding of philosophy and the history of thought which was beyond most 'Marxists', especially those without the benefits of a liberal university education. Gramsci would fairly soon disown 'The Revolution Against *Capital*' as misinformed and misguided, when he had undertaken a more thorough and accurate reading of the actual texts. Even so, in this rather overexcited and much-derided article, frequently cited against the 'idealist' and 'voluntarist' Gramsci in the coming years of inner-party conflict, there are again elements of his mature perspective, specifically the related commitments to historical fact and political action, the 'absolute historicism' essential to effective revolutionary change, and the need for a disciplined, organized, consciously revolutionary party or 'Modern Prince' to direct it, through education and agitation amongst the popular masses. The end-result – what he was at this early stage referring to as 'elevation' (a favoured term in Italian idealism) – would be a purposeful act of revolutionary change enacted by an enlightened, sympathetically and skilfully led proletariat.[9] And his appreciation of the *exceptionalism* of the Soviet Revolution – initially a positive factor in overcoming a relatively weak localized bourgeois hegemony – would be echoed by Lenin's own later and much more ruefully negative assessment of the prospects for proletarian hegemony in one of the least developed economies and societies in the world. The best that could be hoped for in Russia, at least in the short to medium term, was (in Gramsci's prescient words from 'The Revolution Against *Capital*') 'a collectivism of poverty and suffering'. In 'absolute historicist' terms, the Bolsheviks had no choice but 'to take power if the Russian people were not to suffer a horrible calamity', even if this represented (in Lenin's words to the last Comintern Congress he attended in 1923) 'a great misfortune for the international proletarian revolution'.[10]

In effect, the Bolsheviks' radical experiment with history saved and modernized the Russian empire, but sacrificed global proletarian revolution to pay for it. And for the time being capitalism abandoned the East but, partly because of its inherent logic of cyclical crisis and bipolar conflict, flourished in the West. Furthermore, German-style social democracy would prove far more internationally appealing and historically durable than Russian Bolshevism, not least in forestalling proletarian revolution in the countries where it had been most confidently expected; primarily Germany, but also – with a much stronger Labourist hence less 'Marxist' orientation – Britain. This – whether or not something actually, historically, comes to pass (Gramsci argued elsewhere, in his *Prison Notebooks* critique of Trotskyism) – is the ultimate test of a strategy's political value.

'The Revolution Against *Capital*' would prove the most famous, or more exactly controversial, of Gramsci's early articles, but there were others of lasting significance, not least because they also anticipated later themes in Gramsci's more mature thought. The signature theme of the 'national popular' was taken further in 'Socialism and Culture', written for *Il Grido* under Gramsci's customary pseudonym Alpha Gamma in January 1916, which argued that 'every revolution has been preceded by an intense critical effort of cultural penetration'.[11] This 'effort' of acculturation enables the individual change that has to accompany collective struggle if it is to truly and permanently transform social relations: 'Culture ... is the organisation, the disciplining of one's inner self; it is the appropriation of one's own personality; it is the conquest of a superior consciousness whereby it becomes possible to understand one's own historical value, function in life, rights and duties'. This is the basis for what a couple of years later he was describing, in 'Mysteries of Poetry and Culture' published in *Il Grido* in October 1918, as 'critical communism ... the philosophical conception that one "is" only when one "is of oneself" and "has consciousness" of one's own being'.[12]

Elsewhere, he cites 'the Socratic idea of culture: thinking well, whatever one thinks, and therefore acting well, whatever one does,' as an essential ingredient of revolutionary social change. In order to understand and change the world, the basic mission of Marxism, you have to understand and change yourself: 'Will, in the Marxist sense, means consciousness of the strategic aim, which in turn means an exact notion of one's own power and of the means to express this in action'.[13] This was an integrated Marxian 'radical individualism' that would pretty much disappear from left wing discourse under a succession of authoritarian versions of historical materialism: Stalinism, Trotskyism, Maoism, even the rather gloomy structuralism of the Frankfurt School. Radical individualism would re-emerge in a weirdly distorted form as a driving impulse behind late-twentieth-century consumer capitalism, not the only originally radical idea to undergo such mutation (or what Gramsci would later term 'transformism', subtle changes in the ruling ideology to accommodate or absorb opposition). By then radical individualism was the intellectual property of the right, under the ideological rubric of Thatcherism and Reaganomics, and the organized political left was embarked upon its long slow decline into marginal irrelevance. A further curious mutation would displace the 'identity politics' of the 1970s, which were firmly focussed on the liberationist movements of gender, race and sexuality, with a new reactionary politics based on regional, national and in some extreme cases racial belonging.

Right till his own end, Gramsci never quite lost sight of his *Open Marxism* – the title of a 1970s American collection of his writings, whose introduction described him as 'uncontaminated by the historical defeat that he did not live to experience' – though he understood from afar and all too clearly (with a crucial and highly formative eighteen months spent in Russia in the critical years 1922–24) the strains it was placed under by the Bolshevik struggle to protect and preserve the achievements of the Soviet Revolution he had so fervently supported.[14] Other early writings address the need for new forms of collective as well as individual consciousness, and for organized, profound and rigorous programmes of education, another theme that would recur in his thinking. His observation, in 'Remembering the History of the Cotton Workers' Struggle' written in December 1916, that a successful and confident proletariat displays 'nothing servile in its gaze' anticipates his later emphasis on the moral attitudes of the masses, the importance of collective responsibility, self-reliance and assertiveness, and the debilitating affects of 'subaltern' mentalities fostered by bourgeois hegemony in maintaining popular consent to capitalist oppression and exploitation. To the same end, Gramsci was involved in founding in Turin a 'Club for Moral Life' loosely affiliated to *Il Grido del Popolo*, with the aim of getting 'young people who become involved in the socialist economic and political movement to become used to the objective, unbiased discussion of social and ethical questions.' As Boothman observes, 'this is the earliest explicit reference to the "intellectual and moral reform" motif, a key concept of the *Prison Notebooks*.'[15]

In 'Men or Machines', written for *Avanti* later that final month of 1916, Gramsci argued for 'a humanistic school' which would impart, systematically but kindly, the values of progressive enlightenment and the technical knowledge needed to apply them to practical reality. His own lingering resentments at his childhood privations are evident in his plea for 'economic independence for the most deserving children if they are to devote themselves to serious study.' But even the less academically able need a broad liberal education if they are to assume a proper adult role in society: 'technical schools should not be allowed to become incubators of little robots aridly trained for a job, with no general ideas, no general culture, no intellectual stimulation, but only an infallible eye and a firm hand.'[16] Working-class education should be about so much more than work. In 'Class Intransigence and Italian History', a relatively long reflection on the nature and role of the modern state published in *Il Grido* in May 1918, there are further echoes of young Antonio's personal experience in his observation that 'teachers, who are drawn from a narrow and unusually needy stratum of society, are not up to the task of national education'. His later conceptions of the educative and directive role of the modern state in any successful economy and society, whether capitalist or avowedly socialist, are prefigured by his insistence that 'a democratic state is not the product of a kind heart or a liberal education; it is a necessity of life for large-scale production, for busy exchange, for the concentration of the population in modern cities.'[17] These themes would be continued further in his prison writings on 'Americanism and Fordism'. There is also the contempt for liberal philanthropy he would carry through the rest of his life, with its emphasis on charity and 'good works', to which in another article he would counterpose 'solidarity and organisation'.[18]Throughout this period Gramsci continued to reside at Signora Berra's, in his comfortable but simple (and more to the point, cheap) attic room. But he spent less time there as his journalistic and political career, and his personal and political relationships, developed. He seems to have avoided the severe privations of earlier winters, and enjoyed relatively good health, even as the economic shocks and sacrifices of wartime made daily life harder for everyone. His improved mood and condition, and his much wider social circle and deeper personal engagement with it, are reflected in his writings. In an unusually personal article written for *Il Grido* shortly after the October Revolution, which offers real insight into what it *feels* like to live through revolutionary change, he wrote:

I talk with comrades, friends and relatives; I sense in all of them something different ... Everyone is unsettled by new possibilities ... Why hide it? I also share this feeling of restlessness and uncertainty. Three years of war have brought about major changes in the world but perhaps the most significant is to make the world *sensitive*. We *feel* the world; before we only *thought* about it. A new moral climate has come about; everything is mobile, unstable and fluid. (AG's italics) [19]

Bertolt Brecht wrote in strikingly similar terms about the requirement placed on his generation of inter-war artists and intellectuals to be both sensitive to artistic, aesthetic and cultural currents, and insensitive to the shocks of economic, social and political adjustment, if they were to produce anything of lasting value; the end result being that 'the productive person had to pay the price of vulnerability.'[20] David Bowie put it another way, as 'a head-spinning dichotomy – the lust for life versus the finality of everything – that produces these moments that feel like real truth.'[21] These existential, ultimately unresolvable, conundrums – how you bring yourself to face the world anew every day; how you live to the full a life which you know will end in death; how you bring to bear your hard-earned past experience on the unfolding course of the present and future – would preoccupy Antonio Gramsci for the remaining twenty years of his life. But for now the solitary student was turning, as much as Gramsci's always ascetic demeanour would allow, into the young man about town. The sense of impending massive social change, of 'a new habit being formed: not being afraid of new facts, at first because things cannot get any worse than they are, and later because we become convinced that things will get better', was beginning to socialize *him*.[22] His concerns, reflected in his journalistic output, were as much cultural as political, though in these years of revolutionary upheaval the distinction (itself, according to Gramsci, an artifice of bourgeois hegemony) was thoroughly blurred. This was, according to Forgacs, 'a period when "culture" in the dominant senses attaching to the word in Italian at that time (including "education" as well as what the jargon of idealism called "activities of the spirit" such as philosophy, art and literature) was a large part of his routine existence.'[23]

The artistic movements converging into what would subsequently be identified as modernism – futurism, constructivism, their more *outré* offshoots of dada and surrealism – were at this stage explicitly and purposefully political in their aims and interventions, driven by disgust at the carnage of war and the old imperial order which had brought it about. This mood would condense into what Willett calls 'a particular constructive vision originating at the end of the First World War, a new realism that sought methods of dealing both with real subjects and with real human needs, a sharply critical view of existing society and individuals, and a determination to master new media and discover new collective approaches to the communication of artistic concepts.'[24] Gramsci would enthusiastically take this approach – relatively unusually, with the degeneration of Futurism at the onset of war into a militaristic propaganda tool and early ingredient of Fascism – in Italian cultural discourse, and carry with it an appreciation of the 'Americanism' which became synonymous through the 1920s and beyond with this new, expansive and practical cultural mood.[25]

At a time when European theatre criticism was, according to Willett, of unparalleled quality and impact as an essential medium between experimental artists and their appreciative audiences, almost an art-form in its own right, Gramsci built a substantial local reputation as a critic. A large number of his thousand-plus newspaper articles were in fact reviews of plays and exhibitions – over two hundred theatre columns for *Avanti!* alone between 1916 and 1920 – and many others alluded to cultural movements and artistic events as part of broader surveys of the era. Much of his time and attention would have been spent at theatres, salons and galleries; not an unpleasant way of life for an unattached young man in his later twenties, pursuing what in 1915 he had called 'the possibility of feeling beauty wherever it is'.[26] Even when he was invited to lecture to one of the growing network of study circles in and around working-class districts of Turin, which would culminate in co-founding a full-blown Institute of Proletarian Culture in 1921/22 consciously modelled on the Soviet Proletkult, he was as likely to talk about a new novel as a current political controversy: 'an historical episode, a newly published book or a new play could all be valid pretexts for the dissemination of ideas.'[27]

He was often far ahead of his time in his appreciation of new cultural forms and themes. For example, he championed Luigi Pirandello's 'virtuosity, literary ability and verbal sparkle … exceptional plasticity and clarity of fantasy … art which captures the grimace more than the smile of life', at a time when the playwright (whose most famous and enduring work *Six Characters in Search of an Author* is a key text of the Theatre of the Absurd) was widely considered facile and incomprehensible if not downright mad.[28] While fiercely critical of the dramatic failures of Pirandello's experiments with plot and staging – 'philosophical squibs worthy of a provincial schoolmaster', actors reduced to 'stage puppets', 'sermonizing morality and pointless verbosity' – Gramsci was one of the first critics to take them seriously and see in them the basis for a new, modern theatre capable of addressing contemporary moral dilemmas and crises. At least part of the appeal for Gramsci was Pirandello's unapologetic use of his own native Sicilian dialect, and the life-affirming 'efflorescence of naturalistic paganism where life, all life, is beautiful, work is joyful, and irresistible fecundity springs from all organic matter.' These innovative methods and quite novel artistic sources had helped make Pirandello into (for Forgacs) 'a barometer of cultural change'.[29] Gramsci was more critical of the conventional tastes and expectations of Pirandello's hostile bourgeois audiences, who 'needed blood or a marriage, and so did not applaud.' Many years later, writing to his sister-in-law Tatiana from prison, Gramsci would recall with some pride that 'I wrote about Pirandello from 1915 to 1920, enough to put together a book of 200 pages. At the time my judgments were original and unprecedented; Pirandello was either amiably tolerated or openly derided.'[30]

In March 1917, Gramsci wrote a highly favourable review of Ibsen's *A Doll's House* in performance at the Carignano Theatre in Turin, with Emma Gramatica in the lead role of Nora Helmar, against a generally cold reception.[31] This derived, he wrote, from facile Latin *machismo*, a reaction to the new feminist sensibility which sees women and men as more than just muscle, nerves and skin, but as persons, and the family as more than a mere economic institution ... woman is more than the female of the species, whose function is to bring up children and drown them in palpating carnal love. She is also a human creature in her own right, with a mind of her own, her own inner needs, her own human personality.

This clear-sighted northern European artistic sensibility, exemplified by Ibsen, was in stark contrast to the Italian tendency to render characters 'pleasant and loveable, latinizing (them)'. Gramsci's Ibsenesque proto-feminism would be both reinforced and tested by his own romantic relationships, which were strangely anticipated in another review three years later of a play by the Russian dramatist Leonid Andreyev. *Anfisa*'s plot, Gramsci wrote, revolved around 'three female figures, or rather one single figure in all of them: the being who lives on the love and domination of a man, to the point of personal sacrifice, loss of self, hatred, crime'.[32] This was a full eighteen months before he met the first of the three Schucht sisters who would – one after another and in their very different ways, but perhaps best understood from his persistently confused perspective as 'one single figure' – come to dominate every phase and facet of his own adult emotional life.

True to his own deepening Marxism in what some would call his culturist period, Gramsci was as concerned with the social relations and industrial economics of cultural production as with their artistic output. In the summer of 1917 – as the pace of events in the war and Russia quickened, and just a month before Turin experienced its own poorly led and viciously suppressed insurrection prompted by food shortages and other wartime hardships, with more than fifty people killed and over two hundred wounded – he got embroiled in a debate in *Il Grido* over the 'industrialization' of the theatre in Turin under the influence of owner/ impresarios the Chiarelli brothers.[33] He accused them of displacing serious drama with operettas, variety shows and vaudevilles, pandering to vulgar popular tastes for easy entertainment, all in the spirit of 'the autocracy of monopolized capital'. Giovanni Chiarelli replied indignantly with a list of theatre companies they had engaged, not to mention 'various lectures, concerts and French companies', which Gramsci duly rubbished with his own list of variety shows and operettas that had predominated over recent months. Finally, in his own summation, he cites another newspaper's observation that 'The theatre owners have formed a consortium along commercial and industrial lines; they protect only their own interests, and care nothing for art'. He called again for 'state intervention' to redress the balance and prevent such 'monopolistic excesses'.

Eventually, after the arrest of virtually all the other staff following the riots and reaction of August 1917, Gramsci was editing *Il Grido* almost single-handedly. He was also made one of twelve members of an *ad hoc* executive committee of the Turin Socialist Party, after its official bodies were dissolved and its offices in the Corso Siccardi were occupied by the military. It is perhaps a measure, at this moment of crisis, not so much of his ascendancy as his own lowly status that he was not himself arrested, and joined the local movement's leadership by default. Under conditions of repression and censorship, the committee was able to do very little but meet clandestinely, debate and pass a resolution on free trade and tariff protectionism, long a concern of Gramsci's since his days of *Sardismo*. He continued to lead informal discussions among groups of activists. More significantly, he shifted the orientation of *Il Grido del Popolo* away from the rousing propaganda and simplistic explanation favoured by Maria Giudice, and towards what Piero Gobetti would call appreciatively 'an incitement to free initiative from below'.[34] Gramsci commissioned translations of key Bolshevik texts, and published them regularly and prominently, confronting what he called the national way with European ways, and turning 'an evangelical propaganda weekly with some local news (into) a little review of socialist culture, developed according to the theory and strategy of revolutionary socialism.'[35] He managed to keep *Il Grido* going for another year, with its last issue appearing on 19 October 1918, but its shape and focus would provide a model for his next, most famous and successful venture into periodical publication.

Chapter 6

INTO THE STRUGGLE: *L'ORDINE NUOVO* AND THE FACTORY COUNCILS

This early phase of Antonio Gramsci's political career, between the end of the war and his departure for Moscow in 1922, has proved in many ways the most contentious. For their own distinctive polemical and political reasons, competing heirs to the Gramsci legacy have tended to make more of it than it merits. For example, leftist opponents of the Italian Communist Party have exaggerated his role in the 'two red years' and the factory council movement, as well as the significance of the 'Soviets in Italy' themselves. The postwar, mass membership *PCI* itself under Palmiro Togliatti built its own foundation myth around Gramsci, striding purposefully and necessarily with his fellow communists out of the quagmire of reformist and maximalist Italian Socialism, whereas Gramsci himself always had a decidedly mixed and rueful view of the split. Pretty much all sides have cast the journal Gramsci, Togliatti, Angelo Tasca and Umberto Terracini jointly produced throughout this period, *L'Ordine Nuovo*, as a kind of house magazine for the factory councils, and the movement itself as the nearest Western Europe ever came to a genuinely successful, Soviet-style proletarian revolution. But just as the short-lived Turin Factory Councils found themselves almost totally isolated and abandoned by the mainstream Italian workers and socialist movements, and the early *PCd'I* was regarded by the Communist International as a tiny fractious sect who had failed to halt the historical aberration of Fascism, or even take very much of the Italian proletariat with them, the young free Gramsci struggled to make his presence felt in these momentous times. The fact of the matter is that he was always on the margins of political developments, usually in a small minority in the ferocious controversies of the day, or serving as a minor part or ally of a victorious majority. When he ascended to positions of political leadership in his own right, it was usually by default, because of the defection, removal or arrest of other more forceful personalities. Perhaps, as we shall see most clearly in his prison writings, Gramsci's very ordinariness made him more attuned than more stellar comrades to the concerns of ordinary people.

Furthermore, the intellectual qualities which brought him his posthumous fame – organizational rigour, dogged curiosity, openness to traditions and bodies of thought beyond his own and his comrades', acceptance of and almost pleasure in intractable complexity, impatience with ostentation in manner and rhetoric, detachment from the everyday routine of political controversy and an 'absolute historicist' commitment to objective fact and evidence – would have been positive handicaps in the charged political climate of these years and movements. These qualities of reserve and proportion were also essential to his political writings, especially those done in prison, which were always more lasting and vastly more significant than his political actions and anything left by his political contemporaries (with the sole exception of Togliatti). The political journalism of his activist years is either sharply topical, focused on passing events or over-optimistic in keeping with the times. Gramsci's prison notes and letters make very little reference to his own political-activist experience, partly out of awareness of the Fascist censor and the legal ramifications of any sort of admission, not to mention the risks of getting embroiled in the vicious late 1920s/early 1930s in-fighting in the Comintern and the *PCd'I*, but also of the modesty of his own achievements. He is far more likely to draw upon his childhood in Sardinia and his university studies, or even his daily life as a convict, than his time on *L'Ordine Nuovo* or in the Communist Party. Once out of action, which is how he increasingly considered himself in prison, he tended to gloss over his busiest years of activism as something of an interlude. Insofar as Gramsci is our foremost philosopher of defeat, helping to explain how proletarian revolution stalled and fell away in twentieth-century Western Europe, and why bourgeois hegemony has proved so durable all across the world, his personal experience of political failure was far more important than any short-lived and partial success.

So we need to be wary of the established accounts of Gramsci's involvement with the Turin Factory Councils and the influence of *L'Ordine Nuovo*. These were the biggest public events he was ever caught up in, but it's as if the (no longer especially young, at twenty-nine in 1920) man himself disappeared behind them. We have very little sense of what he was actually doing during these momentous times. He very rarely wrote home; years went by without any direct contact with his family in Sardinia. Very few other letters survive, and none of a personal nature, while his public writings concentrated on matters of internal, local dispute in the Turin Socialist Party, the factory councils and the trade unions. The accounts of him by others generally come from recollections many years later, and tend to have a hagiographical bent or contemporary political overlay. We can only assume he was still living in his attic room at Signora Berra's because there is no record of him living anywhere else, and we know next to nothing of his personal relationships in this period.

Following the closure of *Il Grido del Popolo* in November 1918, Gramsci worked solely on *Avanti!*, which was now publishing a separate Piedmontese edition printed in Turin. His theatre reviews, deliciously scathing as they often were, were eagerly anticipated and in some circles feared. He held no formal political office in the local Socialist Party, which had reverted to the control of the old guard returned from the war, exile or imprisonment. He seems to have spent most of his time at the *Avanti!* offices, up a spiral staircase on the first floor of an old reformatory building that had been taken over by the Turin workers' socialist and cooperative movements. His young Socialist comrades Angelo Tasca,

Palmiro Togliatti and Umberto Terracini had returned to Turin from the war and proposed the idea of a new journal, initially with the aim of reporting and propagating the lessons of the October Revolution, independently of the Socialist Party hierarchy. The independence of *L'Ordine Nuovo* enabled its editors to involve other non-socialist activists and intellectuals, such as the Revolutionary Liberal Piero Gobetti, 'most sensible and subtle of all Italian journalists'.[1] Some years later Gobetti would publish a striking pen portrait of his friend Antonio Gramsci during the *L'Ordine Nuovo* days: 'The brain has overwhelmed the body. The voice has a critical, destructive edge, its irony turns quickly to poisonous sarcasm. His rebellion sometimes springs from resentment, sometimes the deeper, pent-up rage of the islander unable to open out except in action, unable to free himself from age-old slavery except by infusing the most tyrannical energy into his commands and propaganda.'[2] Gobetti wrote similar, somewhat overwrought appraisals of the other *Ordinovisti*. These are the estimations of young men, totally immersed in their own small world, slightly over-impressed with themselves and each other and their joint enterprise.

The first issue of *L'Ordine Nuovo* appeared in May 1919, with founding capital of 6,000 lire raised from private sources by Angelo Tasca. Pia Carena undertook most of the administrative duties, and Gramsci was named on its masthead as 'editorial secretary'. On the front page was displayed the rallying cry: 'Educate yourselves because we'll need all your intelligence. Rouse yourselves because we'll need all your enthusiasm. Organise yourselves because we'll need all your strength.' Initially, the journal attracted 300 subscribers and 3,000 readers; by 1920 it had 1,100 subscribers and printed about 5,000 copies, and was mostly distributed in Turin and the region of Piedmont.[3] Gramsci was not initially pleased with *L'Ordine Nuovo*, 'a rag-bag anthology with a strong leaning towards nasty short stories and well-intentioned woodcuts'.[4] He wanted to focus much more precisely on the Soviet Revolution, and what lessons it might offer proletarian revolutionary struggle in Italy. In particular, was there in Italy, any working-class institution which might compare to the Soviets, and assume control of production and the broader economy?

L'Ordine Nuovo identified as embryonic, Soviet-style factory councils the internal committees which had been established in Turin and other industrial centres by the trade unions and the employers as forums for resolving workplace conflicts. To begin with, the committees were elected only by trade union members in each factory. Gramsci suggested that they should be elected by everyone who worked there, on the basis of their shared interests and identities in the production process, and that their ultimate aim should be to take over the running of the factory. This would take them well beyond the traditional trade union concerns of wages and working conditions. An article called 'Workers' Democracy', co-written by Gramsci and Togliatti and published in *L'Ordine Nuovo* on 21 June 1919, argued that the fully fledged factory councils could be a means of turning 'the dictatorship of the proletariat' from a rhetorical slogan into a practical reality, the basis for 'a new, characteristically proletarian state, constructed out of the institutional experiments of the oppressed classes'.[5] The young intellectuals were invited to explain and discuss the proposal at study circles and big factory meetings, with generally appreciative responses from their proletarian audiences. They took with them, and published in *L'Ordine Nuovo*, documents and reports on factory life and workers councils from Russian, French, British and other labour publications, and more theoretical texts by Lenin, Zinoviev, Bela Kun and others. Gramsci made a special effort to publish and popularize writings on culture by Anatoly Lunacharsky, Romain Rolland, Max Eastman, Marcel Martinet, Maxim Gorky and others. He seems to have met a number of prominent individuals in the international revolutionary movement during this period, drawn to this latest upsurge, including (in October 1919) Sylvia Pankhurst, who contributed to *L'Ordine Nuovo* several 'Letters from England' translated by Togliatti.[6]

As postwar unrest intensified, and (often inaccurate or partial) news of the Soviet Revolution filtered through to Italy, Gramsci and several other self-proclaimed revolutionaries were elected to the Turin executive of the PSI, and began to spread the agitation beyond the factories. Gramsci was briefly arrested on 20 July, and held for a few days in the city gaol, his first experience of imprisonment. A fellow prisoner later recalled how well he got on with the fellow Sardinians amongst the prison guards. Gramsci reported a conversation from the same period between a Sardinian migrant worker and a member of the Sassari Brigade, mostly conscripted peasants who had been brought to Turin from Sardinia to help maintain law and order. 'What have you come to Turin for?' 'We've come to shoot at some toffs who are going on strike.' 'But it's not the toffs who are going on strike, it's the workers, they're all poor people.' 'Here they're all toffs, they wear collars and ties and earn thirty lire a day, not field labourers like us on one and a half lire a day.' 'But I'm a worker and I'm poor!' 'That must be because you're Sardinian …'[7] Perhaps not surprisingly the Sassari Brigade were withdrawn to Rome before any serious trouble started.

Early in September 1919 the first factory council was elected by the 2,000 Fiat workers at the firm's Brevetti branch, followed soon after by another larger council at the central Fiat factory itself. *L'Ordine Nuovo* continued to cover developments, and to publish supportive practical and theoretical articles in translation from across Europe, with the aim of a new form of proletarian self-government drawing openly on the syndicalist tradition of Georges Sorel, the International Workers of the World and (a particular interest of Gramsci) the British shop stewards movement, as well as the more topical example of the Soviet Revolution. Predictably, this line of argument was not well received by the mainstream and generally reformist trade union leadership. Similar alignments and disputes were taking shape in the Socialist Party. The party was now split roughly in three ways, with Turati's moderates on one side, Amadeo Bordiga's Napoli-based far left on the other and Serrati's maximalists seeking some form of pragmatic, unifying compromise in the middle. Ostensibly, the matter at hand was the party's approach to the forthcoming parliamentary elections, with Turati supporting whole-hearted participation, Bordiga arguing for principled abstention and Serratti proposing token involvement purely for the more intensive propagation of communist principles. But the political divisions went far deeper than electoral tactics, and represented much broader strategic differences. Bordiga wanted to turn the party into an openly revolutionary, Bolshevik-style Italian Communist Party and to expel anyone who supported liberal democracy and opposed the use of violence in pursuit of class war; 'A good split lets the light in', declared his faction's periodical *Il Soviet*.[8] At the PSI's national congress in October 1919, a month before the elections, the electionist wing won 48,411 votes, the centrist or unitary maximalists 14,880 and the abstentionists just 3,417.[9]

The Turin *Ordinovisti*'s position in all this was not entirely clear, even amongst their central core of Gramsci, Togliatti, Terracini and Tasca. In the run-up to the Congress, most of them had supported Serrati's conciliatory line of unitary maximalism, but at least two of their numbers at the Congress itself were swayed by Bordiga's abstentionism. Gramsci attended a conference in Florence of Bordiga's communist faction, but his argument that abstentionism was not a sufficient basis for the foundation of a separate Communist Party predictably won him and *L'Ordine Nuovo* little support. Over the previous year the Turin young socialists seem to have been almost entirely preoccupied with the local development of the Factory Councils, which in turn aroused little sympathetic interest in the national party. If they paid the council movement any attention at all, all three PSI factions tended to be critical and on occasions downright hostile, either because for Turati it wanted to grant a say even to unorganized workers and thereby subverted the role of the trade unions, or for Bordiga because its focus on industrial and technical matters left intact capitalist control of the State and political power. Some measure of the political isolation of Gramsci's group within the PSI, locally as well as nationally, is that in the November 1919 general elections, the party did very well in Turin and won eleven out of eighteen seats in the area, but not a single candidate came from *L'Ordine Nuovo*.

Nonetheless, the factory councils continued to grow and spread around Turin. By the autumn more than 30,000 engineering workers were involved at the automobile works of Fiat and Lancia. The councils were clearly and confidently going beyond the limitations of corporatism and industrial labourism, and taking an interest in how their firms were run and their products produced. Gramsci reported proudly to the executive of the Communist International in July 1920 that 'they forged links with the office workers and technicians to get hold of financial and industrial information'.[10] Furthermore, solidarity and organizational discipline ran deep. In response to a local Socialist Party request to oppose a Fascist rally, 'the factory councils were able to mobilize one hundred and twenty thousand workers inside an hour … this proletarian army fell like a landslide on the centre of the city, sweeping the nationalist and militarist rabble off the streets before it'.

The authorities and employers were plainly unnerved by the rise of the Factory Councils, and seeking to quell what threatened to be a serious albeit strictly local uprising. Their pretext came in the form of an apparently minor dispute over the introduction of a new official Italian clock time, which would start the twenty-four hours from midnight instead of sunset as previously. At one of the Fiat factories, the union shop stewards argued for the status quo, and were promptly sacked for their insubordination. All across Turin, engineering workers went on strike in solidarity, and began to occupy the factories. On 29 March 1920, the employers imposed a lockout and called in the army to enforce it. In subsequent negotiations, they raised their objections to the new factory councils and what they saw as interference in the prerogatives of management. The officials from the trade unions and the Socialist Party were decidedly ambivalent in their response.

On the face of it, national union and party membership had boomed during the war years and its aftermath. The PSI had grown from 50,000 in 1914 to 300,000 in 1920, and there were now over 2 million trades union members, up from half a million before the war. At the 1919 general elections, the Socialist group of MPs had grown from 50 to 150. But, according to Fiori, this rapid expansion only served to dilute the party's ideological clarity and political effectiveness, and to promote 'to positions of leadership quite out of proportion to their talents ... demagogues without theoretical background or experience'.[11] This resulted in 'paroxysms of verbal revolutionism' with no practical strategy or prospect of realization, and what Angelo Tasca called an atmosphere of 'monomaniac, inoffensive delirium' and 'an orgy of words'. Tasca and the other *Ordinovisti*, embroiled in the pre-revolutionary turmoil in Turin, could only complain, as Gramsci wrote in a document submitted to the local party section, that 'The Socialist Party looks on like a spectator at the course of events, never proposes policies the masses can understand and accept, never makes effective use of the revolutionary ideas of Marxism or the Communist International, and never tries to impose a general line that might unite and concentrate revolutionary action'.[12] Arguing for 'a communist solution (of) proletarian control over production and distribution, disarming the mercenary armed forces, and control by the organised workers of all local authorities', Gramsci anticipated two possible outcomes: 'the conquest of power by the revolutionary proletariat, or a terrible reaction on the part of the property-owning class and the governing caste'.

In April 1920, Gramsci reported in *Avanti!* that Turin was an armed fortress, with 50,000 soldiers in the city, gun batteries on the hills, reinforcements on standby in the surrounding countryside and armoured cars roaming the streets. In the suburbs reputed to be particularly rebellious, machine guns were trained on the residential streets, all bridges and crossroads and factory gates. With the factories shut and empty, the city was effectively under martial law. On 13 April, the councils proclaimed a general strike demanding control of the production process. It lasted just ten days, and ended with a negotiated settlement and reluctant return to work which amounted to a serious defeat. In an attempt to re-establish managerial authority and normal production, the employers closed the factories on the night of the 30 April. Next day the workers occupied them round the clock, with the Factory Councils taking control of what production was possible. At the main Fiat factory, they managed to produce around half the normal daily output of cars, despite a shortage of materials and the absence of nearly all technical and office staff. *Avanti!* boldly announced that 'the labouring, instrumental class has become the ruling class', and for Piero Gobetti the Turin workers were constructing a new order. The *Ordinovisti* and the other *PSI* factions in Turin were all heavily involved. But again, these more advanced struggles were confined to Turin, with the national party and trade union leaderships keeping their distance. Some factories continued to function relatively efficiently, but others ground to a halt. A further dispute, this time on a national scale and more narrowly focussed on wages and union recognition, broke out in August, mostly taking the form of downing tools while still turning up for work in the morning to prevent a lock-out. The normal order of things was finally and fully restored by October, brokered by Giolitti's national government with compromise on both sides. The Factory Councils would never again take productive control; by the autumn of 1920 this latest radical experiment with history was roundly defeated.

In the bitter aftermath, the various local factions of the Socialist Party set about blaming each other, either for acting too short-sightedly or too rashly. Gramsci and the other *Ordinovisti* sought some common ground that was distinctive from either Turati's reformism, Bordiga's abstentionism or Serrati's maximalism, but in the process only succeeded in further isolating themselves from the national party and the trade unions. As Gramsci reported later to the Communist International, the Turin comrades had the labels 'anarchist' and 'adventurist' hurled at them from all sides. What's more they began to fall out with each other, with Terracini and Tasca aligning themselves with electionism, and Tasca in particular arguing for reorientation towards the mainstream trade unions. Gramsci and Togliatti tended at this stage towards abstentionism, with Gramsci trying to rise above it all by arguing that any political party should be founded on wide contact with the masses and wholly new forms of organization like the factory councils. He wrote to his *Avanti!* editor Serrati in February 1920 'I am not the editor of *L'Ordine Nuovo*', and explained pointedly that 'the question of editorship has been put off until May Day 1920, in order to remove any power I had to consign articles to the waste paper basket'.[13] His account of relationships on the journal suggests a good deal of internal conflict. He described Terracini's position as 'a cheap hackneyed formula' and threatened that his own response to it would eschew 'kid-glove treatment'. His own abstentionism was 'not a matter of principle', and was subordinate to maintaining party unity, but the finer points of this unitarian-abstentionist argument – just like his elaboration of Mussolini's active operative neutrality – won very little support. It had been obscured by a visit to Turin by the purist firebrand Bordiga to bring back into the fold those led astray by *L'Ordine Nuovo*. In his letter to Serrati, Gramsci downplayed the role of the journal in the political and industrial disturbances around Turin

> we have never wanted … to acquire the reputation of 'initiators' and 'promoters'. Our work has been directed towards persuading the Socialist Party branch and the Chamber of Labour to take on the task of initiating and guiding the Factory Council movement, and in this we have succeeded. We want neither 'credit' nor 'responsibility' for a movement of this type, which has value only in so far as it is the expression of the broad masses. The only 'responsibility' we can assume is an intellectual responsibility regarding those who challenge us and a political responsibility within the party.

Finally, offering an apology to the senior Socialist politician for 'having offended you in some way', he conceded 'I have a lot, even too much, to learn.'[14]

The arguments between the erstwhile comrades continued in the pages of *Ordine Nuovo* through the summer of 1920. As the Socialist Party strained under the pressures of its own internal conflicts and rising political tensions across the country, most alarmingly expressed in widespread Fascist agitation and violence in its most thuggish phase, demands for a formally constituted Communist Party grew louder and factional divisions hardened. Gramsci set up a communist education group in an attempt to deepen the debate and steer some kind of strategic middle course and to emphasize the point that mass politics – education, agitation and propaganda – must precede revolutionary insurrection. Elections – to take part or abstain – were an entirely secondary consideration, which had already consumed too much time and energy. The group recruited only seventeen members, amongst a local party membership of many hundreds. When the Turin party chose a new executive in the early autumn, the electionists won a clear majority with 466 votes, the abstentionists won 186, and Gramsci's communist education group just 31. In fact, the announcement of Gramsci's name to the meeting provoked loud hissing and widespread booing. The 1914 article in support of Mussolini was again brought up, and Gramsci was served the arch-insult in Socialist circles of being an 'interventionist'. According to Angelo Tasca's later account, Gramsci had made a lot of enemies in the Turin *PSI* over the previous four years, mainly because of his harsh personal manner and way of conversing, and they saw this as a chance to air their hostility. Furthermore, 'Gramsci was no great public speaker, and was really known and liked only within a restricted circle of intellectuals and workers.'[15] If his political fortunes were now at a low ebb so were his personal ones. After being many years away from Sardinia and having intermittent contact with his family in Ghilarza, he received a telegram in November 1920 to tell him that his sister Emma was seriously ill with malaria, contracted while working on the construction of the Tirso dam in a notably malarial region of the island. By the time he got back she was dead and buried. He stayed a few days with his grieving family, but made little effort to re-establish relationships. They were alarmed by how gaunt and exhausted he looked. He was certainly, aged 29 and in always precarious health, no longer a young man.

Chapter 7

GRAMSCI THE COMMUNIST

At this stage Gramsci's Marxism was strident and sweeping, marked by youthful exuberance; the zeal of the recent convert; and the mechanistic, formulaic dogmatism to which universalist systems of thought are prone. Like all left-wing political activists of his generation, the Soviet revolution served as the lodestone, all the more overwhelming for having been grasped late and unheralded, especially in Italy. There were not really very many other sources of inspiration for a young socialist of this era. Social democracy was stale and divided (for Laqueur) 'in a kind of permanent stupor'.[1] The grand old men of the Second International's 1890s/1900s heyday had been tainted by compromise with capitalism and indecision over military intervention in their countries' imperial adventures and the Great War. They were further burdened with their peculiarly stuffy, inert, official version of Marxism, a passive strategy of wait and see, which in practice didn't go much beyond trades union organization, cooperative mutualism and class solidarity in pursuit of a better deal for the proletariat from capitalism, and for themselves and their closest supporters a foothold in their national parliaments and state machines. Someone as attuned as Gramsci to culture, in its most seriously experimental forms and socially conscious, modern movements, would be further repulsed by the aesthetic traditionalism of mainstream social democracy, 'dimly reflecting the taste of the enlightened middle class of some decades earlier'.[2]

Even in the maximalist iterations of socialism in southern Europe, the fiery rhetoric and moral exhortation were coupled with a complete lack of transformative programme or even much by way of distinctive practical policy. Latin social democracy promised distant utopia but little actual change towards it. The *PSI* was especially inclined to botched compromise and procedural muddle, its maximal objectives consisting of far-distant hopes and dreams, while its minimal demands fitted comfortably into whatever parliamentary fix Prime Minister Giolitti, the dominant personality in Italian politics for this whole formative period, was able to cobble together. Like many other values-based social democratic and labour parties, the ultimate aim of an ill-defined socialism served more to hold together disparate political forces within a broad church for generally mundane purposes than to guide purposeful action towards long-term permanent change. It was more a faith than a politics, as Gramsci would frequently observe, for all its (at least in Italy) anti-clerical posturing.

The similarly once-vibrant assorted movements of anarcho-syndicalism, which had emerged out of the same mid-nineteenth-century First International seedbed as social democracy, had achieved very little of note apart from employers' counter-organization, vicious state repression and a whole catalogue of gallant martyrs and ignoble traitors. The black reaction of Fascism was one response to these frustrating, sterile dead-ends, adding fierce nationalism, ritualistic symbolism, macho militarism, corporate statism, populist rabble-rousing and the cult of the strong leader to an ill-defined, selectively anti-capitalist socialism. It is an uncomfortable historical fact that *Il Duce* Mussolini had enjoyed a meteoric rise and spectacular success within the *PSI*, before over-reaching himself with his 'active and operative neutrality' policy and being forced to go his own way. During the factory council period, some time *after* the formation of Fascism, 'he even arranged a secret meeting with the workers' representatives and hinted to them that he might be the man to lead them to victory'.[3] Throughout his career, he would continue to flirt with the rhetoric and postures of revolutionary socialism, and on occasions seek formal pacts of reconciliation and alignment. Furthermore, Lenin – the undisputed figurehead of Third International communism – is known to have chided the Italian Socialists for allowing Mussolini, whom he (and Trotsky) had met and regarded as a highly talented and effective agitator, to slip out from under their banner. Much later, well into the 1930s, Mussolini continued to flirt with Stalin, by then firmly established in his own personal dictatorship.

All Gramsci and the other self-styled Italian communists had to go on for political guidance in 1920 was the Russian blueprint, and a strong sense that their own immediate responsibility was to protect the young Soviet revolution against foreign intervention by their own and other hostile governments. Even then they had very little reliable, detailed information about what was actually happening in Russia or the rest of Europe or the wider world. Likewise they had no real understanding of the historical background to the Bolshevik seizure of power, and of its peculiarly sudden and localized character, or how some kind of comparable proletarian revolution might be conducted in Italian circumstances. Within that confusion, the classic tropes of ultra-leftism were unsurprisingly prominent in Gramsci's *L'Ordine Nuovo* commentaries, such as the tendency to blame failure and defeat, or even caution and hesitancy, on the treachery and disloyalty of established party and trades union leaderships, and to imagine that the masses were simply waiting for the right personalities, signals and slogans before they could emerge from their befuddlement, overthrow their oppressors and stride confidently towards a new society. Moving beyond that narrow, condescending, ill-informed leftism, and towards a more mature conception of how class rule is exercised in modern society and how ordinary people lead their lives within it, would be Gramsci's central intellectual project of his prison years, primarily in his master-concept of hegemony.

But the habits of factional politics formed within the latter-day *PSI* were hard to shake off. Even amongst the Soviet-supporting communists, sectarian intrigue was rife. In Turin, Gramsci had helped to engineer an alliance between the local branch of the Socialist Party and Bordiga's Naples-based abstentionists, causing further rupture with the electionist and trades union-aligned Angelo Tasca, and leading to the election of a Turin *PSI* executive committee of eight abstentionists and three *ordinovisti*. This went some way towards easing his own and the *L'Ordine Nuovo* group's isolation, but it had the effect of immersing their own distinctive communist educationist or culturalist position within the abstentionists' far more simplistic and superficially appealing stance, and in the process sharpening their own internal conflicts. Arguably, Gramsci and his erstwhile comrades had no choice but to collaborate with Bordiga if they were not to fade away completely, but it substantially reduced their political and theoretical impact. In one of his very few recorded speeches from this period, to the conference at Imola of the *PSI* communist fraction on 29 November 1920, Gramsci aligned himself clearly with Bordiga, and in the process likened Serrati's 'Unitarians ... to the Social Revolutionaries in Russia', at that point under fierce attack by the Bolsheviks for being 'petty bourgeois opportunists'.[4] What's more, Gramsci 'did not share the idea of a social democratic phase in Italy', the standard reformist route to socialism of Second International Marxism; 'We are, he said, much nearer the phase of the conquest of power by the proletariat.' This was the generally understood current Leninist strategy of immediate transition from autocracy to the dictatorship of the proletariat, propounded at the Second Congress of the Communist International in July 1920, and codified in the twenty-one points for admission of Socialist Parties to the Comintern, which included renaming themselves Communist and expelling their reformists. It had been consistently promoted in Italy by Bordiga and his followers for some years, with the emerging Soviet state as a shining example. The Bolsheviks had proved that proceeding straight to proletarian rule and the construction of socialism was entirely possible, or even essential if the momentum of revolutionary change was to be maintained. As long as communists were in the ascendancy almost everywhere in the immediate turbulent aftermath of the war, this seemed an entirely plausible strategy.

With the ebbing of the international revolutionary tide over the coming years, and the emphasis in Russia shifting from revolutionary advance to state survival and national reconstruction, Lenin himself would qualify Leninism significantly before his death. Already in 1920, in his pamphlet *Left Wing Communism: An Infantile Disorder* aimed primarily at Bordiga and other intransigents in the Communist International, Lenin was criticizing the policy of abstention from parliamentary elections and proceedings. He argued that abstentionism ignored the need in many countries to carry on the struggle to destroy parliament within parliament itself, not to mention the opportunities for political advance offered by liberal democracy. At the Second Congress of the Comintern that year, Lenin also famously singled out for praise *L'Ordine Nuovo*'s account of the Turin Factory Councils, much to the disgust of the *PSI* delegation, which consisted entirely of unitary maximalists under Serrati and abstentionists under Bordiga. *L'Ordine Nuovo* had been brought to Lenin's attention by a Comintern functionary in Italy, a certain V. Degott, who in a later vivid memoir reported meeting Gramsci in Rome, 'a little hunchbacked man with a large head (almost as if it did not belong to him) and penetrating, intelligent eyes'.[5]

But there were always hints of a deeper, more mature understanding in Gramsci's early political writings, especially when he allowed his newly acquired dialectical materialism to be inflected with the idealism of Benedetto Croce he had grown up with, and to look something like the absolute historicism of the philosophy of praxis he would later espouse, with its emphasis on the importance of factually considered, historically informed and tactically flexible political agency.[6] So, revolution and the establishment of the proletarian state was not 'a one-off event on a particular day' but 'a continuous process of development towards a realm of freedom that is organised and controlled by the majority of citizens'. Education, conducted with 'rigour and discipline', was absolutely crucial if the proletariat were to use their newly won power effectively and achieve permanent historical change. There would be setbacks, especially in the early stages when 'proletarian institutions remained mainly a function of capitalist competition'; this required of 'Marxist communists ... a critical biding of their time'.[7] Even the treachery of established leaderships had to be understood in their particular national and historical contexts, especially when set against the counterweight of established liberal and parliamentary democracy, which was always capable of neutralizing and absorbing opposition. These themes would all recur in his later, more measured prison writings.

Gramsci also understood very early on the epochal dangers of Fascism, warning as early as 1919 of

> irresponsible groups of armed men, no longer bound by any State discipline or controlled by any responsible central authority, who are striving to establish local Praetorian powers and possibly a national military dictatorship; coalitions of pseudo-political forces, who have no vital and long-term interests to defend or aims to propagate, but only their own individual and contingent interests and goals ... This is the hour of the charlatans, of the confidence tricksters, of the grand promises that will never be fulfilled.[8]

At the time this was an unusual and highly suggestive insight, a long way from the purist intransigence of Bordiga, the complacency of Turati or even the unitary maximalism of Serrati. In these early days of emergent Fascism, the dominant Socialist factions were more practically concerned with their own sectarian fortunes within the Socialist Party than with the wider, disturbing developments in Italian society. Fascist violence could be seen as just another aspect of society in chaos, which would be swept away by the right kind of proletarian revolution. If it did for the old corrupt liberal parliamentary circus of Giolitti's *Italietta* ('Little Italy') in the process, with its respectable veneer over the harsh realities of capitalism, so much the better. That would leave the way clear for a proper Soviet-style proletarian revolution.

For the most part, especially after the defeat of the Turin Factory Councils, Gramsci himself accepted the need to establish an Italian Communist Party, either through transformation of the Socialist Party or, increasingly more likely, as a separate breakaway. A meeting in early October 1920 united all the self-styled communists, including the Turin *Ordinovisti* and the far larger and better organized national abstentionist grouping under Bordiga, behind a common manifesto which was endorsed at the Imola conference on 28–29 November. But substantial differences remained, primarily over the timing and severity of the breakaway, which Bordiga advocated immediately and without compromise, while Gramsci argued that there was still some realistic prospect of taking over and transforming the Socialist Party. This time the balance was tipped decisively in favour of Bordiga by a further, contrasting intervention from Moscow, where Lenin was now pushing hard for the imposition of the Comintern's 21 points in every national circumstance. In particular, he expressed frustration at what he saw as prevarication in Italy: 'If one has reformists within one's own ranks, it is impossible to win a proletarian revolution.'[9] The communists should break decisively with Turati and the reformists, then for short-term purposes seek a cross-party alliance of the reconfigured left. Further, this newly hard line urged the need 'to remove otherwise excellent communists from positions of responsibility who are liable to waver over "unity" with the reformists'. The situation in Italy was 'precisely the same' as the months before the October Revolution, when a number of prominent Bolsheviks had misguidedly urged caution and compromise. At this point, in late December 1920, Gramsci seems to have accepted Bordiga's 'Leninist' direction towards immediate foundation of an Italian Communist Party, though more in defeatist resignation than supportive enthusiasm: 'It would be silly to whine uselessly over what has happened and cannot be remedied', he wrote in a private letter.[10]

Again, his local journalistic responsibilities would have kept him more than fully occupied. The last weekly issue of *L'Ordine Nuovo* was published on 24 December 1920. The Piedmont edition of *Avanti!* which Gramsci had worked on for the last four years was renamed *L'Ordine Nuovo*, and became the official organ of the Turin communists, with Gramsci as editor on a respectable monthly salary of 1,100 lire. The first daily issue appeared on 1 January 1921, with a quote from Ferdinand Lassalle as its motto: 'To tell the truth is revolutionary.' The editorial board included Palmiro Togliatti, Alfonso Leonetti and other long-term associates of Gramsci's. Piero Gobetti was entrusted with Gramsci's old role as theatre critic. On 14 January, Gramsci helped to found an Institute of Proletarian Culture as an offshoot of *L'Ordine Nuovo*, affiliated to the Russian *Proletkult*.

The political crisis inside the *PSI* finally came to a head at its 17th National Congress in Livorno on 15 January 1921, which Gramsci attended but made no recorded contribution to. The leadership elections illustrated the party's determined shift to the left under the magnetic attraction of the young Soviet state, with 98,028 votes for the unitary maximalists (still declaring allegiance to the Communist International), 58,783 for the 'pure communists' (no longer avowedly abstentionist since the Comintern's 21 points stipulated participation in bourgeois parliaments where they existed), and only 14,695 for the reformists. But it stopped short of wholehearted endorsement of affiliation to the Communist International, expulsion of the reformists and formal transformation into a Communist Party. The following day, the communist minority around Bordiga met in the San Marco theatre in Livorno and constituted the new *Partito Communista d'Italia*, with a nominal founding membership of around 60,000 (actually nearer 40,000, and set to fall dramatically in coming years). Bordiga was much the most dominant personality in the early *PCd'I*, while Gramsci's position remained marginal and uncertain. His candidacy for the new party's central committee was loudly and vigorously opposed, with more talk of his alleged interventionism, or even (according to Togliatti's later recollection) a complete fabrication that he had fought at the front (Togliatti had actually volunteered, and served as a medical orderly, though this never seems to have been used against him). Gramsci was elected to the central committee, but not to its executive, which was dominated by the formerly abstentionist 'pure communists' around Bordiga. Gramsci's retrospective private view of the *PCd'I*'s foundation was expressed in an unsent note to Togliatti just two-and-a-half years later – most likely unsent because he was unsure of its likely reception – when he was reconsidering his position in the party leadership. He derided 'the attitude of "misunderstood geniuses" we have adopted up to now', and concluded in no uncertain terms that 'The Livorno split, which detached the greater part of the Italian proletariat from the Communist International, was without any doubt the greatest single victory won by the country's reactionary forces'.[11]

The unitary maximalists under Serrati continued to declare support for the Communist International and apply for affiliation, while hesitating to leave the Socialist Party or seek to expel its reformists. Yet another *PSI* faction had coalesced around a trio of old Socialists known as the Maffi–Lazzari–Riboldi fraction, also pledging allegiance to the Third International and hence dubbed the *Terzini*, but described by Gramsci in a memorandum to Comintern President Zinoviev as marginal and ineffective. Serrati's group and numbers of *Terzini* would eventually be absorbed into the *PCd'I*, but by then the Fascists had already seized power. The Italian experience gave early warning of how sectarian divisions on the left could facilitate the supremacy of Fascism, partly because of failure to take the emerging threat seriously. The new party under Bordiga clung to the view that Fascist or military dictatorship was impossible in Italy, with just two mentions of Fascism in its first substantive political statement, the Rome Theses of March 1922.[12] Fascism was little different to what had gone before, according to the theses, 'a natural and predictable stage of development in the capitalistic order'. In the Congress debate, Bordiga called it 'merely a change in the governmental team of the bourgeoisie'.

For now, it seems, Gramsci had no choice but to suppress his reservations and go along with Bordiga. The other ex-*Ordinovisti* Togliatti and Terracini were at this stage fully, sincerely Bordigist, while Tasca was embarking on the long and painful process of disenchantment which by the end of the 1920s would take him out of the Communist Party altogether, and reach a sad and dispiriting end as a functionary in the wartime Vichy regime in Southern France. Gramsci was included on the *PCd'I*'s list of candidates from Turin in the April 1921 general elections, when the new party won just 290,000 votes nationally, compared with over 1.5 million for the extant *PSI*, but he was not elected to the two local seats won by the party. The sympathetic Comintern official V. Degott, who had commended *L'Ordine Nuovo* to Lenin, observed that at this point Gramsci 'has little direct influence over the masses. In the first place he is no orator; and secondly he is young, small in stature and hunch-backed, all things which affect audiences unfavourably.'[13] Gramsci's daily routine was unvarying. Every day, at about 2 or 3 o'clock in the afternoon, he would get up and set off for work, escorted by a bodyguard, Giacomo Bernolfo, an ex-artillery sergeant who was supposed to protect him from possible fascist attacks, and sometimes by an out-of-work Ghilarza man, Titino Sanna. They would go to Via Po, or to a milk bar in Via Santa Theresa where Gramsci breakfasted. Or else (more often) they would go to the home of Pia Carena, before going on to the newspaper offices in Via dell'Arcivescovado. There Gramsci would work steadily with only a short break for a meal in the evening, until dawn of the following day, and go home as the first cafes opened along Via Roma and Via Po. He was in effect working a night shift, according to the exacting publishing timetable of a daily newspaper of the time.

Perhaps unsurprisingly, Gobetti and a number of other contemporaries observed a certain 'inertia' on Gramsci's part, with Gobetti going so far as to describe 'sterility in ideas and activity'.[14] This seems also to have afflicted the now daily *L'Ordine Nuovo*, just one of what Gobetti called 'three unreadable newspapers', published daily by the *PCd'I* and all 'obliged to follow Bordiga's party line'. The daily *L'Ordine Nuovo* lacked 'the theoretical boldness, the imagination and creative *elan* which had once distinguished it' as a weekly journal. On occasions Gramsci dismissed early proofs as worthless garbage, and frequently ordered re-writes of articles. His health was also suffering, with further bouts of illness and exhaustion. There was trouble in the Gramsci family in Sardinia, with Antonio's older brother Gennaro refusing to marry the mother of his child Edmea, who was taken in and raised by Signora Peppina. His younger brother Mario had joined the Fascists in the far north-western mainland town of Varese where he had settled, married and set up in business. Antonio went to see Mario – they had been close as children – to discuss his new political affiliation, without much effect. Years later he wrote to his mother that this visit gave him 'an accurate picture of the milieu in which he (Mario) is some kind of hero'.[15]

The Third Congress of the Communist International, held in Moscow over June and July 1921, ordered yet another change of emphasis in *PCd'I* strategy, back towards *rapprochement* with the Socialists in defence of liberal democracy. This time Bordiga resisted, on the basis that going along with it would imply that the recent Livorno split had been a mistake. Furthermore, the following August the reformist-dominated *PSI* parliamentary group signed a 'conciliation pact' with the Fascists, hardly an endorsement of any kind of left alliance, even if the Fascists reneged on it soon afterwards.[16] Bordiga's resistance earned him a personal reproof from Lenin, and reinforced the common Comintern view that the Italians were just another of those artificial parties called into being by the distant glowing beacon of the October Revolution but with no real historical or social roots in their own societies. But the Second Congress of the *PCd'I* itself, held in March 1922 in Rome, endorsed what Togliatti later described as Bordiga's sectarian conception of the Party. The Congress rejected the Comintern's call for a common front strategy, with only a small right-wing minority around Angelo Tasca in opposition to the Bordiga leadership. Gramsci remained entirely silent in these fierce debates, at least in public; Togliatti later recalled private reservations about Bordiga's majority line. Gramsci seems to have supported a common front approach to work in the trade unions, but not amongst political parties, on the basis that this would represent a more meaningful bottom-up unity rooted amongst the popular masses, rather than some kind of top-down stitch-up. Notwithstanding these finer points of dissent, Gramsci's broader acquiescence to Bordiga's hard line, along with some lingering personal prestige in the International derived from his editorship of *L'Ordine Nuovo*, earned him the position as the Italian party's representative on the Comintern's executive committee in Moscow. Having already travelled on behalf of the Comintern to Lugano and Berlin in January and February 1922, this latter being his first recorded trip outside Italy, he would leave for Russia at the end of May.

Chapter 8

AT SEREBRANYI BOR

Antonio Gramsci set out for Russia from Turin on 26 May 1922. The Fourth Congress of the Communist International was scheduled to begin in November, after many months of intensive preparation. Gramsci travelled with fellow Comintern delegates, party leader Amadeo Bordiga and the agronomist Antonio Graziadei, on a circuitous route into Russia via Latvia. They finally arrived in Moscow on 2 June, a whole week after setting out. The very next day, Gramsci and the Comintern President Zinoviev dispatched a letter to the *PCd'I* executive committee in Italy, urging them to 'launch among the masses the slogan of the "workers government" (as) a call to the workers of all parties', yet another attempt to promote fusion with the Socialists.[1] Bordiga soon returned to Italy, but Gramsci and Graziadei were to stay much longer. On 13 June Gramsci was elected to the Comintern Presidium, and nominated to defend Lydia Konopleva, a young Social Revolutionary charged with offences against the Soviet State. Before the trial began, Gramsci fell seriously ill with what was initially diagnosed as 'a fever due to malaria'.[2] His physical symptoms consisted of convulsive trembling and what he himself described as 'ferocious-looking' fits, cold shivers and then tightness in his chest, 'as if the heart were being grasped inside a hand, or a supple octopus was fastening its tentacles around it'.[3] Inside half an hour of initial observation, his temperature fluctuated between 96 and 100, several degrees either side of the normal 98.6. He saw the alarm in the eyes of the huddle of people gathered around him, and later recalled thinking to himself, 'They know I'm Sardinian. Maybe they think I'm about to knife someone!'

The German communist Hugo Eberlein was assigned to provide Comrade Gramsci with a doctor, necessary treatment and proper nutrition, and organized a recuperative spell in the sanatorium reserved for party members and state officials at Serebranyi Bor, set in a forest of silver pines (which gave the place its name) about ten kilometres north-west of Moscow. There Gramsci was diagnosed with neurasthenia, or nervous exhaustion, a currently common and almost fashionable diagnosis for the illness and inertia afflicting individuals all across the Western world in the aftermath of the Great War, revolutionary struggle and related social upheavals. The Soviets prided themselves on the quality of their care for this oddly modern epidemic, both symbol and product of the progress of civilization. Neurasthenia was especially prevalent in Russia, with widespread physical and mental fatigue from two revolutions, the Great War and the civil war, capitalist blockades, famine and disease and the massive epidemics and fatalities that followed. It was even blamed for a wave of suicides among young men worried about sexual dysfunction as a consequence of excessive masturbation. It was also regarded, somewhat perversely, as a measure of the social advances being made by the world's first proletarian revolution. Whereas in the West, nervous illnesses were confined to brainworkers from the so-called advanced races and upper classes, in the Soviet Union they were found all across the population. This was taken as a sign of growing equality and of upward social mobility, with the clinical name of 'Soviet nervousness', *iznoshennost'* or *utomlenie* in Russian. It was especially prevalent amongst active Communist Party members and Red Army veterans.[4]

Gramsci began to feel much better at the sanatorium, even if only from the effects of good and regular meals, enforced rest and (for him, a lifelong insomniac) relatively sound and undisturbed sleep. He began to enjoy some respite from the headaches which had blighted his adult life. From a rare photograph of the time it seems that, at the age of 31, Gramsci decided to grow a moustache too (but not for long; photos taken a year or two later show him clean shaven). Initially, he was able to continue light political duties from the sanatorium, corresponding with other party officials in Moscow and Italy, attending a Comintern Presidium meeting on 6 August, and the following day delivering a speech to the Twelfth Congress of the Russian Communist Party, where he drew somewhat tendentious parallels between the Social Revolutionaries and the Italian Fascists. His attendance at meetings was sporadic, and on occasions caused muddle and complaint and several recriminations from Bordiga in Italy about the apparent inactivity of the *PCd'I* delegation, but he continued to write letters and reports from the sanatorium and when he was well enough from the Comintern in Moscow. Much of his correspondence had an intermediary purpose, seeking to explain to the International the situation in Italy, or to the *PCd'I* the perspectives and expectations of the International. It was not an easy task.

In September he received a request from Trotsky for information about Italian Futurism, for inclusion in a collection of articles on *Literature and Revolution*. He responded fully and informatively, in what may have provided some light relief from the political grind. Years before, Gramsci had thought the Futurists promising enough to prompt an article proclaiming their most prominent personality 'Marinetti the Revolutionary!'[5] He was still able to report that 'before I left, the Turin section of the Proletkult invited Marinetti to a futurist art exhibition … he accepted enthusiastically, and declared that the workers understood futurism far better than the bourgeoisie … during the show, the workers defended the futurists against the physical attacks of semi-aristocratic and bourgeois youth.'[6] But now the futurists were glorifying war and sucking up to the Fascists. Even their art and poetry, once so modern and adventurous, was showing signs of conformity and contrivance. Gramsci would later conclude from prison in 1930 that the Futurists were like 'a gang of naughty schoolboys who escaped from a Jesuit boarding school, whooped it up in the woods, and were brought back indoors under the policeman's stick.'[7]

At Serebranyi Bor he also made the acquaintance of Evgenia Schucht, middle in age of the five Schucht sisters, three of whom – Evgenia, Julia and Tatiana – would come to dominate the rest of his personal and emotional life. Evgenia (known to her family as 'Zhenya') was confined to a wheelchair at the time, on account of her own nervous debility, which had induced partial paralysis of the legs and kept her bedridden since 1919. None of the doctors at the Schucht family home in Ivanovo Voznesensk, at the specialist institute in Moscow or here at the sanatorium had yet been able to diagnose the cause in anything other than the vaguest terms. It might have had something to do with her service in the Red Army rifle corps during the civil war, and the lasting effects of shell shock from exposure to battle. But it might also stem from other, less experiential and more psychological causes. Evgenia's paralysis had begun soon after her acceptance into membership of the Communist Party of the Soviet Union, under Lenin's personal sponsorship. This was at the behest of his wife Krupskaya, who knew the Schuchts rather better than her eminent husband, and to whom Evgenia had briefly served as personal secretary. In the decades before the Revolution, their families had been part of the small itinerant band of obscure anti-Tsarist intellectuals going in and out of exile across the vast Russian landmass and the more congenial sanctuaries of Western Europe.

The contrast between the Schuchts and Gramsci's own family was stark. Hers was a cosmopolitan, multilingual bevy of five wandering daughters and a solitary son, the youngest child Victor. This large brood was loosely overseen by their mother Julia Grigor'evna and supported by their father Apollon Alexandrovich's substantial inheritance from illustrious and enterprising forebears. This included a semi-derelict farm in Switzerland, and a family plot – where Gramsci's own ashes would eventually be interred – in the beautiful Protestant (or 'English') cemetery in Rome. The Schucht fortune was wearing a bit thin these days, in the aftermath of war and revolution, but it still just about kept the large family going, topped up by whatever extra earnings the girls and Victor could bring home. As German Catholics fleeing persecution during the Reformation in the early 1700s, their antecedents had been received at the court of Catherine the Great and absorbed into the Russian aristocracy, which was when and how the German family name *Schacht* was Russified into Schucht. Apollon's grandfather had owned a watch factory in St. Petersburg. His father Alexander was a cavalry major, killed fighting the Turks in 1878 and buried with great military honours in Constantinople. Alexander's wife Ottilija, Apollon's mother, was the daughter of Franz Xaver Winterhalter, a celebrated court portrait painter who had received commissions from most of the European monarchies. Under the pre-revolutionary Tsarist order, Apollon was formally designated a noble of the Byelorussian city of Mogilev, and followed his father into the Imperial cavalry. However, in the 1880s he was drawn towards revolutionary ideas, and dropped out of military school to undertake musical training at the piano and in composition. Apollon was also widely read and a capable author and critic, fluent in Russian, German, French and Italian. In 1885 he married his wife Julia, the daughter of a prominent Ukrainian-Jewish lawyer in St. Petersburg, Grigorij Girschfeld. Her brother Osip was a fellow student of Lenin at the University of Kazan. Under Russian law Julia had to convert to Orthodox

Christianity in order to marry Apollon. In 1887, the young couple were involved in *Narodnaya Volya* ('People's Will'), alongside Lenin's older brother Alexander Ulyanov, and were swept up in a wave of arrests following the failed attempt on the life of Tsar Alexander III. Ulyanov was sentenced to death, and hanged with three other conspirators a month after turning twenty-one, the basic hurt which sparked his younger brother's revolutionary career. But because Apollon had repudiated the revolutionary terrorism of the Narodniks and argued against the assassination attempt, he received the lesser sentence of exile to Tomsk in Siberia. The Schuchts' first three daughters were born there in quick succession, Nadina in 1885, Tatiana in 1887, and Evgenia in 1889.

After several years of relatively comfortable exile in Siberia, the Schuchts were allowed to move south to the rather less harsh climate of Samara, where they became friends of the progressive Regional Governor. There they met up again with Lenin, who had also been exiled with his family and acted as godfather to the Schuchts' fourth daughter Anna. In 1894 the Schuchts moved to Geneva in Switzerland, where Julia was born in 1896. She came to be known within the family by the Russian diminutive Julka, partly to distinguish her from her mother, Julia Grigor'evna, and partly because she was the youngest daughter. Finally, Victor was born in 1899. In 1904 the family moved to Montpelier in France, then to Rome in 1908. Along the way the children absorbed Apollon's passion for music and literature, and Julia's for natural science and philology. All of them switched easily between most of the major European languages, and excelled at music or science. Between them they were able to play duets and quartets, expertly led by Apollon at the piano, and as The Schuchts they could draw sizeable gatherings to their recitals.

In the great yawning late-nineteenth-century historical chasm opening up between revolution and reaction, and the throes of class conflict over the spoils of industrial capitalism and rapacious imperialism, people in this intermediate social milieu could go either way. The Schuchts had made their choice early on, pursuing Apollon's chosen destiny of international communism. Their internal exile in Siberia and Samara under the Tsar was almost fashionable at the time, and now after the revolution conveyed enormous retrospective prestige. But even in exile they had managed to avoid the poverty and degradation of the local, mostly poor peasant population, and live comfortably if never prosperously. During their sojourns, they had never really bothered putting down permanent roots anywhere, beyond stylistic affectations and vague nostalgic yearnings, for their relatively prolonged and pleasurable stay in Rome in particular. The family had felt settled there, insofar as they ever settled anywhere, for some nine years in all, the first six of them in the pre-war golden era of old Europe. That was when they acquired their facility in Italian, and where Apollon took on his one and only regular job, teaching Russian to officers at the Ministry of War. In the autumn of 1913 the sisters began their own independent travels, to Warsaw, Switzerland, and finally for Evgenia, her sisters Anna and Julia and their mother Julia, to Moscow. The rest of the family joined them there in 1917, just in time for the later phases of the Soviet Revolution. Apollon was not closely involved in the October Revolution, but assisted in the nationalization of the banks shortly afterwards. In 1919, at the height of the civil war, he helped to oversee the education and rehabilitation of prisoners of war and refugees. Now, in 1922, the Schuchts had settled in the textile town of Ivanovo Voznesensk, 250 kilometres north-east of Moscow. They were heavily involved in the Bolsheviks' political struggles, most notably against the Social Revolutionaries who had been making trouble in the town's mills and factories.

Apart, that is, from Tatiana (or 'Tanya'), who had stayed in Italy to pursue a medical career and pretty much lost touch. The last they had heard of her, from a family friend in Rome Leonilde or 'Nilde' Perilli, was that Tanya was working at the Policlinico Umberto, nursing children with malaria. Nadina had likewise not been heard of for some time. At this moment of hiatus after the giddy pell-mell of the civil war, she was presumed to be somewhere with her husband in Southern Russia. The other Schuchts could now enjoy some stability and security, as the momentum of revolution slowed and the new Soviet Union settled into something resembling a normal society. With their father's political record of early revolutionary agitation and exile now an asset rather than a burden, they could also begin reaping the rewards of his impeccable old Bolshevik credentials.

In the relative comfort and tranquillity of Serebranyi Bor, Evgenia – an unattached woman in her thirties – must have wondered about Gramsci's feelings and intentions towards her. They seem at this stage to have got on very well, not least because they could converse freely in Italian and shared many political and cultural interests, probably unusually amongst residents at the sanatorium. But their relationship, whichever course it took, would have developed cautiously. For all the reckless post-revolutionary upheaval in the Soviet Union and beyond – with insurrection in the air in Germany and Hungary and lingering hopes for a rapid transition to proletarian dictatorship in Italy, and newly formed communist parties popping up all over the world proclaiming themselves the local subsidiary of Lenin's heroic Bolsheviks – personal relationships amongst communists still moved with a stiff, stately formality. This was partly because of lack of time and opportunity, when there were so many other bigger and more important objectives to pursue and tasks to perform, but also because of a principled obligation to traditional proletarian norms, which would only grow stronger as the first workers state established itself. The freethinkers and free lovers of the *demi-monde*, the soft underbelly of the transnational intellectual vanguard, might feel able or even politically committed to indulge their carnal urges and desires, to fritter away their time on idealistic speculation and romantic delusions, but they were cranks and dilettantes, wallowing in their decadence and aimlessness, and in many cases coming to a thoroughly bad end. Proper communists felt obliged to set an example and avoid causing offence to the workers whose upright morals and respectable values were being elevated and codified into a new global order. Communists must be serious, skilled, disciplined, responsible people, who could inspire confidence in their ability to manage society and the economy successfully, especially in this epoch of scientific progress, industrial productivism, technically proficient management and post-revolutionary reconstruction. They were, or aspired to be, 'red experts'.

In the lingering heat of the Russian late summer, September 1922, Julia 'Julka' Schucht came to Serebranyi Bor to visit her sister Evgenia. Julia was living with her mother and father and her sister Anna in Ivanovo Voznesensk. She had been working as a music teacher at the *Lycee* there until the year before, when she was assigned a job as a translator of documents for the NKVD, the Soviet Interior Ministry. This allowed her time off to play her part in agitation and propaganda in the factories. She had been the first of the Schucht siblings to join the Bolshevik Party in the summer of 1917, and played a full and honourable part in the October Revolution. Apollon and Mother Julia Grigorev'na Schucht were able to come to Serebranyi Bor whenever they chose, usually fortnightly but sometimes weekly, and stay at one of the Moscow hotels commandeered by the party for its officials and leaders and luminaries. Julia could only visit Evgenia when she had the time for the long round journey and the overnight stay in Moscow, which generally meant holiday periods or the occasional weekend. This was her first visit since Easter, and her first encounter with Evgenia's new friend and comrade Antonio Gramsci. She would have observed a small man, barely five feet tall and a good six inches shorter than herself, with a heavy head, a high broad brow and thin lips, on a square-shouldered, hump-backed body. But she would also have been deeply impressed to hear that Comrade Gramsci would be attending the Fourth Congress of the Communist International as a delegate of the Communist Party of Italy. What's more, he would be sitting on the Comintern's *Ispolcom* (its executive committee) and its Presidium.

Julia Schucht was tall and fair and slender, with shoulder-length auburn hair, and large almond-shaped eyes in a perfectly proportioned oval face, which Gramsci found immediately appealing. He considered her the ideal blend of Jewish delicacy and refinement, from her mother presumably, and sculpted Teutonic angularity from her father, with high cheekbones beside a noble, slightly upturned nose. The combination gave her the finest features of Slavic beauty, evident throughout her long life, even during periods of serious mental and physical illness. By contrast, from the few surviving photographs of the period, Evgenia seemed to have inherited their parents' coarser features: high forehead rather than cheekbones, and a larger, much more prominent nose. Gramsci later recalled that when he had first set eyes on Julia at her sister's bedside she looked to him like a Byzantine Madonna.

Between the family visits to Serebranyi Bor, Gramsci still sought solace or diversion in Evgenia's company. They discussed politics as if their lives depended on it, which of course they did, though in ways which they – with the optimistic, urgent enthusiasm of the Revolution still in its expansive phase – might not yet appreciate. There was the forthcoming Comintern Congress, and daily accounts in *Pravda* and *Izvestia* of the preparations; 'A new world to win!', as one of the Congress slogans put it. A widening range of delegates were making their way to Moscow from all over the world, in pursuit of the Bolshevik recognition that might propel them from obscure clandestinity or bourgeois absorption into the vanguard of history. Draft reports and resolutions were being circulated on the rapidly improving economic situation in Russia, and distributed all over the world through *Inprecor*, the Comintern's news bulletin. At last there was some sign of let-up in foreign support of the counter-revolutionary White brigands and mercenaries, even if only because the British and French had troubles of their own to contend with at home. There was even talk of America, that other young society in dynamic upheaval, recognizing the Soviet state.

In contrast, the situation in Italy was worsening by the day. The Fascists were getting bolder and more violent. Ever weaker Liberal governments cobbled together by Giolitti and his cabal came and went, in an atmosphere of failed national unity.[8] A general strike called by a broad-based Labour Alliance, which included the communists alongside the reformist Socialists and the trade unions, collapsed in ignominy and recrimination. To make matters worse, the faction fighting inside the *PCd'I* was intensifying. The comrades were now arguing not just over the correct way forward but over what was to be learnt from the recent past. Gramsci was trying to stay above it all – Bordiga refusing to collaborate with the reformists and maximalists of the residual Socialist Party, even Serratti's unitarians and the pro-Comintern *Terzini,* and Tasca arguing for a United Front of all anti-Fascists based on the trade unions – but finding it increasingly difficult. The perennial dispute continued over whether the *PCd'I* should contest parliamentary elections, as Tasca advocated, or stand aside from what Bordiga called the 'bourgeois democratic charade'.[9] It didn't help that the Comintern and Lenin himself – for all his global reputation as ruthlessly decisive – kept changing position during these crucial formative years, usually based on the shifting emphases in Soviet domestic and foreign policies and the prerogatives of the young state. They had earlier, as we've seen, supported Bordiga's call for a sharp split. Now they strongly supported Tasca's line of collaboration with the reformists and whole-hearted electoral involvement. Gramsci's half-hearted attempts at a more nuanced, longer-term and deeper-rooted middle course, with his customary emphasis on cultural and educational work amongst the masses, achieved little support or purchase.

Lenin remained sympathetic, at least in private. A letter which only came to light in 2008 records a meeting with Gramsci on 24 October 1922, where 'the two men discussed the overall situation in Italy, including the assessment to be made of Fascism, and were in agreement that Bordiga's position – bourgeois State against proletarian State, with little or no account taken of the specific nature of Fascism – was … far too rigid.'[10] But publicly, Gramsci stuck to the Bordigist party line. On 22 July he wrote to Karl Radek, the Secretary of the Comintern, attacking the 'maximalist rump' of the Italian Socialist Party under Giacinto Serrati and arguing against their admission (under serious consideration within *Ispolcom*) into the International.[11] Serrati – who just a couple of years earlier Gramsci was fretting about having 'offended in some way' – was now subjected to vitriolic personal abuse: he did not have one single worker of the masses behind him, just his own party fraction, which itself was not even made up of workers but of trade union officials and local councillors. Serrati could not speak in public; he was shouted down by all the workers, not just the communists. In a report to the *PCd'I* two weeks later Gramsci wrote, 'We consider Serrati and the heads of his fraction to be enemies of the Communist Party.'[12] At the end of August, he reported to Zinoviev that 'Serrati is continuing to play a most perfidious double game … the polemic against the reformists has been softened and there is no longer any talk of a split.'[13]

His personal life was, for the moment, rather less fractious. In notes and letters Gramsci regularly expressed his devotion to Evgenia and sometimes love; or at least the Italian phrase *le voglio bene*, which she could have understood to mean 'I love you' (it actually has a rather vaguer meaning, of a more generalized affection, literally translated as 'I wish you well').[14] But as far as we know, he made no move to take the relationship forward, towards real emotional intimacy or any kind of physical consummation. She knew him to be shy, and awkward in company, but she could be forgiven for thinking that they knew each other well enough by now to go beyond respectful formality in their personal relations. She would also know from what he said that he was lonely and isolated, and deeply troubled by aspects of his past. Perhaps he simply sought her company for solace and distraction, with no particular romantic interest in her. Some element of confusion on her part would have been entirely understandable, especially when she could observe the growing interest and intimacy between Gramsci and 'Byzantine Madonna' Julia on her younger sister's occasional visits over that autumn and winter of 1922–23.

In early October 1922, into his fifth month at Serebranyi Bor, the doctors pronounced Comrade Antonio Gramsci rested and well enough to resume limited political activities and official duties. From the sanatorium, he would be allowed out to attend preparatory meetings at the Communist International. He could also, so long as it did not take him too far away and demand too much of his precarious health and delicate constitution, contribute to public education and agitation on the purposes and importance of the forthcoming Congress. His first excursion was as part of an official visit to the Soviet State Library in Moscow, where in the building of the State Publishing House GIZ he watched a beautiful new Russian language edition of Rudyard Kipling's *The Jungle Book* under preparation. Gramsci had always delighted in the story of Rikki-Tikki-Tavi and the boy Mowgli who was brought up by wolves, and would make repeated references to it in his notes and letters.

His next engagement was to be a factory meeting in Ivanovo Voznesensk, which he had chosen from a list circulated among the Comintern delegates. To help him, he engaged the younger Julia Schucht as his translator; perhaps gratuitously, given his own improving fluency in Russian, sufficient at least to deliver a scripted speech. Ivanovo lay beyond the city of Vladimir amidst low-lying countryside most notable for its several substantial rivers. Things were generally picking up here and everywhere else, under the 'New Economic Policy' to revive the market economy within the strict framework of the young state's socialist norms. The Bolsheviks had finally realized that Trotsky's 'War Communism' could not go on forever, with the military discipline that was required to make people turn up to work for irregular wages of questionable value, not to mention its starvation rations, requisitioning expeditions into the countryside, and widespread famine and typhoid. There was one story that was often deployed, in hushed tones, to illustrate the horror of those times, about mutinous peasants slitting open a commissar's belly, packing it with grain and leaving him by the roadside as a lesson for all the others.

NEP allowed freedom of trade and production by craftsmen, and concessions on attractive terms to foreign capital, in effect a partial restoration of capitalism. Trotsky and his supporters might rail against it, and call instead for permanent revolution, but after a few months of NEP, the economy had rapidly and visibly improved. Factories and workshops resumed production at something like pre-Revolution levels. Workers returned to their jobs, willingly and productively. Proper wages were restored, and people went back to spending them. Restaurants were open again, and – according to Victor Serge, whom Gramsci befriended later in this period – pastries which were actually edible were on sale at a rouble apiece.[15] The business class now known as 'NEP-men' had been tasked with getting stuff back into the shops, earning themselves a tidy profit in the process. They admirably succeeded, in spite of Lenin's strictures of only a couple of years earlier that the hated business class, what he had called saboteurs in the first and second class carriages, should all be arrested and shot.

All we know for certain about Gramsci's factory meeting in Ivanovo, and his first substantial time alone with Julia Schucht, is that at the end of it she presented him with a written contract for her services. It's unclear whether this was down to general meticulousness on her part, or a particular desire to impress her new acquaintance. We do know from their later letters and other accounts that over the following weeks and months of the Moscow winter and spring, from 1922 into 1923, they got to know each other much better, and found themselves increasingly attracted and attached. Gramsci was also gaining a rather different account from Julia of the Schucht family history than he would have had from Evgenia. The family wanderlust, for example, had been much more disruptive and burdensome for Julia, who after her peripatetic childhood spent almost all her adolescence settled in Rome and would clearly have preferred to stay there, like her sister Tatiana. She also told him about her training at the Santa Cecilia music school under the famous violinist Ettore Pinelli. This was where she had first learnt to play the violin, and to express herself in ways that never came easily to her in words. Her application to join the Bolsheviks in September 1917 had been processed and accepted unusually quickly because of her musical prowess and spreading reputation. Soon after, at New Year 1918, the first new year of the socialist state, she had given a violin recital at the Alexeev School in Moscow attended by 8,000 people. She had played Wienawski's Legende Opus 17, one of her very favourite pieces, 'not least', she said (according to Gramsci's later recollection), 'because when they first heard it in 1865, the composer's future wife's previously reluctant parents agreed to their marriage!'[16] She received a very warm review in *Izvestia* by the prestigious critic Alexander Serafimovich.

Since then, she had performed regularly at party cultural events and private gatherings, usually in a duet with her sister Anna. Their rendition of Bach's violin concerto was especially renowned, though she feared Bach was going out of fashion. She had also composed her own musical settings of Russian poetry, of which her favourite was Lermontov. Her audiences were especially appreciative of her setting of 'On the Death of the Poet', about Pushkin's fatal duel: 'He could not bear the burning shame, The petty calumnies, the stain, they sought to put upon his name … Alone he stood, and now is slain!'[17] Later that summer of 1918, as the war staggered to an end, Julia had contracted Spanish flu (so-called because as one of very few non-combatant countries, Spain had openly acknowledged the epidemic and taken steps to deal with it). Unlike millions around the world, including a number of her friends and comrades in Ivanovo, she had survived and recovered, but the illness had weakened her and left her prone to blackouts and fits, during which she stared blankly for minutes on end. In the years to come, this would be cited as the likely cause and initial manifestation of her own much more serious 'nervous debility'; or more exactly, psychological disturbance and mental illness.

Antonio and Julia began to correspond, still formally and tentatively, as autumn turned to winter and Gramsci and his doctors considered his full discharge from the sanatorium. Julia called him Professor and largely confined her remarks to safe subjects like the weather – 'Today I found the sun! It seemed to have gone missing' – in letters which (she later confessed) underwent as many as five careful drafts before she dared send them off. Meanwhile, he continued to address her with the formal Italian 'Lei' rather than the familiar 'tu', and took care to maintain a rather impersonal business-like tone.[18] It was as if they had to keep reminding themselves and each other that their relationship, if such it was, was for the moment entirely comradely. Gramsci was working hard at his political duties, and still not entirely recovered from the nervous exhaustion with which he had entered the sanatorium, manifested now in faint-inducing anaemia, bouts of amnesia and his perennial insomnia. But Julia would have detected another layer of reserve in his behaviour and character. Much later, in a letter to her, he would attribute this tendency to withdraw inside himself at moments of uncertainty to patterns formed in his own childhood and background – 'I became used to hiding my feelings behind a mask of hardness, or an ironic smile' – and ask for her forgiveness for subjecting her to that same hands-off treatment. 'I suppose my only excuse is that I was trying to gauge your interest in me.'[19]

From her point of view, he would have represented a genuinely fascinating and engaging personality. He had a range of experience and insight well beyond his age and his physical stature, or anything she would have ever encountered in the narrow *milieu* of cosmopolitan malcontents, dispossessed nobles and utopian dreamers she had grown up and lived amongst in her father's *émigré* circles. This man seemed to have grown from, and remained firmly rooted in, the real world, where people made and grew things and truly belonged to places and other people. He was also of course, and despite his own deep personal reserve and coruscating rationality, vigorously and boldly Italian. Whenever Julia picked up her violin, Gramsci later observed, the music itself seemed to bring back to her the warmth and the light of Italy. Over time the contact between Antonio and Julia assumed greater intimacy. It was quite clearly now a dalliance, if not yet a relationship. So clearly in fact that he accused her semi-seriously of standing him up when illness had prevented her from joining a family visit to Serebranyi Bor. Here was a man who, for all his physical frailties and deformities and his manifest romantic inexperience, was used to getting his own way; a glimpse of what had enabled him to attain his present status in the *Partito Communista d'Italia* and the Comintern, a seam of iron in his will. She would be sure to make definite arrangements in future, she wrote back, and to let him know of any last-minute alterations; again, a sign of their growing attachment. They took to walking out together around the grounds of the sanatorium. And when it was time for her to leave, he accompanied her to the main gate and the road back into the city. They both felt, they later disclosed to each other when their intimacy was well and truly established, the wrench of separation and the delicious tingle of anticipation for their next meeting.

Meanwhile, the situation in Italy was rapidly worsening. Mussolini and his Fascist *squadristi* had set about restoring order to the cities and the countryside, with the active connivance of the King and the offices of state. These behind-the-scenes negotiations and manoeuvres had culminated in the grotesque pantomime of the March on Rome on 22 October 1922, with thousands of Blackshirts converging on the capital mostly armed with sticks and whips and even, it was rumoured, toy rifles and revolvers carved from wood. The march took place two days *after* Mussolini had been invited by the King to form a government, with the participation of right-wing mavericks from the Popular Party and the Liberals, and could have had no purpose other than political show. If this was any kind of revolution, as Mussolini described it to his enraptured followers, it was being imposed from above on a cowed nation and populace.

Gramsci spent his final days at Serebranyi Bor preparing an article on 'The Origins of the Mussolini Cabinet' for the Communist International's bulletin, *La Correspondence Internationale,* which was popularly known and read around the world as *Inprecor.*[20] This would be his most extensive historical survey so far of the factors behind Mussolini's coup d'etat. He dug beneath the newspaper headlines and radio bulletins, and the absurd grandstanding of the Fascists themselves, and tried to expose the class character and the political contingencies of the crisis. He began by explaining the historical weaknesses of the Italian bourgeoisie and their failure during unification to achieve a properly modern, integrated national state in the face of the quasi-feudal alliance between the big landowners and the Vatican. Industrial development had been slow and partial, and concentrated in the north. National politics had been dominated by issues of land ownership and related rural issues, which meant that the emergent Socialist Party had been strong in the countryside but weak in the cities: '60 per cent of the Party's members were peasants; of the 150 socialist MPs, 110 had been elected in the countryside; of 2,500 local councils won by the *PSI*, 2000 were exclusively peasant.'[21] In the resulting political vacuum, the liberal Giolitti had assembled a shallow social coalition of city dwellers and agricultural wage labourers. Through parliamentary manoeuvre and paternalistic concessions, all the old tricks of what was known as *trasformismo*, Giolitti had managed to organize a series of precarious government majorities behind his programme of industrialization, free trade and social harmony. This fragile settlement had lasted around twenty years in one form or another, from one century into the next, but was finally blown away by imperialist misadventure and world war.

But for all their mass peasant membership, the Socialists were incapable of concerted political action. Rather, these maximalists engaged in noisy pronouncements in Parliament, in sticking up posters and in songs and fanfares. They were all sound and fury, but no systematic organization or mass education. Meanwhile, the small Italian industrial working class went largely unorganized and unrepresented, outside their few bastions in the northern cities. Italian workers remained politically ineffectual when compared to the other developed countries of Western Europe, with their huge and highly effective trade union movements and Labour and Social Democratic Parties. Proletarian struggles like the Turin Factory Council movement were left isolated or even blamed on irresponsible agents of the Moscow government, and suppressed by Socialist Party officials and trade union leaderships protecting their own positions. The European wave of post-war agitation and upheaval might have swept Italy along in its wake, with wildcat strikes and massive rumbustious demonstrations, but they achieved very little beyond local inconvenience and anxiety, and their participants soon grew confused and demoralized. In March 1920, the industrialists, bankers and landowners began their counter-offensive, with feverish counter-revolutionary organization and action, and the active assistance of the state. Demobilized army officers were allowed to keep four-fifths of their pay if they joined the *Fasci di Combattimento*, previously a small organization of socialist, anarchist, syndicalist and republican eccentrics who had supported Italian participation in the war. These interventionists – previously 'leaders without a following', as Gramsci dubbed them – were suddenly flooded with money and recruits. This provided the armed nucleus for Mussolini's campaign of terror. For all this ex Socialist's revolutionary phrase-mongering and bombast, he was for the moment merely a willing tool of the most reactionary elements of the Italian bourgeoisie who had furnished him with money, arms and men.The article was published in *Inprecor* on 20 November 1922, and brought Gramsci many kind words and nods of praise around Hotel Lux in Moscow, where he was now re-installed while he resumed his official duties at the Comintern. Comrades from other European parties and beyond made a point of stopping Gramsci in the corridors and dining rooms and asking when the next instalment would appear. He was even approached by the Hungarian *Ispolcom* member Matyas Rakosi (whom he had little respect for) and asked to become leader of the Italian party in place of Bordiga. Gramsci knew that Rakosi wouldn't have approached him without some kind of authorization from higher up, but he also knew that at this stage it was not politically practicable. It would split the Italian party in two, he figured, and as things stood Bordiga – with his 'sect mentality' and 'catastrophic' attitude towards the Socialists, whom he compared 'to a corpse which must be cleared out of the way' – would take most of it with him.[22] 'In any case,' he wrote to Julia, 'in terms of general capacity for work, Amadeo is worth at least three of any of us ... I couldn't possibly replace him.'[23] He continued, 'Most of the time I feel like I'm walking on hot coals, with Amadeo ranting away on one side about the need for purity and hardness, and people like Angelo Tasca on the other arguing for immediate and total fusion with the Socialists. Or else I'm wriggling like an eel to find some kind of compromise.'

He had eventually come up with one, whereby the Socialist Party *Terzini* faction under Serratti, which fully accepted the twenty-one founding principles of the Communist International, should be merged into the new Communist Party. This was much better than trying to absorb the Socialist Party as a whole, large parts of which would never accept the tenets and practices of Bolshevism, or even much of Marxism. Even Bordiga, in private gloomier and more quarrelsome than ever, had felt obliged to accept this half-way house.

Chapter 9

AT THE HOTEL LUX, MOSCOW, 1923

The Hotel Lux was a squat four-storey building, at 36 Tverskaya Street in Moscow. Originally called Hotel Frantsiy, it was commandeered by the Bolsheviks and used to house foreign officials and delegates to the Communist International. Despite its name, it was by no means luxurious, even by Russian standards. Originally designed for no more than a hundred guests, during Congresses and other official events it struggled to accommodate many hundreds from all over the world. Some became more or less permanent residents of what they called their golden cage, wholly reliant on their Russian hosts, as revolutions failed or conditions in their own countries made it impossible to return home or they proved more politically useful in Moscow. There were always lots of Germans staying at the Hotel Lux, even when their own political star was on the rise. They set up their own Karl Liebknecht School, after the KPD leader was assassinated alongside Rosa Luxemburg in 1919, to educate (in German) their children. Guests were lodged according to their place in the Comintern hierarchy, and in most cases had to share rooms with several others. Heating was erratic. People clustered round primus stoves in their rooms, and small fires were a common hazard. Hot water was only available twice a week, and people had to shower in groups, as many as four at a time. There was much ribald humour about communal life under socialism, and how the poor privileged capitalists had to do these things all on their own. Children played in the corridors and meeting rooms, or in the street and alleyways outside. In the communal kitchens, pots of food were cooked right next to boiling pans of nappies. The place was infested with rats and cockroaches, and required the regular laying of poisons and traps in a half-hearted attempt at pest control.[1]

During his longest stay at the Hotel Lux, for the final months of 1922 and into 1923, Antonio Gramsci shared a small room with his Italian comrade and near namesake Antonio Graziadei, with whom he had travelled alongside Bordiga to Russia from Italy back in May. Given the standard of his accommodation over the past dozen years in Cagliari and Turin, Gramsci would have been rather more comfortable at the Lux than his room-mate. Graziadei was an aristocrat, a fully fledged Count, who had been a prominent member of the Socialist Party and joined the Communist Party in the Livorno split. Tall and imposing, he wore a substantial moustache with waxed ends. Socially and politically, he and Gramsci could not have been more different. Graziadei had a persistent and comprehensive distaste, common among Italians of his intellectual background, for all things Italian, which were almost automatically in his opinion inferior to those of other nationalities. He could go on for hours about how shiftless, cowardly and socially inferior Italian people were. Gramsci found this odd, and sometimes annoying; a direct counterpart to the fond, indulgent Italophilia of the Schuchts and most of the transnational bourgeoisie. It was a kind of anti-patriotism, derived (he thought) from distant and no longer respectable class hatreds. Graziadei had simply found in communism a new outlet for his aristocratic disdain. It always threatened to revert to a general contempt for all the lower orders, even when (as now with Graziadei) it had found a clear focus for scorn in the reactionary politics and mean-minded moralism of the Fascist-supporting petty bourgeoisie. Graziadei had made an academic career, before his membership of the Communist Party, in political economy. He had held several university professorships, and there always seemed to be several others in the offing, which he could defer indefinitely or graciously take up when the fancy took him. He was the new party's principal expert on land reform, and closely identified with the minority Right faction led by Angelo Tasca and its policies of United Front with the socialists and the contesting of elections. He was to advocate and represent these policies at the Fourth Congress of the Communist International.

Gramsci got on well enough with Graziadei, for all their political and social differences and the inevitable irritations of living in the same small room for several months. They had a shared love of the theatre, and spent enjoyable nights together at the Meyerhold, the Bakhrushin and the Bolshoi, watching superb productions of new plays by Gorki or Sukhovo-Kobylin, or radical new settings of Lermontov or Hoffman, Aristophanes or Shakespeare. Some evenings they preferred to go slumming it, as Graziadei would put it to Gramsci with an inviting sneer, at the Variety Theatre or even the various circuses erected in tents on scrubland on the city's outskirts. They were especially fond of the magic acts at the Variety, which offered a delightful combination of guilty pleasure and innocent childlike wonder, all the more delightful for the free tickets Graziadei was able to procure through what he called his connections. They might also have found common cause in fond reminiscences of the Italian climate and cuisine (if not of Italy's people and popular culture) – lying in their hard beds late at night recalling city strolls or trips to the seaside, or reciting recipes and menus – and in sardonic revulsion at the grey freezing damp of the Moscow winter and the unsavoury conditions of the Hotel Lux.

Evgenia Schucht was now finally showing signs of full recovery, after almost four years at the Serebranyi Bor sanatorium, and of the restored capacity to walk unaided. She still had to lean on walls and furniture every few metres but this was a marked improvement on leaning on people. In a few weeks or months at most, her doctors had said she would be discharged back to the care of her family. But this did not seem to improve her mood, and aspects of her behaviour continued to concern her family. Gramsci was still feeling the lingering effects of his own illness and nervous exhaustion, a lethargy that would afflict him for days on end, and blinding headaches if he pushed himself too hard. He was always wary of anything that might threaten his fragile equilibrium, and this would surely have included Evgenia's irritability. She became really angry on one visit when he dared to criticize her embroidery. The swallows and other ornaments and even the monograms she sewed into handkerchiefs, he observed, always ended up looking more like lizards. She responded in fury. There were also incidents that suggested lingering, deeper disturbances in Evgenia's mental state, such as the discovery of a cache of mouldy eggs stored in her room from months of uneaten breakfasts. This might explain her lack of friends outside her immediate family circle and why, at the age of 34, she remained doggedly unmarried. And of course, it would also encourage Antonio's growing attachment to her younger, more attractive and ostensibly much healthier and better adjusted sister Julia. He clearly felt real affection for the shorter plainer Evgenia, and a lingering bond from their months together at the sanatorium. They were near-contemporaries in age and experience, and had much in common in temperament and outlook. There had been occasions at the sanatorium when they had played together with the innocence of children. For example, he took her for rides around the grounds in a Sardinian-style cart or buggy he had bashed together out of some old pram wheels and planks of wood. One of Gramsci's final notes to Evgenia Schucht at Serebranyi Bor, sent through the Comintern post early in 1923, told her: 'We'll soon have you jumping over streams!' At the very end of the letter, before the customary 'tender embrace' with which he concluded all his written communications to the females in his life, he reassured her 'you mean so much to me'.[2]

Gramsci had other personal worries that winter and spring of 1923. His older brother Gennaro was beaten up and seriously wounded by the Fascists in Turin, losing a finger and a lot of blood. Eighteen other comrades were murdered in the city on the same day, including workers Antonio knew from the car factories. The Fascists also shut down *L'Ordine Nuovo* and charged the staff with subversion and possession of arms and explosives, without proof or evidence. It briefly caused uproar in Italy, but for Antonio the most personally disturbing aspect of the incident was that the Fascists attacked Gennaro because they mistook him for Antonio, his younger brother. There was another unsettling story circulating in Antonio's absence, that Gennaro had been drawing his brother's salary from the party account all these months he'd been at the sanatorium and in Moscow. Antonio was less bothered about the money than the dishonesty. For his part, Gennaro seemed to be blaming Antonio for the beating. All in all, this was another unpleasant turn in the brothers' frequently strained relationship. Elsewhere Antonio described 'Nannaro (as) a strange character. He was a sergeant-major in the 21st Sappers at Monterosso, Montenero and Caporetto. As a miner underground, with only a thin partition separating his tunnel from the Austrian one, he could hear the enemy trying to set off a mine to blow him to pieces', and how he came back from the war even more cold and irascible than before.[3] It's easy to see how such a man might have resented the consequences for himself of his little brother's political notoriety. Ironically, Antonio heard years later that their younger brother Mario, the Fascist big shot in Varese, had been beaten up by communists at around the same time.

Things were no better on the political front. The joint committee that had been established at the Comintern Congress in November to promote fusion with the *Terzini* socialists was threatening to fall apart, with Bordiga refusing to have anything to do with it and everyone else struggling to attend meetings either in Italy, where they risked arrest, or abroad, from where they might not be allowed back into the country. *Ispolcom* was seriously concerned about the worsening situation, calling meetings repeatedly, at the most unlikely hours, which Gramsci struggled to get to. Much of the *PCd'I* leadership were arrested, including Bordiga, on 3 February 1923. A warrant for Gramsci's own arrest had been issued in January, which meant that, for the time being, he would not be able to return to Italy. There had been no hard news sent to Moscow for many weeks about what exactly was happening. There was just one letter (attributed by Hoare to Umberto Terracini), which simply said that everything was destroyed, that the party leadership would have to be reconstituted '*ab imis*' (from the bottom up), and (according to Gramsci) 'created the impression that the party only continued to exist in (the author's) person'.[4] When *Ispolcom* sought Gramsci's opinion about what to do about the *PCd'I* leadership's failure to plan for such an eventuality, he was embarrassed by his lack of hard information. All he could think of was effectively dissolving the party and somehow reconstituting it from outside.

He further suspected that the Russians – 'less centralist than it seems', and always inclined towards manoeuvres of their own – knew more about it all than he did. *Ispolcom* sought further information from Italy and received a reply from 'Tito' (Bruno Fortichiari, a close ally of Bordiga, who had been put in charge of the party's underground activity) that 'the party's internal apparatus had remained completely intact'. It was hard to know who to believe, Terracini and whatever remained of the established leadership, or 'Tito' who (for Gramsci) represented a subordinate and only partially controlled activity, and who could unless known personally be taken for just some confidence-trickster. 'Tito' was summoned to Moscow, clearly furious that his own account had been disputed, to be made aware of Terracini's much more gloomy assessment. 'It then became clear', according to Gramsci, 'that the two centres (the recognised leadership and the underground network) operated entirely independently … defaming and discrediting each other'. The discrepancy in the reports was never properly cleared up, further organizational muddles came to light, and from the outside the party looked like an embarrassing shambles. The substantive issues – especially relations with the Socialists – went unresolved, and (Gramsci recalled) at times the arguments turned into actual brawls or scuffles. While ostensibly at the centre of things, he must have felt his own political isolation ever more acutely.

In the middle months of 1923 Antonio Gramsci set about consciously and doggedly courting Julia 'Julka' Schucht. He had just turned 32, no longer a young man; ready at last, he might have concluded, for a serious romantic attachment. Julia responded; not eagerly – this would not have suited her natural reticence – but willingly. He continued visiting her at Ivanovo Voznesensk, and on a number of occasions she came to see him in Moscow. With her an active and committed Bolshevik, their conversations would have been about the political issues of the day as well as personal matters. Julia's work at the NKVD may well have furnished more immediately and locally sensitive topics. At around this time, Gramsci was trying to protect an old anarchist friend from Turin who had ended up in the hands of the Soviet secret police. There was little Gramsci could do to get the old fellow off the charges of subversion, which he cheerfully admitted, but he might just manage to get the sentence commuted from summary execution to expulsion from the country. They would just as surely have discussed developments in the Schucht family. Evgenia was having some difficulty adjusting to life outside the sanatorium. She had refused to look for work, despite her previous substantial school teaching experience and extensive qualifications, and spent much of the day in her room with her popular novels and her embroidery or even, as far as anyone could tell, simply asleep. Anna Schucht had moved with her husband Theodore Zabel into lodgings of their own, which gave the family more space, but Julia may well have begun missing her nearest sister and musical partner.

During the summer Julia began to stay overnight with Antonio at the Hotel Lux. Graziadei had returned to Italy in the winter, and been replaced as a room-mate by Egidio Gennari, a respected organizer and much less of a character, who presumably made arrangements to stay elsewhere when necessary. Antonio later recalled in a letter to Julia, with some amusement, how hard he worked to make the room clean and tidy and congenial. After that they spent as many nights and (work permitting) afternoons together as they could, stealing time from the revolution. He wrote to her 'I'm not sure yet if I can come on Sunday. They are chasing me hard for a report on our trade union strategy, but I will try to tear myself away. I must, I absolutely must have you go on loving me.'[5] Another time a telegram came from Italy, warning him that a further warrant had been issued for his arrest and advising him not to return home. The messengers went with it to the Lux early in the morning. He was not there, and none of the other Italians had any idea where he might be; he had left no word. They went the rounds of Moscow by car, but could find no trace of him. Now deeply worried by his disappearance, fearing kidnap or worse, they called in the secret police to help. When Gramsci finally turned up at the Lux, having spent the night with Julia at Ivanovo, he was greeted like someone who had returned from the dead.

In a later letter, he asked her, 'Did you come to Moscow on 5th August as you told me you would? I waited three days for you. I didn't dare leave the room for fear of missing you like that other time … You didn't come to Moscow, did you? You would certainly have come to see me, at least for a few moments … Will you come soon? When can I see you again? Write to me. Everything you say to me does me good and makes me feel stronger.'[6] There was in this note a tone of urgency, a neediness bordering on desperation, with an unmistakeable undertow of rebuke. It would have given Julia some pause for thought, before she wrote back that political work and violin practice for a forthcoming recital had kept her in Ivanovo. She apologized for not letting him know earlier, but this cancelled visit had only been a vague arrangement. This interchange offered a premonition of the tone of much of their later correspondence, only slightly softened by the outcry of romantic yearning. Very much later, in very different circumstances, he would write to her that he'd been going over it all again in his mind, over all the memories of their life together, from that first day he saw her at Serebranyi Bor and didn't dare go into the room because he felt so timid – 'Yes, you made me feel timid, and today I smile as I remember it' – until the day she went away on foot and he went with her as far as the main road through the forest, 'and stood motionless there for so long watching you grow smaller and smaller down that road, carrying a bundle across your shoulders on your way back to the great and terrible world outside. Then those few blissful months in Moscow, when we finally gave in to ourselves and each other.'[7]

The experience of falling in love for this first (and, as far as we know, only) time had a profound effect on Antonio Gramsci, and it would haunt him for the rest of his life. He had never felt like this before in any of his dealings with other human beings. As he wrote to Julia, she had given him the greatest, most beautiful, most powerful reason in the world to go on living. He felt a wide-eyed joy he had not known since his early childhood, before his father's imprisonment and his family's disgrace, running around the hills near Ghilarza with playmates or communing with his latest tame bird or furry animal. He discerned in his own *weltanschaung* a sense of the future which almost amounted to reasoned optimism, a temperamental luxury he had never previously dared to allow himself. But over all of this there would be a shadow: a sense of personal vulnerability, projected onto Julia in fits of protective altruism, so that he worried for her too. Falling in love was a dangerous business for everyone involved. He was not only exposing himself to the risk of being hurt, but exposing another person he cared for deeply to his own tendency – all too manifest in his everyday dealings with comrades – to coldness, callousness and even cruelty. The witty remark, rewarded by a hearty round of laughter, could so easily topple over into barbed insult, sharp intakes of breath and uncomfortable silences, and for those on the receiving end wounded pride and hurt feelings. This was what Piero Gobetti had called Gramsci's tone of irony turning in no time to a blowpipe of lethal sarcasm in his early profile.

Gramsci clearly found the simple everyday uncertainties of love very difficult to cope with. Did this other person feel the same, and to the same extent? How could they possibly know, or communicate something so ethereal? After a life of study and action, he was bewildered by the chaos of his own feelings. He often likened himself, especially during still frequent bouts of illness and exhaustion, to a bear with a sore head, retreating with a scowl and a growl into its hole in the mountain. Well, this old bear had been well and truly enticed out of its cave and into the bright open sunlight of the plains. What would it do now? It bothered him deeply that he had not the faintest idea. Yet he knew that the cave bear would find it very hard to go back up the hill and into the darkness. Now that he had found love, he simply had to go through with it, as much for political as personal reasons. Was it possible to love a collective mass when one has not been deeply loved oneself by individual human creatures? Hadn't this had some effect on his life as a militant? Had it not tended to make him sterile and reduce his quality as a revolutionary by making everything a matter of pure intellect, of mere mathematical calculation? One cannot divide oneself into fragments and make only one part function. Life is a whole, and each activity is strengthened by all the others. Love fortifies the whole of one's existence. It creates a new equilibrium, and intensifies all other feelings and sensations.

On 21 September 1923, the reconstituted *PCd'I* executive, surprised by the police in a worker's house on the outskirts of Milan, was arrested *en bloc*. They were accused of conspiracy against the state, and though they were eventually acquitted on the basis of inconsistencies in the evidence presented by the still fledgling Fascist legal apparatus, would spend three months in prison. This would further disrupt the small party's fragile networks and communications. The old leadership around Bordiga was also separately on trial during this period, though they too would be acquitted on 26 October. The acquittals were all achieved on judicial technicalities, and were not received with any great political triumphalism. Everyone knew that these were just opening salvoes in what was beginning to look like a remorseless and very one-sided civil war. The Fascists would drag their opponents back to court as soon as they had brought the law sufficiently in line to make their vague charges of subversion stick. The *Ispolcom* decided that Gramsci should move to Vienna, as near to Italy as he could safely go without risking his own arrest under the warrants issued earlier in the year. From there he would coordinate the party's faltering domestic operations and attempt to rebuild its shattered infrastructure. He would leave Moscow as soon as the necessary transit arrangements were made. Train tickets and a passport were procured by the OMS office, along with a residence permit which his old Italian Socialist comrade Angelica Balabanova undertook to organize in Vienna.

Antonio and Julia were married on 23 September in a simple ceremony at the Moscow Registry Office. It would have been, in the manner of the brisk new morality of the proletarian state, hardly a ceremony at all, simply a formal public recognition of their private relationship, with no obligation to each other or anyone else beyond what they chose to offer freely. They paid over a small fee at the cashier's kiosk at the entrance to the building. The certificate they received in return from the smiling registrar might look impressive, with its stamps and state letterhead and flourishes of signature, but really it carried no more weight than any of the other paper documents dished out by the offices of the new dispensation in an attempt to convince the world that the revolution was permanent.[8] Julia came to live with Antonio at Hotel Lux. She kept her job, but was allowed to reduce her hours and responsibilities in the light of her new status. They moved to a new room reserved for married couples, and set about establishing the daily routines of an established relationship. They would rise in the lifting darkness at 7 am. She would prepare breakfast while he collected the newspapers and any mail from the hotel reception. When he left for work at the Comintern, she would tidy and clean the room, then herself leave for work. When he came home, often late into the evening after a day of meetings and report writing, he would find her reading or darning by candlelight, or simply sitting in her chair and welcoming him home with her beautiful smile. They prepared a meal in one of the wretched communal kitchens, and caught up with each other's news and feelings as they ate.

During this period, late 1923, the big political topic was the defeat of the German revolutionary movement. With it went the prospect of some kind of link between German industry and Russian agriculture that would break the isolation of the Soviet economy, drive a stake through the faltering heart of the capitalist system and establish a new global order of proletarian socialism. The Comintern and the *Kommunistische Partei Deutschlands* had set the date of insurrection for 25 October, the sixth anniversary of the Bolshevik takeover of Petrograd (actually it wasn't; they neglected the two-week difference between the Russian and Western calendars), as if they could make an appointment with history. It turned out to be a complete fiasco, called off at the last minute because they knew they didn't have enough arms and men to defeat the army and topple the Social Democratic government of the early Weimar Republic. Except in Hamburg, that is, which failed to receive the order to abort the revolution in time. Three hundred poorly armed communists took over the city centre, but were easily defeated by the army and the reactionary nationalist *Freikorps* militia. Elsewhere in Germany there was just a vague sense of atypical disorder and indiscipline, which was as much to do with economic collapse and hyperinflation as any serious prospect of revolution. People scoffed in the Comintern corridors and canteens about how German workers would form an orderly queue to take power, and insist that any breakages be paid for. A story circulated about the looting of a shoe shop in a working-class district of Berlin, where people had emerged empty-handed if they couldn't find anything in their own size.[9] Law and order were quickly and easily restored, and the German economy soon for the moment restabilized. Shortly before Gramsci left Julia for Vienna, the couple conceived their first child. He wrote to his mother in Sardinia: 'My companion shares my ideas completely; she isn't Italian, but she lived for a long time in Italy and studied in Rome. She is courageous and has a strong character. You will all like and appreciate her when you get to know her. Next summer or autumn I hope to come with her to Sardinia for a few days, and introduce you all to her.'[10]

Chapter 10

A VIENNESE INTERLUDE

Antonio Gramsci left Moscow at the end of November 1923. He had been in Russia for a year and a half, played a small but significant part in the affairs of the Communist International and a rather larger one in the *Partito Communista d'Italia*, grown a moustache then shaved it off, met and married his wife, lived with her for nearly two months in relative comfort and privacy at Hotel Lux, conceived their first child (without as yet knowing it), learnt to read and converse and write rudimentarily in Russian and grew in personality and confidence more than during any comparable period of his life. But if he resented being parted from his wife and her puzzling family, and from the other emotional and personal attachments he had formed in Russia, he did not let it show. It was commonly understood and accepted that such personal sacrifice was necessary, for the greater cause of proletarian revolution and international socialism.

After a complicated five-day rail journey, multiple changes of trains with either a few frantic seconds or long idle hours to spare, and several fraught border crossings, Gramsci arrived in Vienna on 3 December. The city was recovering from its own post-war privations, under the stern control of the Austrian Social Democratic Party, much more steadily than NEP-era Moscow or, to the north-west, the early Weimar Republic of hyper-inflation and Versailles treaty reparations. Everywhere he looked Gramsci would have seen solid blocks of workers' flats being built by the Red Vienna city council for their million proletarian supporters. These pioneers of municipal socialism, with its complex moral economy of favour and obligation, negotiation and compromise, could mobilize instant demonstrations of 50,000 solid citizens, dressed in sportswear and surreptitiously armed, to deter opposition and force through some new welfare measure. In more celebratory mood, they organized parades of thousands of cyclists in formation pushing bicycles meticulously garlanded with flowers. The Social Democrats even produced a comic newspaper, *Lachen Links* ('Left-wing Laughs'), full of party-approved jokes for the masses. Teams of council workers toured the city in shiny new vans removing abandoned refuse, stray dogs and neglected children. Here, it seemed, history was still plainly progressing, albeit more languidly and complacently than elsewhere. There was a gaiety in the cafés and streets that seemed quite unforced.

Gramsci stayed a few days with Josef Frei, the General Secretary of the Austrian Communist Party, then took up longer-term residence in a scruffy suburb, in an unheated barely furnished room sublet by an unfriendly Catholic *hausfrau*. She was forever complaining that her communist husband was making her keep a Godless foreigner under her roof, and that surely the *polizei* were on their way right now to arrest them all. After a lifetime of sheets and blankets, it was Antonio's first encounter with a duvet, which (he wrote to Julia) 'keeps slipping off in every direction, so that I'm always waking up with either a foot or a shoulder frozen stiff'.[1] His only immediate colleague in Vienna was his secretary Mario Codevilla, a dim tubercular Italian whose conversation consisted solely of small talk. Codevilla was constantly clearing his throat and tapping his fingernails one after the other on any available hard surface. They spent much of their time together composing letters to Moscow or Rome, 'So many letters! I'm writing at least half a dozen a day. I've never written so many letters in my life as in these last few days!' Gramsci wrote to Julia. Most of them sought or offered explanations of the muddled situation inside the *PCd'I*, still struggling to establish a meaningful presence in Italy in conditions of semi-legality. He also wrote articles for *Inprecor* on the situation; 'They suggested I use a pseudonym, though I'm not at all sure why. At least I got to choose my own mangled version of my name, which no one else has yet come up with. I'm now called, for *Correspondence Internationale* purposes, G. Masci!'

The small circle of émigrés and subversives Angelica Balabanova introduced him to offered little by way of open honest social contact. According to the one person Gramsci became at all close to in Vienna, Victor Serge, they all seemed to be running away from something, and always on the lookout for whoever or whatever might be following them. In some cases, marked out by a rather less haunted look, they were following someone else. This alone, Serge observed, revealed much about the present state of the international revolutionary movement. Conversations were conducted in whispers and codes, with one eye over your shoulder and another over your partner's. Introductions were always draped in suspicion, and arrangements to meet again necessarily provisional because 'you never know ...' People went to extraordinarily elaborate lengths to devise signals – a folded or unfolded newspaper, a tug on a right or left earlobe – to indicate that they were or were not being followed or watched.[2]

To Serge, and by implication Gramsci, it all seemed faintly preposterous, especially when compared to the real conditions of violent repression in Italy or social upheaval in Russia. It wasn't so much a requirement of the current political conditions of stolid if brittle parliamentary democracy across most of Western Europe, as a leftover from the tangled undergrowth of pre-revolutionary conspiracy and repression. All these subterfuges really had no place in the brave new world of socialist reconstruction and developing proletarian hegemony. Of course there was a need for care and trust, but there were also heavy doses of preening self-importance and nostalgia for simpler times and polarities in all the furtive nudging and winking and whispering and signalling. These revolutionary class warriors were much more comfortable, it seemed, in permanent revolutionary discomfort. People would somehow appear as if out of thin air, in cafés or apartments or meetings, and then just as mysteriously disappear, never to be seen again. Everyone else would then spend weeks and months trying to figure out whether they were police spies or secret agents – and if so which branch or agency they had been working for, one of a bewildering array of acronyms and abbreviations – when in most cases they almost certainly weren't. They were probably just dissolutes or dilettantes or displaced bohemians or congenital conspirators and lifelong intriguers, people who spent their days attaching themselves to one vaguely interesting cause after another in the absence of anything better to do.

Much of the conspiracy and intrigue in Red Vienna emanated from the ancient intractable enmities of the Balkans, all those broken countries of craggy mountains and fertile valleys to the sun-seared south, for which the Austrian capitol had been an imperial centre and now provided a point of access to the sympathies, attentions and resources of Western Europe. Outsiders like Serge or Gramsci might seek explanations in the cafés and meeting rooms of just what the latest feud, assassination or bomb plot was actually about, only to find their heads spinning within minutes from the torrent of accusations of betrayal, corruption and genocide by one ethnic or political group against another. They were basically a set of tribes, dignified by grand ideals and organizational networks, each with their own growing band of heroic martyrs and alleged traitors, busily filling up their calendars with macabre anniversaries and holy days. Their customs and codes were interesting in their own right, from a strictly anthropological perspective, but (according to the self-confessed cynic Serge) of no great historical or political importance.

The atmosphere in émigré Vienna was further poisoned by news of the constant factional turmoil back in Russia, where it really did count for something. It was getting worse with Lenin's illness and decline, which threatened what Gramsci called (in a letter to Togliatti, Terracini and others) the delicate 'topography of tendencies, with Radek, Trotsky and Bukharin occupying a left position, Zinoviev, Kamenev and Stalin a right position, and Lenin in the centre acting as arbiter'.[3] Gramsci's sponsor Angelica Balabanova herself was under a cloud, having fallen out with Lenin and Zinoviev and been expelled from the Comintern, which she had briefly served as its first Secretary in 1919. That's how she'd ended up in Vienna, unwelcome either in Moscow or in Italy where she had spent most of her earlier life in the glory years of the *PSI*. Even here in Vienna, according to Serge, she seemed incapable of settling anywhere. She was constantly moving from one small furnished room to another with her only personal possessions: a spirit-stove for tea, a small pan for omelettes, three cups for her guests and several huge and ferocious portraits of the famous old Italian maximalist Socialists she had learnt her politics from in the last decades of the nineteenth century. In that earlier, pre-revolutionary period she had reportedly introduced the rising star of Italian Socialism Benito Mussolini to Lenin, who was duly impressed. She had been Mussolini's assistant during his brief, tumultuous editorship of *Avanti!*, and rumoured to be his mistress, though she would later deride him as a false revolutionary, driven 'by egotism and a thirst for personal revenge'.[4]

Victor Serge is the central figure in the only surviving photograph of Antonio Gramsci in Vienna. Serge is holding an unidentified child, who is not much smaller than Gramsci (or Serge, who was also a small man), and both are grinning broadly.

Gramsci took great care to refer to Serge in his conversations and correspondence only as 'a/the Frenchman', because Serge was already under suspicion of oppositionism among the Comintern majority. He was an extraordinary character, an almost exact contemporary of Gramsci's, and seemed to have already packed several whole lifetimes into his thirty-three years. He had been, successively, the child of displaced Russian revolutionary intellectuals, a juvenile delinquent in Brussels, an anarchist convict in Paris, a trade union militant in Barcelona and an active participant in the first, harshest but purest years of the Soviet Revolution. Because of his skills and experience he was made a senior official in the Comintern, working directly for its President Zinoviev (whom he quickly came to loathe), despite never actually being a member of the Bolshevik Party. Most recently, Serge had been dispatched to support the various failing revolutionary causes around Western Europe, in Berlin, then Prague and finally here in Vienna. He had only accepted the posting because it got him out of Moscow. He was thoroughly disillusioned, horrified by the descent of the Soviet state bureaucracy and security apparatus into what he was already calling unaccountable and coldly vicious totalitarianism. He had spent most of the previous two or three years trying to save friends and comrades from arrest, imprisonment or execution by the thugs and heresy-hunters of what he still referred to as the Cheka, the old immediately post-revolutionary name for the Soviet secret police, some of whom had simply switched allegiance from the Tsar to the Bolsheviks. Serge said he understood and accepted the need to eliminate the enemies of the revolution. The problem was that the Bolsheviks had lost any clear sense of who *were* their enemies, and by corollary their friends. They now had all the hallmarks of an exclusive, contemptuous elite.

Serge retained a profound sympathy, respect and admiration for their leaders – Lenin and Trotsky in particular – but saw clearly the historical contradictions overwhelming their best intentions, and bringing out their autocratic tendencies at the expense of their democratic ones. Serge now believed that much of this degeneration was inherent in the Bolshevik model of organization that Lenin above anyone – 'proud of what he has destroyed, not so proud of what he has created' – had brought about.[5] Lenin stressed that the dictatorship of the proletariat was a truly ruthless dictatorship and at the same time the broadest possible workers' democracy. Serge drew a telling parallel with one of those proletarian revolutionaries, spouting workers' power to the workers in the factory then going home to beat his wife, a democrat in the workplace and a dictator at home. Lenin had old friends and comrades jailed or dismissed because they confronted him with embarrassing objections. Even while proclaiming the restored economic liberties of NEP, he continued to deprive his critics of their political and personal freedom. The revolution remained the only hope for mankind – under the leadership of 'our sick Party; sick, but what else on earth is there?' – and for the uncountable millions ground into dust by capitalist profiteering and imperialist warmongering. But it was exacting a very heavy price for historical progress, not least in the honesty and integrity of its leaders. 'If you keep trying to face all ways, you just end up spinning around in circles and getting dizzy.' It took incredible fortitude and intelligence, which only one or two truly possess, to keep your eye on the main prize in the distant future. Once Lenin, already 'a shadow of his former self', had gone, the party unity that only he could maintain would shatter.

When the great man finally died in mid of January 1924, Serge noted the quarter of a million workers who were enrolled at one stroke into the Russian Communist Party on the day after his death. How much were these proletarians worth, he wondered, if they had to wait for the death of Vladimir Ilyich before coming to the Party? Further, Serge argued, these were uneducated, inexperienced, completely uncultivated people, ignorant of the ways of the world, of Marxist philosophy and Leninist political practice. Their communism was just another religion to replace the Orthodoxy of the Tsarist autocracy, or worse, a simple career move. Their dull dead weight would swing the balance of power inside the party firmly towards the bureaucrats and careerists and opportunists in the leadership. Serge's misgivings were deepened by the farce over the embalming and interment of Lenin's corpse, 'an outrage to any self-respecting historical materialist, surely including Lenin himself'. It was only done to placate the backward masses who had travelled in their millions to Moscow to view the body of this new saint in its coffin in the Kremlin, and kept on coming even after the end of the official state period of mourning. Lenin himself had apparently left no clear instructions. Allowing this absurd sanctification to happen, and not specifying a simple burial in the family plot, was 'the final oversight of an ailing and overstretched leader'.

Gramsci until this point was a relatively loyal and orthodox communist. He would have been troubled by Serge's revelations and insights into what was really going on in Russia and the higher echelons of the Bolshevik Party. They would have served to undermine his own previous convictions and hasten his disillusionment, while at the same time delineating and reinforcing some of the doubts he had begun to feel in Moscow. But Serge was famously good company, very well-read and connected, with a wealth of anecdotes and encounters to relate from his revolutionary career. He was already writing and publishing stories, and beginning work on the series of novels which would make his name and reputation. Serge later described Gramsci himself, with the *élan* of the novelist (and, it must be said, a readiness to embellish the literal truth), as

> an industrious and exotic exile, late to bed and late to rise … His head was heavy, his brow high and broad, his lips thin; the whole was carried on a puny, square-shouldered, weak-chested, hump-backed body. There was grace in the movement of his fine, long-fingered hands. Gramsci fitted awkwardly into the humdrum of day-to-day existence, losing his way at night in familiar streets, taking the wrong train, indifferent to the comfort of his lodgings and the quality of his meals.[6]

In fact Gramsci left his lodgings with the Catholic *hausfrau* as soon as he practically could, but not before receiving a harsh lesson in Austrian anti-Semitism and (from 'the Frenchman') some judicious advice on how to deal with it. A comrade from the Soviet embassy who had heard Gramsci was moving asked him to reserve the room for his wife. The pinch-faced landlady agreed, but wanted to know if the new tenant was Jewish: 'I don't let to Jews.' The Soviet diplomat's wife was in fact a Ukrainian Jewess. Gramsci asked Victor Serge what to do. There was only one solution: 'to tell the old woman you couldn't decently ask the new tenant if she was Jewish, but that you know she's a secretary in one of the embassies.' Serge explained that the Austrian petty bourgeoisie might hate Jews, but they worship the Diplomatic Corps far more. Sure enough, the landlady replied, 'Of course she can have the room. I know you can't go asking Embassy people if they're Jews or not.'[7]

Gramsci really didn't take to Vienna, which (he wrote to Julia) seemed very sad and depressing compared to Moscow. There were no sleighs jingling cheerfully along the white streets, only the dreary rattle of street cars ploughing through slush. He spent most of his spare time alone, reading or composing long love letters to his wife. He felt their separation keenly, and a deep sense of loss after their two short months of living together in Moscow. He begged her to come and join him, even though it would mean giving up 'the interesting, active life going on around you. I am too much alone … it's like living in mid-air. I think constantly and with infinite longing of the times we spent together, so close and giving endlessly of ourselves. I can almost feel your cheek against mine, and my hand caressing your head, telling you how much I love you even while my lips are silent.'[8]

In late February 1924 Julia informed him in her latest letter from Russia, unceremoniously and almost in passing, that she was twelve weeks pregnant. He responded that he was overcome with desire to hold her in his arms and feel for himself the new life uniting their two lives even closer than before. But the subsequent letters he received from Moscow, where Julia was back living with her parents and Evgenia in an apartment near Hotel Lux on Tverskaya Street, were not encouraging. The middle months of her pregnancy were difficult, and on several occasions she feared she had lost the baby. Weeks went by without any communication, until a terse note from Apollon or Evgenia informed Antonio that Julia had been unwell in some unspecified way, and implied (in a foretaste of later correspondence between the older Schuchts and Gramsci) that his written bombardment wasn't helping. He could feel Julia – the beautiful, fragile, brittle young woman only he had come close to reaching – drifting away from him again. When she was well enough to write to him herself, her letters took on a curiously dissociated tone, as though she was mechanically recording some formula she had picked up elsewhere. They were dull and dutiful, with very little detail or intimate disclosure or sincere endearment, always indicative of low spirits and growing distance. She also took to signing off as Julia, something she had never done in their previous correspondence, where at least since their very early contact she had referred to herself (and encouraged him to) as Julka. In general, her explanation for not joining him in Vienna was that she could not leave her family. But again there was no specific explanation, beyond some vague sense of daughterly duty. The clear implication was that only they could be trusted to look after her properly and that he couldn't. He might have understood better if she had argued that her pregnancy would make the long arduous journey from northern to southern Europe even more difficult than it would be otherwise, but she didn't. She made no reference whatsoever to the fact that she was carrying his child.

He picked up on her depression, and began to argue that living with him would lift it. He'd find lots of ingenious ways to cheer her up and make her smile again: making cork clocks, papier-mâché fiddles and wax lizards with two tails; his full repertoire of Sardinian folklore. He'd tell her stories of his wild and woolly childhood, so different from her own, each tale more fantastic than the last. He had hoped that her pregnancy would lend her strength, and help her overcome the crisis which he'd long felt was latent inside her, and all bound up with her past, her childhood and her whole intellectual development. 'During that brief period when we were utterly happy, I did think very definitely that our happiness would be completed if you were to have a child, but after you told me you were expecting you have said no more about it.'[9] In the meantime, he felt no cheerier about his posting. Vienna in 1923–4, long after its *fin-de-siècle* heyday as the vanguard of modern European civilization, might sit comfortably in its middle-aged social democracy, but there was a very definite sense of trouble brewing in the surrounding hills and countryside. It had been the capital of an empire of fifteen nationalities. As it crumbled and dissolved in the ruthless contest of European imperialisms and the internecine squabbles of the Hapsburgs, the capital city had enjoyed its final heyday, as a bubbling melting pot for all their cultural elites. In the last days of the nineteenth century and first of the twentieth, all the experiments and innovations that would come to define modernity and modernism had emerged here first. But by the 1920s, the Vienna of Klimt and Schoenberg, Mahler and Freud, Hoffman and Schiele had been shattered and scattered.

It may not have made a particularly congenial place of residence for Gramsci, but it offered a perfect vantage point from which to observe the ebbing of the international proletarian revolutionary tide, if not (at least for Gramsci) to do much about it. The news from Russia was vague but always disturbing, especially when filtered through the jaundiced accounts of willing or not so willing exiles like Serge and Balabanova. Lenin had been shot and seriously wounded in 1918, paralysed in 1922, struck dumb in 1923, and died soon after on 21 January 1924. Over those four years, his previously unwavering revolutionary determination had been tossed this way and that by the vicissitudes of the young Soviet state and the desperate struggle for its survival. As Gramsci wrote ruefully in a letter to the party in Italy just a couple of weeks after Lenin's death, 'The Statutes of the International give the Russian party *de facto* hegemony over the world organization.'[10] Comintern strategy under Lenin's faltering leadership altered almost by the week, and left its weaker components – most obviously but not only the Italians – struggling for clarity and direction. Even Lenin's final serious political act, the famous testament which amongst other things presciently warned the party about Stalin and Trotsky's weaknesses and ambitions, had been suppressed and denied any immediate impact. Now the great man was dead, the other leading Bolsheviks – Trotsky, Stalin, Zinoviev, Radek, Kamenev, Bukharin et al. – were fighting bitter, outwardly incomprehensible and endlessly shifting factional struggles over his legacy and who should succeed him. From a distance Gramsci found it all bewildering, and confessed to feeling misled by his ignorance. He wrote an editorial obituary for Lenin in the relaunched and refashioned

L'Ordine Nuovo, headed *Capo* ('Leader').[11] It was followed a fortnight later by an editorial headed *Contro il Pessimismo*, arguing against the mood he himself was beginning to feel overwhelmed by, and pleading for calmer and more congenial dealings amongst the Soviet comrades.[12]

There was a venom in it all he just could not begin to comprehend, and which friends like Serge could not begin to explain in anything other than metaphysical or even mystical terms. It all came down, apparently, to thoroughly un-Marxist intangibles like the 'Russian soul' or the necessary blood-letting of revolutionary upheaval. They all seemed to find their historical reference-points in the French Revolution, with its Jacobin terrors and Thermidor purges. There were endless discussions about who might be the Russian Robespierre or Danton or Bonaparte, as if history was a piece of theatre that was simply re-staged every hundred years or so, with the same plot and cast of characters updated for a new century. There was a lack of historical specificity in these discussions which Gramsci would have found deeply frustrating, in his own words 'hellishly complicated'.[13] Whatever was going on, it threatened to consume them all in biblical-scale catastrophe. If the Bolsheviks were set on destroying each other, why did their capitalist enemies abroad or even at home need to bother? They simply had to bide their time while the revolution tore itself apart.

The quite separate factional battle inside the tiny, shattered Italian Communist Party continued to rage, a blurred miniature compared to the angular iron monument of Soviet Bolshevism. The majority group in the Italian leadership, loyal to the imprisoned Bordiga, were still refusing fusion with the Socialists, 'accepting the decisions of the International formally, then beginning factional activity designed to draw from these decisions the greatest possible advantage for our group', as a secret factional memorandum of 12 July 1923 put it.[14] Gramsci was not involved in this latest formation of Bordiga's leading group, which was designed to evade the strictures of the Comintern majority. In this poisonous atmosphere, each wing of the party was intercepting and publishing letters and documents which exposed their opponents' subterfuges and deviations. Bordiga proposed from prison that the *PCd'I* should split from the Communist International altogether. When the round-robin reached Gramsci, he (alone of the non-right wingers) refused to sign it, as much because of its sectarian tone as its inevitably destructive consequences. His principled stance didn't do much good, but simply served to illustrate and deepen his political and personal marginality inside the *PCd'I*.

Bordiga remained the party's dominant personality, 'stubborn and inflexible to the point of absurdity', as Gramsci put it in a letter to Alfonso Leonetti, at that point his only close comrade inside the leadership.[15] All Gramsci's inquiries and surveys indicated that Bordiga retained overwhelming support in what remained of the party inside Italy, with 'the sectarian and one-sided spirit proper to Italians'. A large majority of local and regional officials and activists was still attracted and swayed by Amadeo's incendiary rhetoric and calls for immediate insurrection, even though anyone with any sense could see this would mean the final and total destruction of the party. Meanwhile, the right of the party were ever more determined to engineer fusion with the Socialists on any terms, and active collaboration with any other anti-fascists to restore constitutional norms to Italian government. All Gramsci could propose in order to resolve the conflict was 'a clear, frank argument which goes right to the bottom of things'. It must have sounded inadequate as he wrote it, and pathetic when he received his own copy of the memorandum. He wrote to Togliatti on 27 January 1924, 'I will not hide from you that in these two years I have spent out of Italy, I have become very pessimistic and wary.'[16] He resisted Leonetti's suggestion to reconvene the old *L'Ordine Nuovo* group from Turin as the core of a new leadership, because 'it would only look like a clique reassembled around my own person for bureaucratic reasons … It would all end in personal feuds over the right of inheritance to a legacy of mere memories and words.'[17] What's more, as if to confirm his view that '*ON*'s basic ideas are anachronistic', he had received no response to his many requests for articles for the latest edition. To Mauro Scoccimaro he wrote, 'The main force which holds the party together is the prestige and ideals of the International, not the bonds which the specific action of the (Italian) party has forged.' Faced with the lack of practical unity, amongst and between party members in exile and at home, and between leaders and members, he confessed, 'I do not know yet exactly what to do … Probably I shall remain alone.'[18]

Nonetheless, he worked hard to bring the party round to a position distinct from the two polar extremisms which had so far dominated the debate, mainly by correspondence, urging a united front from below of mass revolutionary action radiating out from the workplace. This was, he argued, the only strategy which promised to stop Fascism in its tracks and revive any prospect of proletarian revolution. What's more, it had the support and authority for now of the Communist International, which had declared the Bordigan stances of the Rome Congress completely inconsistent with the resolutions of its own Third Congress. Gramsci's counter-arguments demonstrated 'that we are not becoming crystallized in an attitude of permanent opposition, but know how to change our positions as the relations of forces change and the problems to be solved are posed on a different basis'.[19] Only that way could the party move beyond its difficult birth, 'and stop being nothing more than an external faction of the Socialist Party'. This process had to start with a full and proper understanding of what had happened in Russia, and what aspects of it *couldn't* be expected in Italy and the rest of Western Europe. First, 'the political conception of the Russian communists was formed on an international and not on a national terrain'. Almost all the leading Bolsheviks had spent their formative years in prison or far-away internal or external exile, and only returned to Russia once revolutionary change was already under way. Second, Russia had lacked the labour aristocracy which dominated trade unions and social democracy in Western Europe, 'the political superstructures created by the greater development of capitalism. This makes the action of the (western) masses slower and more prudent, and therefore requires of the revolutionary party a strategy and tactics altogether more complex and long-term than those which were necessary for the Bolsheviks in the period between March and November 1917'.[20]

At the same time, Gramsci was beginning to form a clearer view of what was distinctive about the Italian situation, and of the strategy required of the *PCd'I* if it was ever to transcend the Bordigan viewpoint of an international minority and approach things from the viewpoint of a national majority, suited for political action in specifically Italian circumstances. Gradually, the other party leaders were won over, or at least pacified. In the process, Gramsci wrote sardonically to Togliatti, 'I have involuntarily won a reputation as a fox of devilish cunning.'[21] A new leadership group was reconstituted around Gramsci as Party Secretary, who agreed 'to put all I can into this group. I won't be able to do all that I'd like to do, because I still go through periods of atrocious feebleness which make me fear a relapse into the kind of stupid coma I have suffered from in recent years.'[22] The party press was revived inside Italy, taking full advantage of the relatively liberal atmosphere the Fascists had sustained since coming to government in an attempt to prove their respectability and keep the bankers and industrialists on their side. On 12 February 1924 the first edition of the new *PCd'I* newspaper *L'Unita* was published in Italy, with a name suggested by Gramsci to consciously echo the great southern intellectual Salvemini's earlier publication, and by June circulation had risen to 50,000. A fortnightly *L'Ordine Nuovo*, a rather more conventional political review than in the heyday of the Turin Factory Councils, and rather more sustainable than its more recent daily version, appeared in March, soon selling 5,000.

These were real measures of revival, especially when possession of communist publications could be used as evidence in criminal proceedings or excuse for a Fascist beating. The struggle between reaction and revolution was still in the balance: History might still be got back on track, Gramsci wrote hopefully in *L'Ordine Nuovo*. On 6 April the *PCd'I* won 270,000 votes in a general election. Nineteen communist MPs were elected to the Italian parliament, including (in his absence) Gramsci representing a constituency in the Veneto region. They would be massively outnumbered by the 'national list' led by Mussolini and the Fascists, who had won a parliamentary vote to change the electoral law so that the largest single bloc would automatically gain two-thirds of the seats. This gave the National List 374 out of 535 seats, provided a constitutional veneer to the Fascist dictatorship and 'effectively guaranteed the permanence of Fascism in power'.[23] But at least Gramsci's parliamentary seat gave him immunity from arrest if he returned to Italy. Victor Serge reports a further incentive: 'When the crisis in Russia began to worsen, Gramsci did not want to be broken in the process, so he had himself sent back to Italy by his Party.'[24] Throughout this period, Antonio continued to correspond with the Schuchts, with very little direct response. To Julia he wrote on 13 April, 'Will I ever be able to stick my tongue out at you again? We're serious persons now and mustn't set a bad example to the children ... When I'd read your last letter I began to feel sure you must have arrived in Vienna, and that I would bump into you in the street ... Darling Julka, you are the whole of life to me, for I had never felt what life was until I loved you.'[25] He received no direct reply from his wife to this or any other of his subsequent letters from Vienna.

Chapter 11

LEADER BY DEFAULT

Antonio Gramsci returned to Italy on 12 May 1924, nearly two whole and very eventful years after leaving, to be met with horror stories from the time he had been away. Comrades had been murdered or savagely beaten, with that peculiarly methodical technique – force-feeding large quantities of castor oil, sometimes mixed with petrol, and kicking or beating with cudgels on the kidneys – the Fascists had taken as their own.[1] Offices, meeting rooms and printing presses had been smashed to pieces or burnt down, including most of the places in Turin where Gramsci had worked during the war and the red years afterwards. People had been forced out of their homes and families, or targeted simply because – like his own brother Gennaro – they were associated with known communists, socialists or even Liberals. All you needed was a record or even suspicion of opposition to the Fascists, and you were fair game for the *squadristi*. The worst thing was that the entire machinery of the modern state, above all the police, was being absorbed into this apparatus of terror. The *carabinieri* could be relied upon to stand idly by while the Blackshirts went about their business, or even to join in if they felt like it. There was no point complaining afterwards. Collaboration went all the way up to the highest courts, with only small isolated murmurs of misgiving. All the legal, constitutional and moral safeguards of liberal democracy and the bourgeois order, which the comrades of the Socialist and Communist Parties had been so scathing towards during their own ascendancy, but also exploited so assiduously to advance their own cause and protect their own standing and institutions, had simply been cast aside by Mussolini and his sidekicks, with an ease that surprised *Il Duce* himself. Parliament was frequently shut down for months at a time or bypassed altogether.

Gramsci's first formal duty as *PCd'I* Secretary was a clandestine party conference near Lake Como a few days after his return. He travelled there from Rome among crowds of holidaymakers and day trippers, well aware that he was almost certainly being followed, as he would be routinely for the remaining years of freedom. The conference was held outdoors for security reasons, in a lovely little valley, white with narcissi flowers. There were around sixty participants, mostly central committee members and regional leaders. Looking round at their upturned faces, some familiar but mostly not, all of them bemused and anxious and strained, Gramsci must have wondered who and what they were actually representing. Current estimates of national party membership at this time were just a few thousand, and only a handful of those – not many more than those sat in this sunlit field – were in any real sense active. What could they possibly do about the political catastrophe engulfing them and the country, this carnival of reaction? Could they even be relied upon to follow the strategic direction of himself and the newly reconstituted, Comintern-endorsed leadership? The answers to these key questions emerged during the day's debates and votes on the three motions put to the conference. The first was proposed by the new leadership around Gramsci, still known as the 'communist education' group after the study circles the original *L'Ordine Nuovo* had organized for the Turin Factory Councils. It was supported by four central committee members and three regional secretaries; seven votes in all. The second motion, from the right-wing minority calling for a broad anti-Fascist alliance and the restoration of constitutional democracy, won four votes from the central committee and six from the regional secretaries; ten votes in all. The third motion, communicated from Bordiga in prison by his solitary remaining acolyte on the central committee, called for immediate armed insurrection and transition to proletarian revolution. It won support from that one CC member and no fewer than thirty-nine local leaders; forty in all.

Gramsci would have listened to these debates with mounting concern. It was like the last five years had never happened, and these bellowing extremists had somehow been transported through time directly from the hungry, embattled streets of Turin and Milan and the tumultuous final conferences of the old Socialist Party, with the bright glow of the young Soviet Revolution on the distant horizon. They were still confident of imminent victory, and bathing in its warm seductive allure. They thought they could simply vote an insurrection into being. Nothing had been learned from the failure and isolation of the Factory Council movement, the defeat of the factory occupations by the industrial employers, the big landowners' brutal resistance to peasant land seizures and rural reform, the sectarian squabbles of all the various sects and coteries descended from the Socialist Party, and finally the inexorable rise to mass support and state power of the Fascists. During the lunch break, they retired to a large local hostelry on the southern shore of Lake Como. They pretended to be employees of a Milanese firm on a works outing, singing Fascist songs between courses – the anthem *Giovanezza*, Salvatore Gotta's paean to youth, no doubt providing a rousing finale over the *tiramisu* – and making florid bombastic speeches in honour of *Il Duce*. It was as if five years of pent-up fury and dismay were suddenly being released; catharsis through play-acting. It would help to lift morale for the battles ahead far more than all the hours of windy speeches and arm-waving posturing in the valley of the narcissi.

Gramsci had taken a room on Via Vesalio in Rome in a house occupied by a German family, the Passarges. They didn't know he was a communist MP, and he went to some lengths to avoid them finding out, trying to look and act like an ultra-serious professor. Sometimes, during the long warm evenings and summer nights, he would hear them creeping along the corridor outside his room, while he read without absorbing much, scribbled some note or reference or slept fitfully thinking of his wife and longing for some intimate human contact. After his two busy years in Moscow and Vienna, his demanding job and his brief taste of married life at Hotel Lux, he was living more like a student again. His hours became even more irregular than they always had been, and sometimes he would realize with a start that he had read or written or simply day-dreamed right through the night and that the sun was coming up on the eastern horizon over sleepy, lazy, ancient, reactionary Rome. Unlike Moscow or Vienna, the sun was taken here as a signal to slow down rather than rise up. In retrospect, there was something fundamentally serious and grown-up about the Russian and Austrian capitals. By contrast, Italy just seemed silly and childish, especially with the Fascists parading around like toy soldiers. Friends and comrades, including many of the old *L'Ordine Nuovo* crowd who now felt safer in Rome than in Turin, occasionally visited him at Via Vesalio and talked politics late into the night. He got to know the Sardinian nationalist MP Emilio Lussu, and relished the chance to talk in their shared dialect about developments on the island. As he grew concerned about disturbing or alarming the Passarges, and increasingly embarrassed at the chaotic state of his room, he would arrange to meet people at a restaurant near Termini station. Afterwards, they would stroll around the city talking or, if they felt like being entertained, go to the cinema and catch an *Americano* comedy or melodrama, including the latest, often startlingly inventive Charlie Chaplin. While the cultural life of the Italian capital had markedly declined under the dead hand of Fascist censoriousness, which made Gramsci fondly recall the mad poetic turmoil of Moscow, there were at least plenty of movies to see.

With his encouragement and practical help, *L'Ordine Nuovo* groups began to meet around the city to discuss the latest issue of the *PCd'I* fortnightly review and provide cover for more obviously political activity and organization. Members were very young, in their teens and early twenties, and hungry for information and guidance. Gramsci sensed that were beginning to look through and beyond the crude simplicities he'd encountered at Como, and attended as many and as often as he could, introducing discussions and always trying to prompt responses and other contributions. He exercised his authority as an MP and experienced militant judiciously, so as not to overawe these very much younger and less experienced comrades. They had been children before and during the war, and knew very little of the old Italy before Fascism, that unruly society of sharp political discord and ideological tumult, with widespread class warfare struggling for expression and resolution within a formally liberal-democratic, always fragile legal and constitutional order, now known disparagingly on all sides as Giolitti's *Italietta*, 'little Italy'. Gramsci tried to encourage fresh thinking about how to revive the fortunes of the workers' movement in these radically altered, reduced circumstances. It was very difficult. All these young comrades seemed capable of suggesting was more of the same. More copies of the fortnightly *L'Ordine Nuovo*, and of the *PCd'I* daily paper *L'Unita* and the new weekly *Lo Stato Operaio*, sold to more workers at more factory gates and in more workers' districts of more industrial cities. More outings to the countryside, to spread the word to more peasants. More members of the party, more discussion groups like this one, more public and street corner meetings. Shouting ever more loudly to be heard above the hubbub, rather than educating people, truly changing them and their minds.

He didn't spend much time in Parliament, even when it was in session. Against the Fascists and their 'national list' allies' massive rigged majority, there wasn't a great deal of point voting or even speaking. He and his comrades were happy to leave all that to the windy old buffoons of the Liberal Party and members of the various strands of reformist Socialism who held out some hope for some kind of constitutional resistance and restoration. Nor did they feel any obligation to their notional constituents in the far-flung corners of the Italian peninsula; at least no more than any other MPs, who might deign to return at election times, dispensing smiles and waves and (in most cases) *lire* in return for votes. Most of the communist MPs preferred to devote their limited time and energies, and their parliamentary salaries and privileges, to propaganda and organization, rather than what Gramsci routinely derided as the squalor of parliamentary life. Then came the Matteotti affair, which briefly rocked Mussolini and his friends back on their heels. Giacomo Matteotti was a moderate Socialist MP with an independent streak and a pragmatic approach which had made him a long-time natural opponent of both the flamboyant Mussolini and what Matteotti called the communist secession from the Socialist Party. He had compiled a mass of hard evidence of electoral fraud and financial misconduct by the Fascists in the recent general election, and presented it to parliament on 30 May 1924. He accused Mussolini of being ready to use force if the Fascists had failed to win at the polls. A great clamour of 'Yes! Yes!' arose from the Fascist benches. As he sat down, he remarked to fellow Socialist MPs, 'Now you can prepare my funeral oration ...' A furious Mussolini made it clear in his response that he wanted Matteotti punished for his insolence.[2]

A few days later, Matteotti was beaten and stabbed to death by a gang of *squadristi*. They were led by a certain Amerigo Dumini, who was on the payroll of Mussolini's press secretary Cesare Rossi. They dumped the body in a wood fifteen miles outside Rome, where it lay undiscovered for a further two months. The National List government was badly shaken by the furore over Matteotti's disappearance, as its non-Fascist components took fright at the public expressions of outrage at his assumed murder on Mussolini's orders. The communist daily *L'Unita* ran a full-page headline 'Down with this Government of Assassins!' At the opposite end of the traditional political spectrum, the industrialists of the great northern cities actively contemplated a restoration of the old Liberal order they had less than two years previously helped Mussolini to overthrow. They were known to be holding preliminary discussions with the old Prime Minister Giolitti. Over succeeding weeks and months, Fascism tottered, as its leaders panicked and its hangers-on deserted in droves. *L'Unita* trebled its circulation, and in many localities attempts were made to disarm the Fascists; communist motions on the crisis were passed at factory meetings. The murder of Matteotti also united all the anti-Fascist parties and groups in Parliament, who agreed to withdraw in protest. They would meet separately, and call themselves 'The Aventine Secession' after the Plebs of ancient Rome who once withdrew from the Senate to the Aventine hill outside the city. There they went about their usual business of long-winded debate and empty resolutions, with the small band of communists deriding their narrow parliamentarism.

Personal letters from Moscow were still few and far between. When Julia did write, her letters were brief and cursory, with that same mix of forced cheerfulness and banality – 'the weather here has been glorious!' – that had aroused Antonio's suspicions in Vienna. He tried to break through the formalities with his letters to her, which were full of fond reminiscences, bold declarations of love and pleas for her to join him:

> How I would love to go for a stroll with you so that we could see the beauty of Rome together … I shut myself up in my room. I seem to have become a cave bear once more! I think of you, and the sweetness of loving you, and of knowing that you are very close as well as very far away.[3]

On 18 August 1924, while Mussolini's government tottered in the wake of the Matteotti crisis, Antonio wrote to Julia about the *PCd'I*'s desperate attempts to exploit the public mood of disgust. What he did not know was that his wife had given birth eight days previously, because there had been no word from Moscow. He knew the baby was due between 8 and 15 August. As the days passed he grew more anxious, and wrote hopefully, 'Perhaps as I am writing now the child is already born and lies there beside you, where you can caress him after having suffered to bring him into the world.'[4]

Finally, after a two-week trip to Milan and Turin on party business, he arrived back in Rome on 3 September to find two letters from Julia waiting for him, dated 11 and 18 August. The baby had been born on 10 August, weighing a very healthy three-and-a-half kilos. He had, she wrote, 'a lot of brown hair, and a well-formed head with a high forehead and very blue eyes'.[5] She observed in her second letter, atypically poetically, that 'he looks as if he has been a long time in the sunlight already, like a ripe fruit still attached to its tree'. Julia had called him Lev, for 'Lion', which Gramsci in immediate and joyous reply thought a little ridiculous for 'a tiny baby without a single tooth in his head! But really I don't care what he's called; all that matters is that he is a living child, our son, and that we shall love each other more every new day because we see ourselves in him, only stronger and happier.' He asked her to share with him every phase of the baby's development. He was convinced that the day a child put his foot in his mouth was of prime importance. 'Don't fail to inform me the moment this act is accomplished, symbolising as it does official possession of the outermost limits of the national territory.'[6]

In fact, Gramsci insisted, not long after, that the child's name be changed to Delio after a beloved cousin who had died very young, the son of his Uncle Serafino, whom he had briefly tutored. As the weeks passed, other aspects of their distant liaison also proved troublesome. He found some of her descriptions of the baby somewhat odd – 'He sticks his tongue out at me to make me angry' – while she steadfastly refused to accept his practical and financial assistance, which she mocked as pretensions. He sent her some money via Comintern courier Vincenzo Bianco. It wasn't a huge amount – a small part of his now substantial earnings from journalism and parliament, which he would only otherwise have given to the party press – but he hoped it would make some improvement in Julia and the baby's material conditions. She sent it straight back with Bianco, with a short note saying she could cope perfectly well on her own. This was their first substantive disagreement, and it introduced a new and sour tone to their correspondence. 'I think of all the time we've spent away from each other, of all those aspects of your life I have been absent from,' he wrote, 'There is so little I can do for you and the child, and I would like to do something.' The grinding poverty of his own childhood had made him appreciate the value of even the smallest gifts, 'which create bonds, feelings of solidarity and affection nothing can destroy'.[7] She wrote back that these feelings of personal and family solidarity seemed to her bourgeois, especially when expressed through material objects and money. His gift was an offence to the communist principles by which they were supposed to live and raise their child. All the help she and the baby needed was available from the Soviet state. She described approvingly the Soviet maternity ward where she had lain for the statutory prescribed week while recovering from giving birth, and the children were all brought along in a big trolley before being distributed to their mothers to be fed. He replied, measuring his words carefully but perhaps not carefully enough, that this scene seemed so real to him that he was tempted to provoke her by suggesting that maybe they give a different infant to the mother each time, given that Soviet discipline is so imperfect, and scarcely likely to reign among the nurses in a children's hospital. He brought the awkward exchange to some kind of conclusion with profound regret that he had not been able to share the anxieties and joys of new parenthood with her.

Not for the first (or last) time, Gramsci threw himself into political work as a way to overcome his personal frustrations and disappointments. He tried to convince himself and his party that things were looking up. He reported to the *PCd'I* Central Committee that the Matteotti crime was definitive proof that the Fascist party would never become a normal governing party, and that Mussolini was capable only of striking picturesque poses, not of being a real statesman or dictator. He was no national figure, no Cromwell or Bolivar or Garibaldi and would go down in Italian history as a quaint phenomenon of provincial rustic folklore. Fascism was being propped up by its allies in industry and agriculture, but only as much as the rope held up a man who had just been hanged. In fact, Mussolini soon recovered his composure, and the Fascist 'revolution' its forward momentum. He conducted a purge of his more extremist aides, including those most clearly implicated in Matteotti's murder, and a reshuffle of his ministers to appease his allies and public opinion. Meanwhile, the Italian economy had begun to benefit from the upturn all across Europe that came from post-war capitalist restabilization and the general sense that the proletarian revolutionary tide had ebbed. The big industrial firms were increasing investment and production and exports, and new small companies opening up, all of them encouraged by the Fascists' harassment of the trade unions, the raising of prices and the reduction of workers' wages.

The drastic cuts in secondary school and university places which Mussolini's Education Minister Giovanni Gentile had introduced in 1923 began to bring down underemployment – with less competition for higher-grade jobs – and perhaps paradoxically, to quell disaffection amongst young people, especially the better educated. Fewer new graduates meant more and better opportunities for the older graduates who had struggled to find suitable work. It was a kind of middle-class protectionism, reversing decades of educational expansion, which Gramsci observed to his comrades brought to a grinding halt the upward social mobility through education of tens of thousands of poor, talented young people like so many of them. Along with measures to discourage internal migration from the countryside to the cities, vacuous talk of the rural soul of Italy and the emergence of something called 'super-country' in Fascist rhetoric, which flattered the peasant masses while doing nothing concrete to alleviate their poverty and ignorance, it represented a serious step backwards in the country's real economic development and long-term social progress.

In September Gramsci heard from Turin that one of his oldest and closest friends, Piero Gobetti, had been viciously beaten up, and the family home where he lived with his parents burnt down. On 12 September a Fascist deputy Armando Casalini was shot and killed in a Rome tramcar by a deranged young man, Giovanni Corvi, operating completely alone. For the Fascists this made up for Matteotti, and full-scale repression resumed and intensified. Mussolini felt confident enough to dismiss the 'vociferous nagging' of the Aventine parties.[8] In a speech to Parliament, still occupied solely by his own adoring supporters, he threatened, 'On the day they actually try to do something, on that day we shall make hay of them, and use it as litter for our camps!' Between 3 and 5 October, in front of horrified foreign tourists in Florence, the *squadristi* went on a rampage against the local opposition, leaving several dead and many injured.

Chapter 12

A BRIEF RETURN TO SARDINIA

Gramsci spent much of the autumn of 1924 rushing around Italy rallying the comrades and assessing their capabilities for practical action against Fascism and for the revolution. He was still able to travel freely but constantly aware that he was being followed and on occasions pointed out. His stature and his deformity would have made him even more conspicuous than his politics and occupation. Police surveillance became increasingly blatant. After Casalini's death it got very much worse, as the Fascists recovered their morale and motivation. They had a martyr of their own, and could pose as victims as well as victors. Gramsci felt less and less like he was being protected, as they claimed to be doing whenever he complained, and more and more like he was being watched. Apart from anything else, it made getting about much more expensive, because taking taxis rather than trams was the only way to shake off his 'tail'.

In late October he returned to Sardinia, by boat from Genova, no doubt mulling over the worsening situation on the mainland and wondering what he would find on the island on his first visit in four years. His memories and associations of the island capital Cagliari, where he had lodged with his brother Gennaro while preparing for university, were not especially fond. He was to attend the regional Party Congress to be held clandestinely in a field between the Cagliari salt pans and the village of Quartu. He spent the night on a camp bed in a lawyer's office in Cagliari, listening to the Fascist militia carousing in the street outside while they gathered for the second anniversary celebrations of the March on Rome. The next morning, a Sunday, he was collected by a young factory worker, Antonio Bruno, and arrived at the meeting place at around 7 o'clock. The *PCd'I* had never been big in Sardinia, where progressive opinion was normally channelled towards Sardist separatism, the basis of Gramsci's own politics until he moved to Turin and joined the Socialists. But he was shocked by how few comrades there were here now: just twenty, representing an active membership barely twice that, in a population of several hundred thousand. Admittedly, the island's most adventurous young people, including Gramsci himself and a number he had grown up with, had left for a better life on the mainland or in America, as ambitious youth always had. There had never been much to detain them here by way of education or employment, social and financial prospects. Sardinia tended to get what the rest of Italy didn't want, including its school teachers, who would often show up at village

elementary schools like Gramsci's own and promptly disappear when they saw
where they'd ended up. But with the economic upturn, whose benefits were being
felt even here in Sardinia, the exodus had eased slightly. He would have expected
the Party's vigorous and well-publicized efforts against the Fascists during the
summer to have brought in many more new recruits. It had elsewhere, though he
had his doubts about the quality of the influx.

Gramsci sat in the shade of a large tree and addressed the comrades assembled
around him. He spoke about Bordiga, how his imprisonment had taken him out
of the struggle and out of touch with the true state of the nation and world affairs.
He explained the need to reorganize the party for conditions of repression and
clandestinity, mainly through a network of cells which would not give each other
away, and could if necessary be directed from outside the country. Fascism would
one day topple under the weight of its own contradictions, and having destroyed
its bourgeois rivals leave the nation leaderless. The *PCd'I* needed to be in a position
to step into the breach. For now, the party's strategic priority had to be persuading
the peasants, and here in Sardinia the shepherds and fishermen, to side with the
organized workers across Italy who remained stubbornly resistant to Mussolini
and his empty bluster. His speech was applauded politely in the early morning
sunshine. The comrades were not exactly roused, but they were not disinterested
either. In discussion, only one delegate spoke up for Bordiga, in a hectoring
harangue that seemed to have been modelled on old Amadeo's personal rhetorical
style. To everyone's great relief, the one remaining Bordigist in Sardinia had to
leave early to catch the 2 o'clock (and last) train to the south-west mining town of
Sassari. Those who remained enjoyed a simple lunch of pasta, bread and cheese,
apples and wine, and continued calm and constructive discussion into the evening.

The great Communist politician from the mainland was as interested in
their stories about Sardinian life and folklore as the prospects for international
proletarian revolution. There had been an upsurge of labour militancy in the Sulcis-
Iglesiente mining basin, with even the new Fascist union organizers threatening
a strike against the French mine-owners and managers as part of a countrywide
campaign to pressurize the bosses into accepting state control.[1] Gramsci wanted a
full account, and an assessment of the chances of broadening the dispute beyond
wages and hours onto matters of industrial management and social welfare, which
were just as important to workers and their families, and crucial to the prospects
of proletarian hegemony. But he would have been just as interested in the acts
performing in Cagliari's musical theatres, which he had applauded and heckled so
rowdily as a student, and which particular songs and jokes were proving especially
popular.

The next day Gramsci took the same two o'clock last train down the west coast
to his home village of Ghilarza. This was the first time he had visited his family
there since 1920, when he had returned briefly for the sombre occasion of his older
sister Emma's funeral. He was met by a group of old friends at the railway station
in nearby Abbasanta, and stepped sprightly down from the train. Two other men
had got off the train and stood on the platform, trying hard to look inconspicuous
and disinterested. Gramsci then stepped smartly back into the carriage when the

station master blew his whistle. The two policemen also scrambled back onto the train. As the train pulled away, and his friends pretended to wave him off, Gramsci jumped back down onto the platform and slammed the carriage door behind him, a practiced evasion. The train sped off, with Gramsci's 'tail' safely on board, down the single line towards Sassari and the other grim mining towns beyond. It must have felt like a small victory with which to start the walk home.

Ghilarza would have been little changed since he'd left: the lava-stone houses with plumes of smoke fluttering like pale blue ribbons from their squat chimneys; the orange groves rising from their backyards into the surrounding hills; stamping donkeys tethered to their posts for the night, raising their heads from their mealy bags to investigate passers-by; the smell of dung and baking bread; villagers nodding their greetings at their low doorways or in the narrow streets. Behind him, Gramsci might have heard them muttering about Don Ciccillo and Peppina Marcias' boy, the famous MP. The only surprise was a bicycle coming clattering down the street, ridden by a young peasant boy with a great pile of sheepskins on the back, the first bicycle Gramsci had ever seen here in Ghilarza. In rural Sardinia, there was as yet no sign of radio or too many other symbols of modernity. In fact, he reflected some years later, the place was closer in spirit to America than Italy, because they received more direct, reliable, uncensored news from émigré relatives in New York and Chicago than from anyone on the Italian mainland. Stories about mobsters and hoodlums – many of them of course of Italian descent – or the latest Hollywood sensation would have meant more to these people than what Mussolini's government or the coterie of career politicians who made up most of the opposition were up to. Gramsci barely had chance to greet his mother before a procession of village worthies came to pay their respects to the visiting dignitary. Even the local Fascists came by, revelling in the success of a fellow Sardinian, even if he was a communist: 'The Sardinians are doing well, eh? Good for Sardinia!' A group of labourers from the local Mutual Aid Society asked him all about Russia and the Communist Party. He told them about the October Revolution, and the ongoing struggle to create a society which was equal and fair. The Soviets were creating an economy where workers and peasants were justly rewarded for their labours, and everyone could be sure of enough to eat and a decent place to live. This was a revolution against misery and poverty. The labourers looked puzzled, until one of them piped up 'But Signor Gramsci, why leave Sardinia, which is so poor, then join up with another load of poor people over there?'[2]

Finally, he was left alone with his mother and what remained in the *casa Gramsci* of his family. Throughout the visitations from the local worthies she had sat in the corner or clattered around the kitchen, deeply resentful that after all these years other people still had first call on her son's time and attention. Now she sat him down at the table and they exchanged family news. She delighted in his account of his marriage and Julia's maternity, and made him promise to send her regular photographs and news of every significant development in the child's life. She was pleased they'd called him Delio after Nino's cousin on her side, and said how pleased his uncle was too. She might also have noted Nino's newfound serenity and maturity, with much relief after years of worry over what would become of him, her brightest but most vulnerable child.

After dinner, Antonio played with his four-year-old niece Edmea, Gennaro's child, who amid considerable scandal had been left with her grandmother to raise. She was a quiet, reflective child, but as they played, and Edmea became absorbed in the joy of the game, she came out of her shell. Later he wrote to Julia about how the child had been scared by the sight of some big boiled crabs being prepared for dinner. To distract her he made up a story about 530 wicked crabs under the command of General Chewbroth, with his brilliant General Staff Fieldmistress Bloodsucker, Fieldmarshall Cockroach and Captain Bluebeard, who were foiled by a little band of good crabs Fidget, Thudbang, Whitebeard and Blackbeard. The wicked ones pinched her on the legs with his (Gramsci's) hands, while the good ones came scuttling to her defence on garlanded tricycles, armed with brooms and skewers. The whole house echoed to the whirr of the tricycles, the thump of brooms and conversations between the scampering crabs. The little girl believed it all absolutely, and took the story so seriously she thought up new episodes and twists to it herself. Gramsci concluded that it was all very much more entertaining than receiving the village dignitaries.

Gramsci stayed in Ghilarza for ten days, from 27 October to 6 November 1924. After their opening salvo of news, he and his family struggled to establish meaningful contact. All they really had in common were distant memories, and he was none too sure how accurate they were. He had left Ghilarza as a very young man, in his mind much earlier, while they had stayed where they felt they belonged. Perhaps they had never been that close, and he was romanticizing his childhood, as he was inclined to. There was so much business that would have to remain unfinished, and though they always professed pride in his achievements, they were always uncomfortable with his politics. He and his mother had barely seen each other in thirteen eventful years, either side of the biggest and most catastrophic war the world had ever seen and the wave of proletarian revolution. Many of those years had passed without any form of communication between them. He appreciated the sacrifices she had made for her family, and the true heroism required to hold it together during Don Ciccillo's disgrace and absence. Against all the odds she had enabled her children (Emma sadly apart) to grow up and realize their potential. For the most enterprising of them, and especially him, Nino, that meant leaving her behind. All her best efforts were bound to result in loss. For her part, she was clearly proud of her successful son, but had no meaningful way of expressing it, or any real sense of what his success amounted to, apart, that is, from all the local worthies coming to pay homage as soon as he appeared over the hill.

He was also well aware that his own memories of her and his childhood were deeply unreliable, shrouded in impressions that came from sources other than his own mind or true feelings at the time. The proof of this was that he could never arrive at a settled judgement of his life and place in the family. Was it, as he led friends and comrades to believe, a carefree existence roaming the village streets and surrounding countryside, tracking animals and building ships out of sticks? Or was it, as he had told Julia in a less guarded moment, a sewer of bitterness in which he was made to feel he never belonged or was fully loved, or even worse a burdensome nuisance? Perhaps it was all of these things, foremost at different times or operating at different levels at the same time. As for his father, Don Ciccillo had always been a remote stranger, scowling in the corner if he was actually there at all, and contributing little to the family's upkeep and care. Their shared, all too accurate and reliable memory of his imprisonment and its effects upon the family hung over them all like a dark cloud, always there but never spoken about. It was the one hard reliable fact in their store of family lore, all the more irksome for being effectively unmentionable.

On Gramsci's final morning in Ghilarza, his mother gave him a traditional Sardinian baby's bonnet to give to Julia for their child. All the while Edmea, who had grown quite attached to her Uncle Nino, scampered at his feet and hung on to his coat, making funny noises and faces to attract what remained of his attention. The family assembled awkwardly, embraced and said their farewells. They parted at the foot of the hill where the boundary of the village met the surrounding orange groves. Antonio set off alone for the station at Abbasanta and the long journey back to the mainland, with a final wave before a bend in the road took him from their view. He would never return to Ghilarza or Sardinia, and his parents and sisters and little Edmea would never see him again.

Chapter 13

THE THIRD SCHUCHT SISTER

On 3 January 1925, Mussolini announced that he would no longer be accountable as Prime Minister to Parliament, which he regarded as nothing more than a campsite for his Blackshirts. What he called the fascistization of Italy would now gather pace, with suppression of all political debate and organization. The press and the opposition parties would be subject to state control, and local government would be replaced with appointed officials. From his balcony overlooking the Piazza Navona, *Il Duce* told thousands of delirious supporters that he considered the nation in a permanent state of war. With all constitutional, legal and political obstacles removed, he set about creating the military-industrial system which would sustain Italy's war on itself and in time on anyone else who stood in the way of his plans and dreams. The short-lived Aventine opposition collapsed in a shower of windy rhetoric, futile protest and party machinations. In November 1924 the nineteen Communist MPs had withdrawn, frustrated by their failure to get the other parties to actually do anything, and returned to confront the Fascists in the official Parliament at Montecitorio. The other opposition parties continued to press Mussolini to respect legal norms. He responded with a wave of repression, closing down politically suspect clubs and societies, dissolving opposition parties and movements by decree, ransacking the houses of opponents, arresting their occupants and taking over their newspapers. This time Mussolini did not even bother to blame rogue elements amongst his subordinates, but accepted 'full political, moral and historical responsibility for every single thing that has happened … If Fascism is a criminal conspiracy, then I am the chief conspirator!'[1]

Soon after Gramsci returned to Rome he heard that Tatiana Schucht, the Schucht sister who had been missing the longest and furthest away, presumed by the family to have been left behind in Rome, had finally been located. Since Gramsci had arrived here in May 1924, and bearing in mind promises he had made in Moscow, he had been keeping an eye out for her, or at least for someone matching her description. In truth he would not have not been looking too hard or closely, because he had plenty else to bother himself with. And after all these years away, the family's description of her would have been quite vague: smaller than her sisters, a bit like Julia, a bit like Evgenia, not much like Anna, most like Nadina whom he had also never met. Further, from what they said about Tatiana, or Tanya for short, this second oldest of the sisters was just as troubled and complicated as the rest of them, with her own spells of nervous exhaustion, physical illness and prolonged hospital treatment. She was also, at almost forty and as far as anyone knew, unattached and unmarried. Antonio could have been forgiven a certain sense of caution towards this errant Schucht sister; Julia and Evgenia were quite enough to be going on with.

It wasn't him who tracked Tanya down, and set up their first meeting on 2 February 1925. That was old family friend, Leonilde Perilli, Nilde for short, who traced Tatiana to the Crandon Institute in the Via Savoia, where she was working as a science teacher. Tanya had been out of touch since 1917, when Apollon finally left Rome to rejoin his wife and other daughters in Russia in the afterglow of the October Revolution. For reasons which were never made clear, at least to Gramsci, Tanya had stayed behind. He had subsequently surmised that it was to pursue a medical career of some sort, following her nurse training before and during the war, but no one seemed to know what shape this had taken. From what scraps he heard of Tanya's life in the intervening years, the medical career seemed to have petered out altogether, and been replaced by school teaching and other bits of temporary, mostly clerical work. Nilde told the family that Tanya had behaved very strangely when she had made contact. She was plainly depressed and downcast, and could only imagine that someone in the family had died, so refused to write to them herself or believe Nilde's reassurances that they simply wanted to know that she, Tanya, was alright.

Gramsci's first task would have been to set her mind at ease, and relay the good news about his own and Julia's marriage and their recent arrival. Of all the sisters, Tanya did indeed most closely resemble Julia and rivalled her younger sister's beauty; he told her later that he may well have seen her once before in Rome on a passing tram and, in his reverie of longing for his wife, mistaken her for Julia. When they all briefly lived together in 1926, he mistook them for each other on several further occasions. Tanya was still very recognizably a Schucht, and identifiable from her small size among the gaggle of sisters he had seen in a photo from twenty years ago, hardly any taller than Gramsci himself. But she had aged much more quickly than the others. She had evidently not thrived in solitude, and whatever she had been through in Rome was etched in her pale lined face and superficially brittle manner. Her dress was far from elegant, functionally sufficient, almost scruffy, with patches and rows of stitching on her coat and skirt. Her Slavic features were somehow less clearly defined than either Julia's or Evgenia's, supplicant rather than defiant, cowed rather than haughty. Perhaps the light and warmth of Italy had somehow faded her, like a photograph left on a windowsill.

He warmed to her during their first evening together, as their conversation roamed far more freely than it ever did with her sisters, over politics, their impressions of Rome and their lives here, her work and his. Perhaps there was more to her than met the eye. There must be something about her that had enabled her to strike out on her own and live independently for nearly ten years in a foreign city. They went to eat at a restaurant, and he noticed that she ate as little as the other Schucht sisters, but otherwise appeared to be in good physical health. He had been given to understand that Tanya did not share the family's loyal and thorough-going Bolshevism, but like much else he'd been told about her this was not entirely true. As he wrote to Julia the next day, 'politically she's much closer to us than I had been led to believe … The only things she takes exception to are the denial of free speech to the Russian opposition and the imprisonment of some of their leaders. I was very happy to meet her because she is very like you.'[2]

They met again several times over coming weeks, over *trattoria* meals, and he enjoyed her company as much as the food. She would have reminded him ever more clearly of Julia, but without the secrets and obstacles he always seemed to be confronted with within five minutes of conversation with his wife. 'She's like you in so many of her features and movements', he wrote to Julia, 'The music of her voice is like the echo of your own. She would be pleased to know I wrote "echo", because she objected to my comparing her voice to yours, which she says is very beautiful.'[3] For her part, Tanya was charmed and amused by Gramsci, whom she quickly began to call Nino, and (despite her worries about what it might entail) glad of this unexpected chance to re-establish contact with her family. 'She wanted to buy some shoes for you,' he continued in his letter of 7 February to Julia, 'with the most terrifying heels. I resisted strenuously, insisting that you would certainly never wear such horrors, and pointing out that she would never wear them either. She wants to buy little shoes for the child too. What a terrible woman, with her mania for shoeing the whole world!' Gramsci had told Tanya that he would soon be travelling to Moscow, and she decided that he could take her gifts of fine Italian shoes with him. There was to be a meeting of the full Executive Committee of the Comintern on 21 March 1925, and he was to lead the Italian delegation. It would be the first time he had been to Moscow, and seen Julia, since November 1923, nearly a year and a half ago. He would at last meet his son Delio, a real living child, rather than a faint impression on photographic paper. This time he travelled openly and legally as an MP, which still counted for something, with an ordinary passport which took weeks to arrange but finally came through at the end of February. His tail to the Austrian–Italian border was obvious but discreet and unobstructive.

He arrived in Moscow in early March, with the first hints of spring: traces of blue in the unrelenting pale grey of the midday sky; the steady drip of melt water onto the pavement from the huge iron downpipes on the more prominent public buildings; the occasional warning crack of overhanging icicles and the rushing roar of loosened snowdrifts on pitched roofs; the emergence from the dirty receding snow of snowdrops and bluebells on patches of communal ground that had once been tended gardens; the emergence of those other kinds of 'snowdrops', homeless old people and abandoned children (*bezprizorniki* in Russian) who had died of disease and hunger over the winter, been immersed and preserved in the snow and ice where they fell, and now lay or sat blue-faced and stinking till the city authorities' cleansing squads got round to clearing them away and dumping them in some huge hole in the ground on the city's outskirts.

The Italians left their meagre luggage at Hotel Lux, and were immediately taken on a round of official receptions and public meetings. There was an air of formality and officialdom about proceedings that had not been present when Gramsci was last here. Perhaps this was a sign of the increasing confidence, security and authority of the new workers' state. Similarly with the endless tables of statistics and charts and graphs, demonstrating 'scientifically' that fully fledged communism was within reach by the year 1935, in ten rigorously planned, realistically timetabled and rationally organized years. The great Lenin's legacy would soon be brought to technical fruition, capitalism exposed and overcome as the necessary but now redundant phase in human history it truly was. Socialism would take its place, if necessary in this one country but eventually, when every other laggard country caught up with the helter-skelter pace of change in the motherland of proletarian revolution, across the whole world.

After a banquet for all the foreign delegations at the Kremlin, Gramsci had to attend a late night meeting at the Lux of the Italian delegation, who struggled to stay awake after their long journey and a meal of such unaccustomed plenitude. It was reconvened early the next morning to ratify the statement on Fascism which Gramsci would present to the *Ispolcom* later that afternoon. 'Three o'clock sharp, Comrade Gramsci!' he had been told by the powdered, starched female secretary assigned to the delegation, who came knocking at his door at 8 am. Finally, approaching lunchtime, with the statement agreed by the still drowsy Italians, he managed to hurry down Tverskaya Street to the recently restored apartment block where the Schuchts were now living. Delio, it turned out, had whooping cough. Every breath, in and out, gave off a high-pitched wheeze, interspersed every few breaths with a harsh cough. His feverish, distressed face would have been barely recognizable from the grainy posed photos Gramsci had received every few months. In the hour or so he spent with the Schuchts, the child would also have been wary of this odd-looking stranger they told him was his father. Antonio just about had time to convey news of Tanya, her love and best wishes. At some point, he suggested again that Julia and Delio might join him in Rome. This time, presumably with Apollon Schucht's approval, the family agreed. As soon as the necessary arrangements could be made, Julia and Delio – and Evgenia – would come to Rome.

Official business continued to keep Gramsci busy during his time in Moscow, and he had very little time to spare for the Schuchts. He managed to snatch a few spare hours on the occasional afternoon and, as the child recovered from his whooping cough, would take Delio in his pram down Tverskaya Street to a pretty little garden reserved for Comintern officials and delegates. There he could play the proud father, as comrades peered into the pram at the tightly swaddled child and cooed over him. The other Italians remarked approvingly on Delio's olive skin and bush of thick black hair, and how closely he resembled his Italian papa. When Delio had been given a clean bill of health, Antonio suggested to the Schuchts that they should give their doctor – an especially attentive and competent female paediatrician – a gift to say thank you for helping the child make such a speedy and full recovery. They agreed, and together Antonio and Julia chose a reproduction of Correggio's *Danae* in one of the art shops that under NEP had come back to life near the Kremlin. This would have been about the only time the couple got to spend alone, pushing the pram around the centre of the city like normal, proud young parents, and fussing over the child propped up inside it. When they got back to the Schucht family apartment, they wrote their best wishes on a small card attached to the brown paper wrapping. At the bottom, Antonio and Julia signed their names. Evgenia then stepped forward and signed her own name beneath Julia's, and alongside wrote 'the mothers'. Gramsci chose not to say anything about this most peculiar behaviour, and the strange web of relationships it implied. But later, as he was preparing to leave with the picture to deliver to the clinic, he overheard Apollon scolding the child back in the living room: 'Auntie Zhenya is not your mother! Delio has only one mother, only one mother, only one!'[4]

Gramsci was back in Rome on 28 April. He saw Tanya soon after, and conveyed the news and best wishes from Moscow. In the meantime she had heard from her mother, who wrote that they had found Antonio moody and apathetic while he was in Moscow, that she (Julia Grigor'evna) had been disappointed because he had not brought her chestnuts from Italy, that Evgenia objected to his heavy smoking and that more than once Julia had been reduced to tears by things he had said or done. He responded that he had been understandably tired from the journey and preoccupied with party business; he had smoked no more than usual; and chestnuts weren't in season. He was aware that on occasions he had upset his wife, and felt remorseful about it, but he rarely understood why and to what extent. All in all he would have been left utterly perplexed by this latest encounter with the Schucht family.

He threw himself back into his political work. There seemed to be so much to do, so little time and so few people to do it. He slept little and poorly, startled awake by something he had to do the following day, then lying awake worrying he would be too exhausted to do it. His headaches, which had almost disappeared in Moscow, returned with a vengeance: a constant dull throb, with regular peaks of pain that would lay him low for useless hours on end. At best they were a kind of ticking in his head, corresponding to the beating of his heart. At moments of uncertainty or acute stress they would speed up, so that it seemed that time itself was running out on him and his few scattered comrades. There were always articles to write for the party press; so many articles, whose quality and coherence he fought like a tiger to maintain. In reality, a daily paper, a weekly magazine and a fortnightly review were far too much for a small struggling party like his, as Piero Gobetti had observed, but they couldn't close them down for fear of looking weak, losing influence and capacity, or disappointing their still substantial national readerships. Sometimes he ended up writing, anonymously or under some ridiculous pseudonym, almost entire editions on his own.

He was acutely aware of the low political consciousness amongst those few comrades who remained in circulation and active, and even amongst those older cadres in exile or in hiding, whose substantial experience was no compensation for their lack of information and engagement with the contemporary, constantly changing political scene back here in Italy. If anything it was proving a handicap, because these senior comrades were still thinking and arguing in terms of the situation when they had left or gone underground. The party's other MPs in Rome weren't much use either. They were of variable quality and commitment, and some even bridled at the 10 per cent levy the party had agreed they should pay from their salaries towards its costs. One or two refused to pay altogether, threatening to inform the press about improper use of parliamentary funds, and were promptly expelled from the party. Political organization and influence was limited or non-existent back in their constituencies, so they couldn't be pressured there either. Somehow or other, the quality of party organization, activity and consciousness had to be raised. So Gramsci devised what he called a 'Party School', a kind of communist university, based on correspondence courses in history, philosophy and culture, as well as matters of political theory and organization. Two batches of study material were mailed out in the spring and summer of 1925, both with long introductory essays written by Gramsci and extracts from other Marxist writers edited and translated by him, until it became clear that they were being used by the Fascists – often tipped off by sympathetic *postini* – to identify their communist opponents.

On 16 May Gramsci finally made his maiden speech to Parliament.[5] The Fascists were proposing a new law to restrict public servants' involvement in associations, clubs and institutes. Its stated target was the Freemasons, but the Communists feared it was also designed to bring their own activities under even tighter state control. Fascism would in the meantime reach an accommodation with Freemasonry, which was too weak to resist but too strong to destroy. Parliament was unusually attentive as Gramsci spoke quietly and steadily, with none of the flights of windy rhetoric they were used to. Even Mussolini was pictured in the newspapers leaning forward with his hand to his ear. Fascism was simply seeking to supplant Freemasonry as the main source of patronage for official and civil service jobs, Gramsci argued, the so-called Fascist revolution was nothing but the replacement of one set of favoured administrative personnel by another.

'Then why are so many bankers and industrialists against our revolution?' asked Mussolini.

'There are plenty behind you, and the rest will come over eventually, in order to safeguard their wealth and their jobs,' replied Gramsci. 'They'll join the Fascists *as well as* the Freemasons!'

All this was just a sideshow. The real question was why, although the Communist Party had not been declared an illegal organization, members were arrested every time they were found together in groups of three or more.

'Just like in Russia!' shouted Mussolini, 'In Russia you're very good at rounding people up. Quite right too! At least here we let people out again. We only pull them in so we can get to know them.'

His cronies bayed their amusement.

'You're doing what they used to do in the South before the war,' Gramsci said through the hubbub, 'when they hired thugs to arrest anyone who voted for the opposition ... so they could get to know them.'

From across the chamber a voice shouted, 'You know nothing about the South!'

'I *am* a Southerner,' Gramsci responded, then turned back to Mussolini. In order to exercise power he had to place himself at the head of the class which controls the state. Here was the grain of truth in his muddled, reactionary perversion of

Marxist teaching. He could not be leader of the proletariat, so he became dictator of the bourgeoisie. One day the workers and peasants would unite to consign the bourgeoisie and *Il Duce* himself to the dustbin of history. As he finished, the Chamber erupted in massed shouts of fury, and just a few of acclamation. Over the following days, a story circulated that Mussolini saw Gramsci immediately after the debate, drinking a coffee in the parliamentary bar, and approached to congratulate him on his speech. Gramsci, according to this story, just carried on sipping his coffee and ignored *Il Duce*'s outstretched hand. When the story got back to Gramsci himself, he scoffed and dismissed it. Why was it that Italians had to turn everything into opera, or worse into melodrama? And why did everything have to be black or white, with no shades of grey in between, and every individual a hero or villain, when most people spent their lives wading around the mess in between?

In this case, how likely was it that Mussolini, this proud violent man with his rolling eyes and often stated contempt for the niceties of parliamentary debate, would have risked being doubly mocked by the leader of his keenest adversaries? Or that the awkward debutante MP of a minor and embattled party, winding down over a coffee and well aware of the utter futility of his rhetorical defiance, would have spurned the hand of the most powerful man in modern Italy, for whom he retained a grudging respect throughout his life, from his support for active and operative neutrality in 1915, his 1923 description of Mussolini as one of 'the most intelligent fascists', right through to polite appeals for improved conditions in prison?[6] Not to mention a number of striking similarities in personal and social background, temperament and choice of occupation, over and above their more obvious differences in political outlook and trajectory.[7] For Gramsci it was an early taste of the myth-making and glorification of prominent individuals he would elsewhere ridicule, and repeatedly object to when applied to himself.

He wrote to Julia soon afterwards with a rather more downbeat account. The Fascists had accorded his parliamentary début an unusually favourable reception, heckling rather than just howling him down, so from a revolutionary point of view he had started off badly. He told her he was exhausted, and had to be very careful in his everyday movements. Above all he felt completely alone, partly because of the illegal operation of the Party, which forced everyone to operate individually and independently. As a way to escape this political desert he tried to see as much as he could of Tanya, who reminded him so much of Julia. But there was no real way of making up for her absence. Everything he saw in the world around him reminded him of her and Delio, and so made him more acutely aware of their separation and his unhappiness. He couldn't even bear to look at babies and small children, whom he'd always been so fond of, because they just reminded him of what he was missing. But it would pass, he concluded, because he knew that they were coming to Italy; 'We will recover our energies, and our personalities will grow together as we watch our Delio grow up.'[8]

Chapter 14

THE SCHUCHTS COME TO ROME

The news from Russia was of continuing economic and social upheaval. NEP may have restored the market economy, and got the country moving again, but it had also brought back many of the perennial social ills of capitalism. There was mass unemployment far worse than anything from the Tsar's time, with 150,000 in Leningrad alone, on a dole of 25 roubles a month on average, which was just about enough to live on, and progress of sorts from the days when they'd have starved to death. There were beggars and prostitutes on the streets of the major towns and cities, an estimated 7 million *bezprizorniki* with only enough orphanage places for a few thousand at a time, and even epidemics of suicides and gang rapes amongst the youth which (according to 'the Frenchman' Victor Serge) went almost wholly unreported because the authorities were keen to discourage 'defeatism'. An epidemic of rabies was sweeping the country, with mad dogs in the cities and rabid wolves in the countryside. There were widespread racketeering and corruption: 'Twisters start up a fake co-operative. They bribe officials for credits, raw materials and orders. They become the universal middle men between socialized industry and the consumer, and double the price of everything.'[1] If the Soviet Union was developing into a normal modern society, it brought the problems as well as the benefits of modernity.

Julia, Delio and Evgenia Schucht arrived in Rome in late October 1925. Antonio found out about their impending arrival quite by accident, at a reception at the Soviet embassy, when a secretary happened to mention that she was looking forward to working with his wife, who had managed to secure a transfer within the NKVD. This was the first Gramsci had heard of any of it, the actual date of their arrival or Julia's job, but he tried to exult in the fact that they were definitely coming. As their arrival approached, and his excitement and apprehension mounted in equal measure, Antonio received further unsettling news from Tanya. There had apparently been considerable discussion amongst the Schucht family about their living arrangements in Rome. It had been decided, at Evgenia's insistence, that they would all live together. Tanya was told to find somewhere suitable, and that she should move in with her sisters. This despite the fact that she had lived in her own rooms in Rome for over eight years now, and for the last five years had been comfortably settled in the house of the principal of the school where she taught science. She told Antonio about her forced move as though there was no possibility of her refusing. She said she had already found a furnished apartment on the Via Trapani, with two sizeable bedrooms and – luxury of luxuries, especially compared to what the Schuchts were used to in Russia – its own separate bathroom. This would also have suited Antonio, who presumed he would share a room with Julia and their child, because the Passarges were moving too.

However, Evgenia had further insisted that he, Julia's husband and Delio's father, was not to live with them. She said she had been advised that his presence would constitute a security risk. If his relationship with them were known, the Italian authorities might revoke their visas. This was clearly nonsense. The police already knew that Julia was Gramsci's wife, because he had told them when he was asked to sponsor the visa applications. He decided not to pursue the matter for now. He couldn't risk another crisis, especially when they might still decide not to come. He couldn't force himself upon them either, so he moved with the Passarges to a house on the Via Morgagni. Just days after he had moved with them, the police ransacked his room. The four-hour search was overseen by Commissioner Belloni, the deputy head of the Roman police. Belloni was civil enough, and engaged Gramsci in long conversation about the legitimacy of Italian claims to Corsica and even parts of the French mainland like Nice and Savoy. But the Passarges finally discovered that their lodger was not a Professor after all. There was no question of him moving out, at least for the time being, they said when the police had finally left empty-handed, but they were noticeably less quiet and respectful around him and his room.

Evgenia, Julia and Delio arrived at Termini Station with several heavy chests and suitcases. A comrade with a small motorized van had offered to transport them and their baggage to the Via Trapani. Antonio settled into a pattern over the next few weeks of visiting for dinner in the evening, when he had finished his political duties and Julia had returned from her job at the embassy, and staying there for the rest of the evening. Evgenia had taken on every aspect of the child's care, while Julia seemed to have very little to do with the child. In fact, she seemed to have little interest in very much at all. He understood that it was best not to broach her work, because of its political sensitivity and possible repercussions for their residence status, so that closed down one substantial line of conversation. He tried to consult her about his own work, or propose joint projects like translations between Russian and Italian, but the best he could hope for was dutiful compliance. After the first few sentences of an article or a communiqué, she would complain about its complexity or a growing headache, and didn't he understand that she was tired after a busy day doing just this kind of thing at work?

The whole family – Tanya aside – were not especially interested in the Italian political situation in which he was otherwise totally, daily immersed. It seemed that the petty squabbles and difficulties of his tiny and ineffectual *Partito Communista d'Italia* really were nothing compared to the titanic battles going on inside the Russian Party and the wider efforts to construct the new socialist society of the Soviet Union, with which the Schuchts kept in close and interested contact. Julia relayed news from the embassy much more enthusiastically than anything she might say to him. The Schuchts spoke Russian between themselves at home, with its barked and mumbled pronunciations, even in the presence of Tatiana, whose Russian was even more rudimentary than Antonio's. The words which Delio was beginning to form and utter were all unmistakably Russian. Julia was plainly disappointed in Rome, and found it dull and dowdy compared to the gay sunlit city of her youth or even the NEP-era bustle of Moscow. Antonio offered to acquire a camera for her, so she could at least record outings they might take on fine days, but she seemed uninterested in either the camera or the outings.

She had also given up on her music, saying she no longer found it useful to herself or society, especially now that her livelihood did not depend on it. Antonio found this sad, because she had played so beautifully and derived such obvious pleasure and fulfilment from it. Julia frequently complained that she was tired from her job, that she wasn't used to the work it involved – mainly administrative, with very little translation called for because everybody at the embassy spoke Italian and Russian – or to working full time. She seemed to spend most of her days filing. He tried to show sympathy and support, and suggested that she might try to reduce her hours. This, she said, was out of the question because there was so much to do. She did not want to let down her employers or show anything less than total commitment to their common cause. It might look like dull routine to him, but she was still making a contribution to the proletarian revolution and the building of socialism. He struggled to make sense of the contradictions and inconsistencies. In general, Julia was even more withdrawn and impassive towards Antonio than she had been the last time in Moscow. She refused requests to go out with him in the evening but, he noted sourly, was always eager to go out with her sisters or her old friend Nilde Perilli to shows at the Argentina or Adriano concert halls. He began to take Julia gifts whenever he went to the Schuchts – flowers, sweets, small glass baubles or wooden carvings that he picked up at street markets or in department stores – until one day Evgenia commented pointedly on how much these unnecessary fripperies were costing. Wouldn't the money be better spent on the upkeep of the child and the household? Besides, Antonio soon realized that Julia never seemed too impressed by the gifts from her latest male admirer anyway. She would unwrap them, examine them cursorily and lay them aside, then look at him blankly as if to say, 'What else have you got to offer?' Even the sweets sat there mouldering and unconsumed, in this household of women who seemed to have the diets and appetites of small birds. On several occasions, Delio, rummaging and rampaging around the flat, was found with sticky hands and a mouthful of sugar or chocolate, and forced by Evgenia to spit or even vomit them out. Julia's appetite for flattery and seduction and male admiration seemed to have waned as thoroughly as for everything else in life.

'Mama Zhenya' was in firm charge of the family. She did the housework and cooking, neither of them particularly well, and looked after Delio while his 'Mama Julka' and auntie Tanya went to work. She refused to allow Antonio to smoke in the apartment, which left him – by now a sixty a day man – even twitchier than he would have been in her presence. She called his favourite Macedonian brand 'foul-smelling Turkish donkey shit'. Aspects of her care of Delio disturbed Antonio profoundly. The child was allowed to run riot around the apartment, with no structure or purpose to his time, and no restraints on what he might do or delve into. The mouldy sweets were the least of it. Gramsci regularly had to remove sharp or fragile objects from the child's tight grasp before he broke them or hurt himself or someone else, to the child's howling chagrin, which could only be soothed by 'Mama Zhenya'. There is a surviving photograph from this Italian interlude of Evgenia holding tightly and proprietorially onto Delio in St. Mark's Square, Venice, presumably taken by Julia with the camera Antonio had bought her.[2]

Gramsci recognized the precepts of Rousseau, whom Apollon Schucht was known to admire and espouse, in the upbringing of this 'noble savage'. In fact, when old Apollon came to stay in the spring of 1926, he took one look at the situation – in the household, the city and the country – and promptly returned to Russia. Without sentimentalizing or harking back to some traditional ideal of family life, this arrangement – with Evgenia setting herself up as 'the mother', and Julia and Tanya under her, all three of them self-styled neurotics – just felt all wrong. Antonio would read alarming reports in the paper about the mistreatment or even murder of children, and find himself imagining morbid scenarios of what might happen here. One particular report stayed with him for years, about a woman in Genova who had poisoned herself and her five-year-old grandson, leaving a note saying that she had had to take the child to paradise with her because she could not do without him even there. But the worst thing for Antonio was that Evgenia seemed determined to stand between him and Delio, and to poison whatever relationship they might be able to cultivate in already trying circumstances. To begin with, the child had called Antonio *dyadya*, Russian for uncle. He had clearly been coached by Evgenia, and this went on for several days until an outraged Tanya plucked up the courage to object. Then there were the sleeping arrangements. Evgenia had placed Delio's cot right next to her own bed, on the opposite side of the larger bedroom to Julia's. Evgenia claimed her sister would need all the undisturbed sleep she could get after working all day at the embassy. More often than not Delio ended up sharing Evgenia's bed, because at the slightest murmur she would scoop him out of his cot and in with her. Tanya told Antonio that Nilde Perilli had heard from several of her acquaintances around town that Evgenia was passing the child off as her own. Out on walks with him in the pram, or holding him in shops and cafes, she would talk about aspects of his birth and infancy which could only have been experienced by Julia.

All this time, Antonio received little response from Julia, both to his own feelings and desires and to what was going on around them, in what he would later call 'this peculiar ideological atmosphere'.[3] He just could not seem to break through her fog of reserve. In January 1926, he proposed that they should formally register their marriage with the Italian authorities, in a small ceremony at the Registrar's office in the civic buildings near the Piazza Navona, and she went along with it. He might have hoped that this would reawaken in her some sense of her wifely duties, of the obligations they had publicly made to each other. But there were also further considerations over the Schuchts' legal status in Italy, not quite as stark as the ones Evgenia had raised before, but serious nonetheless. This time, he had heard from a fellow MP who had contacts in the Justice Ministry that the Fascists were reviewing the residence status of foreigners, with a view to tightening up visa requirements and favouring those with some kind of hereditary connection to Italy. This did not include the 'Slavic race' where the Schuchts – for all their other cultural and national affinities – would be formally placed under the newly devised framework of ethnic categorization. In the light of this, it would do no harm for him and Julia to have their relationship formally recognized in Italy. It would also clarify the status of Delio as his child. Tanya's position was straightforward enough; she had after all resided in Italy all her adult life (though when they first met, in the summer of 1924, Gramsci was under the impression that she had registered as a Soviet citizen).[4] Evgenia's situation – she had been born in Siberia, and was much more evidently Russian in her speech and manners – was much less clear.

Soon after this, Julia informed him that she was pregnant again, and that all being well the baby would be due in August, at around the time of Delio's second birthday. Antonio was initially delighted, but early pregnancy added another set of complications to the brittle domestic atmosphere of the Schucht residence. The best times were actually when Julia and both her sisters had gone out for the evening, and Antonio was left alone to look after his son. He was supposed to put him to bed at 7 o'clock sharp, but invariably kept him up beyond that, playing or telling stories or play-acting like he had with his niece Edmea in Ghilarza. They sat at the family piano, now little played and out of tune for lack of use and attention, and plonked away on the keys to made-up songs. To Gramsci's astonishment, the little boy began making animal noises to accompany the notes, 'from the bear's baritone right up to the high notes of the chickens at the other end!' as he reported excitedly to the Schuchts on their return.[5] Or they would work on drawings with Delio's crayons and big rolls of printing paper Antonio had requisitioned from the party press. Delio's pictures were mostly random scrawls of colour which would occasionally and haphazardly assume some recognizable shape, which his father never failed to point out and praise. For the most part, however, Delio was more interested in the complicated patterns and cartoon-like caricatures Antonio was making with his crayons on his side of the roll. He would look up to find the child staring intently as his efforts took shape, clearly fascinated by the process of pictorial representation – summoning up an image out of nothing, literally exercising one's imagination – but quickly look back down at his own drawing when he realized that his father had noticed his interest.

Certain games never ceased to amuse Delio, no matter how many times they were repeated. Almost as soon as Antonio arrived for the evening, the child would urge him to take the wall clock down from the wall – '*Chasy! Chasy!*' in Russian – and move the hands into all their possible positions. To begin with, Gramsci thought the child was learning to tell the time, but when questioned Delio showed no sign of understanding what the time, or time as a concept, might be. He reasoned that it was more likely that Delio, aged barely two, was fascinated by the removal of an everyday household object from its usual place, where it sat untouched, its conveyance to another place entirely and its transformation into a plaything, something you could actually alter with your hands. The process was far more interesting than the object. Gramsci bought Delio a small wooden train for Christmas, with passengers that slotted into their seats in the open carriages and a track which could be reconfigured into lots of different shapes; itself an educative activity which Delio could be engaged in, passing his father rounded or straight interlocking pieces on request or even making suggestions of his own. But the child quickly grew frustrated at his inability to manipulate the small parts and figures, and threw one of the carriages at the wall, where it broke in half. Delio was more impressed and fascinated by the fact that his father, after some mild admonishment of the child's destructiveness, managed to repair the carriage with a few judicious drops of glue.

The political situation continued to deteriorate. There were several bungled assassination attempts on Mussolini in the year between late 1925 and late 1926: in November by a former Socialist MP called Tito Zaniboni, in April by a deranged fifty-year-old aristocratic Irish woman called Violet Gibson (subsequently deported by Mussolini and committed to a mental asylum in Northamptonshire for the rest of her life), and in October by a fifteen-year-old boy in Bologna, called Anteo Zamboni. With each failed attempt, the Fascist crackdown grew more severe, and the myth of Mussolini's superhuman invulnerability ever more inflated, when the only wound he ever suffered was a bloodied nose from Gibson's ancient revolver. Gramsci considered the attacks on *Il Duce* utterly counter-productive and quite mad. As far as he knew, they were the work of isolated individuals, incompetently executed, and nothing to do with the *PCd'I* or any of the other anti-Fascist parties. If anything, he suspected, they were put up to it by dark forces within the state and the Fascist combat apparatus, pursuing the 'strategy of tension', which the far right has always used to consolidate its power.

Meanwhile, Gramsci's efforts to reshape and redirect the *Partito Communista D'Italia* were beginning to bear some fruit. At its third National Congress, held necessarily over the French border in Lyons, he and his supporters won 91 per cent of the votes for the Executive Committee. They won the same overwhelming majority for the main resolution, subsequently known as The Lyons Theses, which Gramsci had put up for debate. Bordiga's faction got just 9 per cent and was reduced to an extremist rump. At subsequent EC meetings, Gramsci's positions on the rebuilding of the labour movement and alliances with the peasants and elements of the middle class – in sharp contrast to Bordiga's calls for armed insurrection – were also endorsed and put into action. He was under no illusions over what had caused this apparently spectacular about-turn in the party's politics in the fifteen months since the disastrous Bordigist jamboree in Como. Above all there was better news from Russia, at least from official sources. The *PCd'I* could now bathe in the glow from the worldwide prestige of the first workers state, which by the mid-1920s was apparently established as a going concern after years of civil war, terror, privation and famine, and rapidly developing under the state-directed capitalism of the New Economic Policy.

The recently renamed USSR was even receiving international recognition from the previously hostile Western powers, most notably that other young country and beacon of modernity, the United States. This served to obscure the increasingly vicious in-fighting amongst the Bolshevik leadership that followed Lenin's death, apparent only to insiders and contained by the rigours of inner-party discipline. But there were other, more local reasons for this new mood of unity and loyalty in the battered ranks of the *PCd'I*. As Tasca and Graziadei and other right wingers repeatedly pointed out during debate, for polemical purposes of their own, the small vanquished party was almost totally reliant financially and organizationally on the Comintern from which the inveterate splitter Bordiga wished to disaffiliate. If he had prevailed, the embattled party would almost certainly and immediately have ceased to exist. Under constant harassment in Italy itself, it kept going on Soviet money and glory; an early warning of the fate of many Western Communist Parties.

But behind the façade of Soviet triumphalism and NEP-boom, the internal political situation was getting worse in Russia as well as in Italy, with the conflict inside the Soviet Communist Party crystallizing into factional struggle between the majority around Stalin and Bukharin and the opposition minority around Trotsky, Zinoviev and Kamenev. It now threatened to break out of the corridors and meeting rooms of the Kremlin and the Smolny, and infect the wider party and the worldwide movement. The substantive issue was the pace of industrialization and the collectivization of agriculture in Russia, which Trotsky et al. wished to hurry on, as against the continued operation of the NEP free market, which Stalin and Bukharin for the moment advocated. But what concerned Gramsci most was the poisonous atmosphere within the Bolshevik Party and the risks to Communist unity. There was a great deal of personal rivalry and animosity, and jostling for the undisputed position of leadership vacated on Lenin's death two bitter years before. The whole shouting match, and the vicious personal denunciations of which it largely consisted, had very little principled political basis. The different sides could amend or even overturn their positions in a moment if it conferred some factional advantage. In October, Gramsci was asked to write on behalf of the *PCd'I* Executive to the central committee of the CPSU about the growing crisis. He wrote that 'you are degrading and may even annul completely the leading position the CPSU acquired under Lenin's leadership. It seems that your absorption with Russian questions is making you lose sight of their international implications.'[6] The Italian party had no desire to tell the Russians what to do, or which course to take in their own internal affairs, but they should always act in a spirit of comradeship and communist unity: 'We would like to ensure that the majority of the CPSU central committee does not go too far, abuse its victory and take excessive measures.'

Palmiro Togliatti, Gramsci's comrade from Sardinia and Turin, was the *PCd'I* representative in Moscow at the time. He had abandoned Bordiga some time before and supported Gramsci's position inside the party. They had collaborated closely on the Lyons Theses for the *PCd'I*'s most recent Congress. But when he received Gramsci's letter to pass on to the CPSU, he considered it ill-advised and withheld it. Far better, Togliatti wrote back to Gramsci, to support the correct (and by implication, winning) position of the majority around Stalin and Bukharin, than dwell on the split itself and its consequences, which might be taken as veiled support for the opposition. Gramsci sent an angry note by return, rejecting Togliatti's arguments and insisting that he submit the original letter to the Russians. Togliatti continued to suppress it. In Moscow, the Stalin–Bukharin majority pressed home their advantage. Trotsky and Kamenev were expelled from the CPSU executive, while Zinoviev was removed from the Presidency of the Comintern. The objections of the Italians or anyone else were brushed aside, in a climate of stifling conformity. There was to be no further direct contact between Gramsci and Togliatti for what remained of Gramsci's life.

At around the same time, Gramsci received a private letter from his other old friend and comrade from Turin Angelo Tasca, who was now living in exile in France.[7] Tasca was still involved in the *PCd'I*, albeit as figurehead of its small right-wing minority faction, and representing the party abroad and in Moscow, but with growing misgivings. He described his present 'state of resigned discontent' and aired his deep-seated suspicion that he was 'unsuited for life as a communist militant'. He said his uppermost concern was his wife and child, their welfare and future prospects, and the health of his relationship with them. He was desperate to avoid becoming the husband and father his own father had become, distant and cold and frequently cruel; Gramsci would have recalled a tall fierce patriarch trapped in mourning for the young wife he had lost at Angelo's sister's birth. For Gramsci, reflecting privately on his altercation with Togliatti and this dispiriting communication from Tasca, and reports of many other good comrades' disillusionment and despair, it must have felt like everything was falling apart. But he resisted suggestions that he himself should go into exile, expressed repeatedly and more forcefully by the rest of the party leadership as the general situation in Italy darkened; he insisted that leaders should remain in place until it became quite impossible. And bearing in mind Victor Serge's earlier assessment, he may have been concerned about the fate that awaited him in Russia. He would come to regret deeply what he would later call this perversity of desire and heroic vanity, and wish he had got out when he could. He and his fellow communists had not yet fully grasped the severity of the latest Fascist terror and clampdown, its radical historical distinctiveness and the political catastrophe about to befall them and their country. Beguiled perhaps by their small local inner-party successes, they underestimated the severity of the gathering storm around them.

Throughout this turbulent period, Gramsci continued to see as much of the Schuchts and his son as he possibly could. But they had not settled in Rome, and were becoming increasingly anxious about the political situation and whether it was safe for them to stay there. Evgenia was making it plain that she wanted to go back to Russia. While Julia continued to work at the Soviet Embassy through the middle months of her pregnancy, she did not dare disagree. Evgenia even suggested that the family's departure would make life easier for Antonio, because he would not have to worry about their safety and would be free to pursue his political duties wherever they took him. Her final and decisive argument was that Julia would be better off giving birth in the special maternity clinic for party and state officials in Moscow, and that her baby would also be better looked after there. Gramsci, well aware of the deterioration in Italian health services under the Fascists, and with no special privileges of his own to confer, found it hard to object.

The problem remained of exactly how they would travel, and get across the border without the appropriate documentation, which would be very difficult if not impossible to acquire. They needed a ruse. So in late July Evgenia, Tatiana, Julia and Delio travelled as holiday makers to Bolzano in the Alto Adige region of north-eastern Italy. Julia crossed the border alone on 7 August, reached Moscow three days later, and gave birth on 30 August to another boy, Giuliano. Meanwhile Antonio had joined the others at Bolzano, and enjoyed a couple of relatively carefree weeks with Delio. He wrote to Julia: 'We played a lot. I made some little toys for him, and we lit fires out in the fields. There weren't any lizards so I couldn't show him how to catch them.'[8] Without Julia there, Evgenia also seemed much more relaxed and unobstructive. There was just one moment of unpleasantness, when he tried to teach the boy a ribald Sardinian song, *Lassa sa figu Puzone* ('Leave the fig alone, bird'), and Evgenia realized the *double-entendre*. She left with Delio for Moscow in early September 1926. Antonio would never see them or his wife Julia in person again, or meet his second son Giuliano at all.

At the end of October, he travelled to Genova for a secret meeting with a representative of the Comintern, Jules Humbert Droz, who was to explain the controversy in the Russian party to the *PCd'I* Executive and try to allay their concerns and fears. Gramsci was eager to attend, to receive a clear first-hand account of what was going on in Russia, and to clarify the *PCd'I*'s position in return. But on the way there, he was intercepted by the Milan police and advised to return to Rome. There had been yet another attempt on Mussolini's life, and the police told Gramsci they could not guarantee his safety. There was a definite sense of the net closing in. On 5 November the government cancelled all passports and ordered border guards to fire on any illegal fugitives. All anti-Fascist publications were suppressed, and parties and organizations dissolved. Opposition MPs were expelled from Parliament, on the spurious grounds that they had absented themselves during the Aventine period (doubly spurious for the Communists because they had returned long before the others).

On 8 November, the police began to round up Communist and other opposition MPs and activists. After an afternoon and evening of frantic messages to make his escape, which Gramsci persisted in ignoring, he was arrested at 10.30 pm at the Passarges' house on the Via Morgagni. He had been under close round-the-clock surveillance for several days, so more than likely would have been followed and captured wherever he'd gone. The MPs' parliamentary immunity and other legal safeguards, which they had thought right up to the last moment would protect them, were wholly disregarded. The 'exceptional measures' were to be applied retroactively, to a time when the Communist Party was still legal and represented in Parliament; a juridical nonsense which summed up the bold and sweeping totalitarianism of this next phase of Fascism. The communists were to be put before special tribunals created by decree for disposing of all opposition to the Fascist regime, superseding all established legal and juridical procedures, and staffed by members of the Fascist militia and army officers. These tribunals were empowered to impose summary terms of *confino* or internal exile for up to five years at a time, a revival of a practice actually introduced by the pre-war

Liberal government of Giolitti.[9] Their conditions would be more relaxed than ordinary prison sentences – with subsistence allowances, provision for private accommodation and even for detainees' families to join them – but crucially would remove them from political life, disperse them to the remotest parts of the country and prevent them escaping abroad. They were 'not allowed a defence lawyer or to produce witnesses and could not appeal to the ordinary courts'.[10] Mussolini was pictured on his balcony overlooking the crowds in the Piazza Navona, smiling widely and rubbing his hands.

Chapter 15

FIRST CONFINEMENT

After his arrest on the evening of 8 November 1926, under the 'exceptional measures' introduced four days before, Antonio Gramsci was taken to the Regina Coeli prison in Rome. For the sixteen days he spent there, he was kept in absolute solitary confinement and subject to the most stringent prison discipline, for his first three days in a filthy cell crawling with bugs, with nothing to read and only basic prison rations to eat. When he was finally and officially put 'on payment', a simple kind of credit that was deducted from the political prisoners' subsistence allowance of ten lire per day paid by the government, he was able to buy food and supplies from the prison canteen. He was then transferred to a cleaner, fumigated cell, with fresh sheets on the bed and simply but adequately furnished. It also had an electric light that, to his considerable annoyance, he couldn't switch off in the night, forcing him to try to sleep with his hands over his eyes. The hour's morning exercise was spent alone in a circular courtyard divided into segments by very high walls, supervised by sneering guards on top. Once, just for a bit of variety, he wrote to Tanya, he was kept out there for half an hour in the pouring rain. The cells were regularly inspected for signs of attempted escape, with guards bustling about checking the window bars and the door hinges. This included a noisy nightly inspection at 3 am, which made it hard to get back to sleep. For nearly three weeks, these gruff strangers were the only people Gramsci saw. All he had for entertainment or simple distraction were scraps of conversation through the walls or from opposite cells, swiftly suppressed if the guards overheard. At this stage he was utterly unaware of how long this would go on, but half-suspected that he was in some kind of holding pen while the authorities decided what to do.

On 19 November Gramsci was informed that he had been condemned to the maximum sentence of five years' *confino*, internal exile under the supervision of the police. There was no further explanation or detail, but he overheard one of the guards say that he would be going to the Italian colony of Somaliland. This would involve a voyage of almost two months in chains, crossing the equator, which he very much doubted he'd survive. In fact he was informed on 24th that he would serve his sentence on an Italian island, at that stage unspecified. On 25th he travelled by train to Naples, in the company of four comrades, linked by chains and manacles. Their *carabinieri* escort were much more respectful and correct than the prison guards, and allowed free conversation and the sharing of food and cigarettes. The group spent two nights in Naples, then on the evening of the 27th went by boat to Palermo in Sicily. There they stayed in relative comfort, in a house overlooking Monte Pellegrino, while other groups of political prisoners gathered for embarkation to their final destinations. Gramsci discovered that he and most of the others, including his old comrade and more recent adversary Amadeo Bordiga, were bound for the island of Ustica, north of Sicily and many miles from anywhere.

Because of rough seas, the voyage to Ustica had to be attempted four times. This was a real torment. The detainees were woken at 4 in the morning, underwent the formalities of handing over money and valuables; then a prison van to the harbour, the climb down to the boat which took them to the ship, then clambering up the ship's ladder to get on deck, then down another ladder to the third-class compartment. All this in handcuffs, and chained to three others. At 7 am the steamer set sail for the hour-long passage towards Ustica, pitching and rolling like a dolphin, then turned back because the captain considered it too risky. They went through it all again in reverse, back to their cells but by then it was past mid-day and too late for lunch, so they didn't eat till 5 pm, having had nothing all day. This whole caper on four successive days, till they finally arrived at Ustica on 7 December. Once there, life settled down and improved considerably. For now, the political internees were pretty much left to their own devices, as if having rounded them up and shipped them to this remote island the Fascists weren't sure what to do with them next. Gramsci gained weight and, for him, slept well. His headaches eased. The island was much prettier, he wrote to Tanya, than it looked in the picture postcards he promised to send, picturesque and colourful. He asked her to convey his good news to Julia. In a photograph taken of him and his comrades on Ustica, which was sent abroad and circulated around the party leadership in exile, Gramsci looked happy and relaxed.

At most there were around thirty communists in *confino* on Ustica. The six most prominent – including Gramsci, Bordiga, Virginio Borioni and Enrico Tulli, who was soon joined by his wife – had a house to themselves, with three bedrooms, a kitchen, a washroom and a terrace overlooking the beach. The weather on this isolated island was mild, but it rained frequently, which created double or even triple rainbows of the most extraordinary size and vividness. They bought their food and provisions with their pooled ten lire a day allowances, and prepared their own meals communally. Gramsci wrote to Julia on 15 January, 'It's my turn today to act as waiter and kitchen-porter. I don't know yet whether I'll have to peel the potatoes, clean the lentils or wash the salad. My début is awaited with much curiosity; for some reason they don't think I'm up to it! Several comrades have offered to take my place, but I'm insisting on doing my bit!'[1] The politicos, as they were referred to by themselves and everyone else, were subject to a loosely enforced night-time curfew. But they were otherwise free to roam the island, an area of around eight square kilometres of mostly scrub and bare rock. Of its permanent population of roughly sixteen hundred, around a thousand were islanders of Sicilian extraction, identified in the old demotic Italian of these parts as *Christiani*. Fully six hundred were ordinary criminals from all over the country, known as *soldati* (soldiers) to themselves. Both criminals and islanders were decent and hospitable towards the *politicos*. It was as though the new ideological dispensation of the mainland had not yet reached this far out, or had tarried at least some way behind its exiled opponents. Ustica had been left behind by the modern world, and by any of its inhabitants that had the means and the gumption to leave. Those that remained, permanently or temporarily, were united in suspicion and contempt for the bosses and big shots of the mainland, by which they were as likely to mean Sicily as Italy.

Gramsci was fascinated by the ordinary criminals or *soldati*, their habits and pastimes, regional identities and moral codes, and sought out their company whenever it was permitted and safe. That usually meant catching them on their own, well away from the prison guards who watched over them loosely, or the fellow convicts who kept a much closer watch. There was no paid work for most of them, he discovered, so they relied on the ordinary criminals' *mazzetta* (state handout) of just four lire a day. Most of this was spent on wine, so drunkenness and alcoholism were common. 'They would sell the shirts off their backs for a drink,' he wrote to Tanya, 'and many appear to have sold their shoes and jackets too.'[2] They borrowed more from moneylenders amongst their fellow prisoners, at a ruinous weekly interest of 30 per cent, so ended up paying over almost all their *mazzetta* every week, with just a single lira retained for basic subsistence of pasta and herbs. It was not unusual to see these particular wretches supplementing their *minestrone* with grass from the fields. The interest was collected in full and on time by the money-lenders, surrounded by hulking lackeys 'who would disembowel their great grandfathers for a drink; so, the indebted convicts are consigned to a downward spiral of obligation and decrepitude'.

As well as a much smaller allowance, the common criminals were subject to much harsher treatment from the police and prison warders, with frequent beatings and solitary confinement. They had to observe a stricter curfew than the politicos, from 5 in the evening till 7 in the morning, locked up for the night in large dormitories, where they played cards for what remained of their pathetic *mazzetta*. There were four distinct subgroups. The Northerners were mostly burglars, pickpockets or petty thieves and fraudsters. The Romans were tightly organized and loyal to each other, even those amongst them who acted as informers. The Southerners were divided into two distinct, mutually hostile subgroups: the Neapolitans and the Sicilians. A convict from Palermo offered Gramsci this ethnographic survey of these distinctive 'subaltern mentalities'. Of particular significance to this fellow were the different groups' attitudes towards knife-crime, which was his speciality. The Northerners had no time or use for it, he said; the Romans and Neapolitans could look after themselves in a knife fight if they had to; but the Sicilians had elevated the use of the knife and the drawing of blood into a highly ritualized code of honour. This fellow, Gramsci wrote to Tanya, was very proud of having inflicted a wound on the boss who was mistreating him. It had been measured as ten centimetres deep, and ten centimetres it was, not a millimetre more or less. This was his masterpiece, and it filled him with intense pride.

There was also a kind of intermediate group, known as the Bedouins, from the Italian colonies in north and east Africa. It was never entirely clear what their crimes were, traditional property theft and personal violence, or acts of rebellion against the colonial authorities. It all seemed to amount to the same thing, a kind of indiscriminate subaltern resistance, very like the old brigandage of Sardinia. They didn't seem to differentiate amongst themselves either, Gramsci observed, between *politicos* and *soldati*. The condition of outlaws in the colonies, as in much of southern Italy, covered a multitude of sins. One particular Bedouin by the name of Haussiet took a fancy to him, would join him for coffee and tell stories from the desert in exchange for tales of Sardinian mountainsides and Russian winters. Their store of anecdotes for the moment exhausted, they would fall into an easy silence. For hours on end the Bedouin would sit and watch Gramsci reading and writing. He especially enjoyed looking at Gramsci's family photos, and complained that his wife was so stupid that she would never think of sending him photos of their son. Gramsci wondered whether this wouldn't offend one of the precepts of Islam, but the Bedouin said it was alright because Kemal Ataturk, the founder of modern Turkey, said so.

Of the indigenous islanders or *Christiani*, what caught Gramsci's attention most was their attitude towards animals. On the one hand their donkeys, their only means of freight or transport, were large and extremely tame. He took this as a tribute to the kindliness of the inhabitants, in stark contrast with his own village of Ghilarza, where the donkeys were half-savage and wouldn't allow anyone near except their own master. On the other hand, on Ustica he witnessed the arrest of a pig which was found feeding illegally in the village street and was led off to prison like a common thief. He found the way of arresting the pig most amusing too. They got hold of it by its hind legs and pushed it forward like a wheelbarrow, with the beast screaming like a fiend. Another time, he tried to buy ten packets of Macedonia cigarettes with a fifty lire note, but the village tobacconist was dumb-founded and struggled with the change. She was only used to selling cigarettes to convicts one at a time, so she had to perform the difficult feat of multiplying the individual price by ten times twenty. The prison authorities quizzed him about a letter from a friend (most likely Piero Sraffa) offering to send him a radio, and for unspecified security reasons refused to sanction it. A few days later, the government-appointed *Podesta* of Ustica himself came to tell Gramsci that the municipality would purchase the radio set for him, because he had been to Palermo several times and seen for himself that it wasn't possible to send outward messages with an ordinary wireless.

Gramsci got on well with his old comrade and more recent adversary Amadeo Bordiga. Their common present plight appeared to supersede their several previous years of bitter animosity and dispute. What had seemed like bombast and self-importance in old Amadeo became in these straitened circumstances kindly affection, good humour and quiet efficiency. Bordiga remarked on Antonio's distinctive step first thing in the morning, that it was the step of a man who has not yet drunk his first cup of coffee, sluggish but somehow impatient at the same time. Gramsci was much taken with this character sketch, and relayed it to Tanya.

He further noted Amadeo's obsession, characteristically Neapolitan, with food – in stark contrast to his own general indifference – and the iron conviction that you could tell from anyone's manner or speech whether their most recent meal was a good one. In the evening, they played cards with their house mates, the first time Antonio had ever played seriously. Amadeo assured him that he had it in him to become quite a dab hand, if not a proper card sharp. They argued amicably about the order and shelving of their rapidly growing library of books and newspapers. Antonio wanted to do it by subject and date, while Amadeo went by size and shape, with the result that Antonio complained he could never find anything in such a dreadful symmetrical mess. Together they organized a school for the other politicos, modelled on the communist correspondence courses Gramsci had organized back in 1925 (and the old intransigent Bordiga had scoffed at). There were three basic levels, depending on students' previous education, consisting of grammar, mathematics and basic science. The students had high intelligence and practical understanding but for the most part little formal education, so they lapped it up like eager children. On top of that there were extra courses in history and geography, French (elementary and intermediate) and German for those who were capable of them. They used textbooks ordered by Gramsci from Sperling and Kupfers, a bookshop in Milan, on an unlimited credit account opened by Piero Sraffa, now an Economics Professor alongside John Maynard Keynes at Cambridge University in England.[3] The courses were open to officials and inhabitants of the island, who also sought and received help in the upkeep of the place. The tower clock, which had not worked for six months, was repaired by a communist watchmaker from Bologna. Electricians undertook to install lighting, and builders planned a landing platform for the ferryboat so it wouldn't have to take its chances against the rocks. From there, they would be able to watch out for its four times weekly arrival (Mondays, Wednesdays, Fridays and Saturdays), with its precious cargo of mail. Its frequent non-arrival due to bad weather was the cause of crushing disappointment and, Gramsci wrote to Sraffa, a certain melancholy settling on every face.

The ferryboat and the post it delivered were of course Antonio's only connection to the vast and terrible world he had recently been plucked from, his fragile link back to his birth family and the new family he had just begun with the Schuchts. At this stage both Julia and Tanya were writing regularly, but with quite different tones and subjects. Antonio's responses were similarly differentiated, easy and flowing with Tanya, wary and formal with Julia, whom he increasingly tended to address, refer to and think of as Julia rather than the previously customary diminutive 'Julka'. To some extent this was governed by Tanya's continued residence in Italy, far away but at least in the same country, and her own distance from her family. This contrasted with Julia's re-immersion in her old life in Moscow, not to mention her stated preoccupation with her two small children. Julia regularly excused the rather cursory, scribbled nature of her forwarded notes by reference to the fuss and racket the children were making. But it also reflected Antonio's growing attachment to his sister-in-law and parallel estrangement from his wife. His own early prison letters to Julia, or 'Julka' if he was feeling well disposed or making a special effort to reach her, largely consisted of homilies and pep-talks ('we two are still young enough to see our children growing up, all of us together') and fond reminiscences of their limited time together – the later months of 1923 and the spring of 1925 in Moscow, the first six months of 1926 in Rome – and of the much more limited periods within them which could be considered truly good times, a few scattered days and weeks which he could list and recall in fine detail. He soon ran out of things to write to her, and had to apologize via Tanya for the infrequency and childish hesitancy of his letters. It was partly, he reasoned, from the dull dispiriting realization that they would pass through at least three pairs of hands and eyes before they reached hers. Over the years this would evolve into what he called a prison style of writing, guarded and stiff, full of hints and allusions he could only hope their recipient would understand or decode.

First there was the prison governor, to whom every item of correspondence with the outside world had to be submitted and, if anything caught his eye, explained. This caused a particularly absurd if amusing incident when Julia wrote to Antonio about Delio's developing sense of direction. She described the child lying in bed in a north–south position, declaring that in the direction of his head lived people who used dogs to pull their sledges across the ice. To the right was China and to the left Austria. His legs pointed to the Crimea and so on. The governor interrogated Gramsci for over an hour, without letting him read the letter, about the secret messages it contained: what was this about Austria? Who were these people whose dogs pull them along? Gramsci tried to explain, still without reading what Julia had written, until in exasperation he finally asked whether the governor was married himself. Surely he must understand how a mother might write to her distant husband about their child. The *Direttore*, married but childless, handed over the letter without another word. Then there was Tanya, who would enclose his letters to Moscow with her own, because he was not allowed to write direct from prison to the Soviet Union. It would be only natural if she glanced at them. Finally, his letters would be scrutinized by the Foreign Relations Department of the Soviet secret police, with any political or otherwise sensitive information referred on to the Comintern and the *PCd'I's* External Centre based in Paris. But beyond all this, there was the censor in his own head, wondering what and how much Julia/Julka could take, and how she would react to any particular item. More broadly, it is hard to write freely to someone you cannot feel sure will actually be interested in you and what you have to say, as by now he generally couldn't with Julia, this beautiful stranger who had seen him at his most open and vulnerable but had given so little of herself away.

When he did write, he tried to reassure her that he was physically fine and in good spirits. He was aware of reports of his poor health or even impending death circulating abroad as part of the campaign of protest against his and the other prominent communists' detention. These politically motivated fabrications annoyed him intensely. As he wrote to Julia, the truth was bad enough; why couldn't they just stick to that? In fact, he insisted, he was probably in better health than ever. His only illness on Ustica, aside from his usual headaches and nervous debility, was a slight cold which he got over in a couple of days. Other comrades were having a much harder time of it, he told her. Molinelli fainted three times in one night and suffered convulsions lasting as long as twenty minutes. His roommate Pietro Ventura had wild nightmares that made him howl and jump about in his bed. He pleaded with his wife for more detailed letters, especially about the children, their development and illnesses, and for any photographs of them she could send. On the other hand, he advised her not to write anything which might cause the letter to be held up even further during its complicated transit.

His letters to Tanya were much franker and fuller, with detailed references to recently shared books and fulsome gratitude for gifts and supplies: when he saw her handwriting on the first bottle of coffee he received, he felt like a little boy again. He even discussed the difficulties of personal writing under censorship, in particular the difficulties of communicating his feelings without sounding like a church elder. She sent him much-needed warm winter clothes, a woollen jacket and socks. This prompted more profuse thanks, as well as mild rebuke that she should stick to what was allowed and not send things like chocolate and gingerbread that would simply be confiscated. He began to outline to her his plans for captivity: (1) To keep healthy. (2) To study German and Russian systematically. (3) To study economics and history. He requested books he felt he would need, as well as personal equipment: a safety razor with extra blades, nail-scissors and a small file; a bottle of aspirin in case the strong winds gave him toothache. He did not spare her the details of his various torments, from his recurrent ailments to his awful journeys between prisons. He complained if she went longer than a week between writing, because she was his only regular, reliable correspondent. In subsequent letters he would apologize for complaining, and beg for her indulgence and understanding.

After just six weeks and two days of tolerable and recuperative *confino* on Ustica, Gramsci was suddenly transferred back to the mainland for trial by the Special Tribunal for the Defence of the State, set up to deal with the detained communists. His first five-year sentence of *confino* would be superseded by a much more formal and no doubt lengthy period of imprisonment, after a show trial which would have all the trappings of the judicial process but none of the inherent uncertainties of its outcome. The Fascists had apparently made their minds up what to do with their opponents. His journey to Milan took nineteen days, as a common prisoner with other convicts, part of it tied on a short chain to a criminal with epilepsy. It exacted a toll on his health and his spirits from which he would never fully recover. The physical and emotional benefits of Ustica were abruptly thrown into reverse. The authorities – probably all the way up to Mussolini, who notoriously took a close interest in such matters, 'sometimes to order leniency; more often to specify that the accused be found guilty after a summary trial' – had decided that the anti-Fascist opposition should be broken as individual human beings as well as collective political threat.[4]

The *PCd'I* leaders in exile were at the advanced stages of an escape plan whose details were known only to Bordiga. The most prominent communists, Gramsci amongst them, were to be collected from Ustica beach on a moonless night by a sympathetic fisherman, and transferred to a steamer which would take them first to French Corsica for registration as political refugees, then on to freedom in exile in Marseilles and Paris. In fact, given the exiled leadership's distance from Italy, and their limited resources and experience at this kind of thing, it was always pie in the sky. They even misread the lunar calendar. Gramsci was removed by the prison authorities from Ustica on 20 January 1927, under a bright, waxing half-moon on the rough sea passage to Palermo, just a few days before the escape plan was to be implemented.

Chapter 16

THE TRIALS BEGIN

Antonio Gramsci addressed his first letter from Milan to 'My dear ones' Tanya and Julia.[1] He asked them to 'Imagine a huge worm creeping from Palermo to Milan, continuously reconstituting itself, leaving one ring in each prison and picking up new ones, shaking right and left before it settles into its next stage.' At each stop, the worm would deposit its cargo of prisoners for two to eight days in pigsties called transits, amidst the accumulated filth and poverty of generations. The prisoner arrived exhausted, dirty, unshaven, wrists raw from long hours in chains, sunken eyes stinging from sleeplessness and the strain of concentration. On leaving he felt dirtier and more tired than ever, and arrived at the next transit with wrists livid from the cold irons and the weight of the chains, and aching arms from carrying his own baggage. So it went on, pretty much the entire length of the peninsula, over a period of nearly three weeks.

The letter was never received, but retained by the prison authorities because of its exposure of prison conditions, and used as evidence of subversion in his trial. For most of the tortuous journey he thought he was going to Rome, and managed to send Tanya a telegram in the hope she might come to visit him there. In fact he was sent to Milan, in a prison transport in the company of ordinary rather than political prisoners. This is why it took nineteen days, because people were joining and leaving the convoy at every stop, in Palermo, Naples, Caianello, Isernia, Sulmona, Castellamare Adriatico, Ancona and Bologna. He stayed overnight in the prisons there, except for two nights in the *carabinieri* holding cells at Caianello and Castellamare, which he described as 'the two ugliest nights of my whole life', surrounded by scowling, feuding convicts and baited by the provincial police as a bigshot red. Peering through the filthy windows of metal railroad cars which still bore the linings of frozen snow they had stood in overnight, and shivering uncontrollably in his thin shirt and threadbare overcoat, he recognized the names of stations from his own travels or in one case – Ravisindoli in the Abruzzo region – from Julia's accounts of Schucht family holidays when she was a child.

He was able to describe the trip retrospectively as an endless film and a fantastic novel, because of its generally nightmarish quality and the extraordinary characters he encountered. At Ancona, a kindly old man of humble peasant origin asked for some soup he'd left. Gramsci gave it to him gladly, 'impressed by the serenity in his eyes and the modesty of his manner, only to learn immediately afterwards that this repellent beast had raped his own daughter'. During the exercise period in Naples, where he witnessed an initiation ceremony for the Camorra, Gramsci met a man called Arturo who said he was forty-six years old and had already spent twenty-two of those years in prison. He was an expert shoemaker, and could cite Nietzsche. Tranquil and smiling, he had skin like yellow parchment or cured leather. Gramsci saw him again in Ancona, but he was a different man, 'hard angular face, sharp icy eyes, chest puffed out, a tense spring ready to snap, like Farinata in Dante's Inferno, in contempt of hell'. In Palermo Gramsci met a formidable anarchist from Turin, who refused to disclose anything to the authorities about himself apart from his nickname, L'unico: 'I'm the only one, that's it …' One evening the other convicts organized a knife-fighting contest, strictly organized with spoons for weapons scraped against the walls, so that hits showed up on clothes as white marks. They fought in regional teams – Sicilians, Calabrians, Neapolitans and Apulians – but not the Sicilians against the Calabrians, because they hated each other so much it would inevitably turn serious. The Apulians were the best knife-fighters of all, and the two finalists were both Apulians, a sixty-five-year old and a young man of amazing skill and agility. In Bologna prison Gramsci was approached by someone calling himself Dante Romani, who also said he was an anarchist, an engine driver by trade who had been arrested after the riots in Ancona in 1920. He had just finished his sentence and was on his way back home, but he seemed strangely well informed for someone who had spent the last six years in prison.

Gramsci finally arrived at Milan prison on 7 February 1927, where he was to await his trial. Though he maintained his correspondence with Tanya and his Sardinian relatives, mainly his mother, he was limited to just two letters out per week, which had to be completed within four-and-a-half hours on a Monday afternoon. For his first six months he did not receive a single visit, primarily because Tanya, the only person within reasonable travelling distance, was in hospital for much of this time, having succumbed to the Schucht sisters' propensity for neurasthenia. In Tanya's case it was complicated by suspected appendicitis. She also suffered an acute bout of phlebitis, painful inflammation of the veins in the legs, but this had recurred throughout her adult life and was fairly easily treated with tight bandages and Aspirin. Tanya's nervous exhaustion was more troubling for Antonio, firstly because she assured him that this was the first time she'd gone down with it, but secondly because he already understood how dependent he was becoming on her, his only close, attentive and reliable relative in mainland Italy. Tanya had taken him on as a kind of cause or project, with what he began to describe as her animal protection psychology, and considerably rearranged her life around him.

He took meticulous stock of his own new life, and the tightly constrained world in which he was to lead it, which he relayed as best he could in his letters. The prison of San Vittore in Milan consisted of eight radiuses extending from a central hub, like the spokes in a bicycle wheel, with cells on either side of broad high corridors. From where they sat at the hub, the guards could see what was happening on every radius and get there quickly if they needed to. It was the typical design for the modern prison, invented by the French for the more humane, scientific containment of opponents of the Revolution; at least, those not consigned to the guillotine. Combined with more recent thinking in criminology, which had established through methodical observation and measurement that crime was more prevalent among certain types, who therefore could not be held personally responsible for their crimes, it created the prison atmosphere and ethos of a holding pen, a warehouse rather than a rubbish dump – notwithstanding Mussolini's description of his harsher penal policy as 'social hygiene' – which was progress of sorts.[2] If there were types, Gramsci wrote to Tanya, these arose from the negative effects of confinement on certain personalities and social backgrounds, so the calmest were the peasants; then the factory workers, then the craftsmen, and finally the would-be intellectuals, who were prone to sudden bursts of infantile raving.

There were fifty cells in each radius, which made for a prison population of at least four hundred, perhaps a couple of hundred more if you took into account the ordinary criminals who were trusted to each other's company and expected to share cells. On the way to his daily two hours of solitary exercise, strictly forbidden to converse with those other prisoners, he had calculated that he was now in the twenty-second cell of the second radius, having been moved (for no obvious reason he could see or that anyone was prepared to tell him) from the thirteenth cell of the first radius. It had a single window, whose bars gave it the look of a wolf's mouth or *bocca di lupo*, its name in prison slang. It was high up in the wall, too high to see any more through it than a patch of sky. A band of sunlight appeared at 2 o'clock in the afternoon, reached about 25 centimetres across, and worked its way around a mid-point on the wall – well above his head – till it fell away in the early evening. Gramsci calculated from this trajectory that his current cell must be facing south-west-west. He compared this ration of sunlight to his previous cell, where the sun shone between 10 and 2 o'clock, and at its highest created a band at least 60 centimetres wide at around chest level. He had been able to stand there for at least an hour every day with the warm sun full on his face, whereas now he could only reach it on tip-toe, stretching his fingertips towards the precious heat.

He slept on a camp bed up against a side wall, with two thin mattresses, one woollen blanket and fresh linen once a fortnight. There was also a small table, a bedside cupboard, a basin and an enamel iron jug and a mirror in which he could shave. He had purchased a small cooking stove and a few aluminium utensils from the stall brought in once a week from a local department store. It really wasn't much worse than most of the places he had lived, and considerably better than some. He habitually rose at 6.30, half an hour before the guards roused everyone else with their shouts and a clanging bell, and made himself his first cup of coffee of the day. Then he tidied and cleaned out his cell and his toilet, washed his face and hands at the basin, and combed through his unruly hair at the mirror. At 7.30 he was brought half a litre of hot milk, which he drank straight away with a few mouthfuls of bread. At 8.00 he was escorted to one of the exercise yards, where he strolled around reading and smoking for two hours. Most recently, he had been reading *The Gentle Peasant Girl* by Pushkin, and learning roughly twenty lines of the original mellifluous Russian a day. The rest of the morning he perused the five daily newspapers and several weekly political papers and cultural reviews he bought and had delivered and, for light reading, the constantly replenished stack of popular novels from the prison library.

Lunch arrived irregularly, at some time between 12 and 3, soup or pasta with a bit of bread and cheese and a quarter litre of wine. Over lunch and afterwards he continued reading. A similar dinner, augmented by meat or a couple of eggs, would be delivered to his cell between 6 and 7. With the state of his teeth, he wrote to Tanya, he could not eat any vegetables, though he could nibble at dates and biscuits. To allay her concerns, he assured her that he drank only three coffees and smoked no more than fifteen cigarettes a day. At 7.30 pm the guards commanded silence with their bell. He would go to bed and read until between 11 and midnight. If he felt like it, he would make himself a cup of chamomile tea at around 9 o'clock, and ruminate on another day of organized pointlessness. All this was paid for from his relatively generous prison allowance of ten lire a day, and brought in from the outside by the Milanese grocers and newsagents who did good business from the prison.

His present cell was, he estimated, about three metres by five, and four metres high, the dimensions of a student's bed-sitting room. It was situated right above the prison workshop, so the throbbing of the machines went on all day and into the evening if there was a job to finish. All of this he consigned to memory, to be recorded later in his letters because he had no means of writing observations down. In the same spirit of petty restriction that pervaded all the Prison Regulations and limited his interactions with other prisoners to a mere glance and a nod in the corridor or staircase, he was not allowed any writing materials outside the strictly timed hours allowed every Monday afternoon for family correspondence. It took him all that time to write the two letters per week he was allowed to send, with a scratchy quill pen on sheets of cheap coarse paper that had to be surrendered when the time was up. During this period of hiatus, his personal letters were mostly an increasingly desperate attempt to keep in touch with relatives he hadn't seen – or in some cases heard from – in years.

In the summer heat of 1927 Gramsci wrote to Giuseppe Berti, a comrade in the *PCd'I* leadership in exile: 'I am undergoing a period of great moral stress because of certain family matters. My nerves are on edge and I'm very touchy. I can't succeed in concentrating on any subject, I have lost all sense of your circumstances, and I have no idea what sort of changes have been going on in the exile community.'[3] Word began to circulate among the communist exiles that Antonio was refusing to put pen to paper because of an exaggerated sense of caution and some kind of family-related moral crisis which, apart from anything else, was leaving him seriously short of money. He was finding it ever harder to buy in provisions from outside with just the government allowance, and for whole weeks was having to rely on the meagre prison fare, which was making his digestive problems worse. With Tanya in hospital and out of circulation, arrangements were made to transfer funds via his family in Sardinia. There was a further round of rumours about Gramsci's health, typically exaggerated as they gathered political force, and culminating in yet another rash of stories in the émigré and foreign press about his imminent death. His old Turin friend and comrade (and now husband of Pia

Carena) Alfonso Leonetti claimed in the Comintern bulletin to have heard 'an anguished cry from Milan jail: Gramsci is dying of hunger!'[4] The party leaders considered another escape plan but, after receiving coded messages from the *PCd'I* prisoners in Milan, it was quickly dismissed as completely infeasible.

The first visit Gramsci received since his arrest in November 1926 was from his brother Mario, in late August 1927. It was a strange encounter, all the stranger for being the least expected or desired by either Antonio or his younger brother. Mario had been an official with the local Fascists in Varese, in the Lombardy region of northern Italy, but he had decided that it was bad for his business to be too openly involved and had withdrawn from active politics. Nonetheless, he was able to use his contacts to persuade the prison authorities to approve a new medicine for the worsening indigestion Antonio had been writing home to his mother about. Antonio wrote to thank Mario for his intercession, giving him more detail about his various, mostly stable medical conditions. Mario's wife Anna had heard the stories about Antonio's supposed illness and looming death. Now armed with his letter to Mario, and with all the dreadful sounding Latin medical terms and complicated chemical compounds required to deal with them, she wrote in wild lamentation to her mother-in-law. Signora Peppina was predictably distraught, and Antonio had to write to reassure his mother that all things considered he was in fact quite alright. All of this upset, made worse by delayed and muddled correspondence the length and breadth of the country, rumbled on for weeks on end. The various parties – Antonio, Mario and Anna, above all Signora Peppina and the others back in Ghilarza – suffered agonies of confusion and worry while they waited for further letters, or for their own to reach their destinations. Each round of letters only seemed to make matters worse.

Antonio finally asked Mario to come to visit him at the prison in Milan, in the hope that this would clear things up and calm everyone down. In fact it had quite the opposite effect. For the fifteen minutes of the visit, Mario was deeply disturbed by the prison environment, jumping out of his skin at the slightest noise or commotion, Gramsci wrote to their mother. Mario was also obviously embarrassed by the incarceration and the dishevelled appearance of his brother, whom he had not seen since 1921, when they had had a similarly uncomfortable encounter, involving discussion of their passionately held, diametrically opposed political views. Oddly, Mario had also visited Tanya in hospital before travelling on to the prison, and invited her to come for a recuperative holiday with him and his wife in Lombardy. Antonio attempted to put Mario at ease with a funny story from his early months in Milan, which he thought he would appreciate. A guard had asked him if it was true he could have been a government minister if only he'd agreed to change sides. Gramsci said a minister would have been a bit much, but he could have been an under-secretary at the post office or the public works department, because that's the kind of job governments gave Sardinian MPs. The guard thought he was serious, and asked him why then he hadn't switched sides.

Antonio remembered Mario fondly as a lively, enquiring and funny little boy back in Ghilarza, doing skits and impressions of teachers and uncles and village elders. Mario had always seemed to be at the centre of a huddle of other small boys, telling some outlandish story or demonstrating some new trick. That would have seemed a long time ago now. After a quarter of an hour, Mario got up to leave, still edgy and embarrassed. Antonio hoped that was the end of the matter. But after the prison visit, Mario wrote a further alarming letter to his brother Carlo in Ghilarza, who set about organizing a trip to Milan for himself and his mother to see their dying brother and son before it was too late. Antonio then had to write to both Carlo and his mother separately – using up an entire week's ration of precious correspondence – to reassure them that really and truly he was fine, and that on no account should they come and see him now, especially his mother, a woman of seventy who'd hardly been outside her village and never made a rail journey longer than forty kilometres.

To the clearly panicking Carlo he wrote curtly that 'your present mood isn't worthy of a grown man' and, drawing on his own experiences of hardship as a student and an activist, outlined the philosophy of self-sufficient perseverance that had got him through all these years of penury and oppression, and would enable him to survive prison:

> When all is lost or seems to be, you have to go back to work, starting from scratch with a cheerful attitude. I believe that you always have to depend on yourself and your own energies, without expecting anything from anyone, in order to avoid being disappointed. You must set out to do only what you know how to do and are capable of doing, seeking your own individual way. Anything else is romantic daydreaming.[5]

It did not occur to him at the time that this stark homily, and the bitter wisdom it contained, might cause further concern to his relatives. Antonio wrote an account of the whole mess to Tanya, regretting whatever he himself had done to create it and resolving in conclusion that he couldn't count on Mario or his precious connections any more. He would just have to make do with the medicines and supplies he could get hold of in prison and that Tanya might be able to procure for him outside and have sent in. He had no further direct contact with Mario, to everyone's evident satisfaction.

His only other visitor and regular, reliable correspondent in Milan was Tanya, who came to see him just a few days after coming out of hospital in early September 1927. She had been there for nearly six months, ever since Antonio had arrived in Milan. He tried to give her an upbeat account of his own health. He felt less nervous tension now than for years. Perhaps he was getting used to life in prison. He guarded against it, but realized it was inevitable, necessary even. He was hungry for news from the outside. How were things in Rome? How was that lemon plant he had left behind? Had someone thought to water it? And how were the Passarges? He knew Signora Clara was unwell, and that his arrest must have come as a great shock to her and her husband. One of his very first letters from prison had been to her, asking for some of his books, but he hadn't received them. Knowing how reliable she was, he suspected she never got the letter. In fact, Signora Passarge had died in the summer, but Tanya had been reassured by a bereaved Signor Passarge that it was not directly caused by Gramsci's arrest, unpleasant though that had been. Tanya had taken his lemon tree into her own care, and it was doing well on her windowsill. She would bring him a lemon on her next visit. For now she had brought him some fresh milk and cheese. She told him she was planning to move to Milan so she could see him more often, and had already found a job at the Soviet trade delegation there. He outlined for her his latest thoughts on a programme of study, something to stave off intellectual degradation and provide a centre for his inner life.

He had in fact been thinking about this for much of the summer, and was anxious to get on with it, badgering the prison authorities for permission to write in his cell, outside the prescribed hours for correspondence, and to order the books he would need, some of them dangerously close to the proscription on political agitation. He believed it would help him to survive his imprisonment, however long that might turn out to be, and have the added benefit of making sense of the failure and defeat of the revolutionary struggle, at least here in Italy. Otherwise he just didn't know what he would do with himself. By taking on grand historical and cultural themes, he would hope to rise above the everyday turmoil of political life, not to mention the dull squalor of prison routine, and create something *für ewig*. This, he explained to Tanya, was Goethe's term for research and writing that had no immediate practical application, and in that sense was disinterested. But for precisely that reason, it would enable him to shed light on the epochal historical changes that had swept across Italy and the rest of the world in the last few centuries. For now, the themes he wanted to explore were firstly the formation of intellectual castes and their role in the creation of national cultures; then something on comparative linguistics, his degree subject before he dropped out of university; thirdly, a study of the plays of Pirandello, which he had reviewed for the socialist press during the war years when no one else was taking the playwright seriously; and finally, a study of popular taste in literature, with a view to identifying just what appeals to those masses of people who devour the serialized stories in the periodicals.

He also shared with Tanya further observations of prison life, which he planned to compile into a fuller account, a separate section of his prison notebooks. It was never completed, but its isolated fragments offer some wonderfully evocative anthropological snapshots. The available company in prison was divided into two strata, he reported: ordinary criminals, with whom conversation could be interesting for two or three weeks, until one exhausted the supply of the picturesque and the typical that was inherent in their condition; and the self-styled intellectuals, referred to in vulgar Italian as *mezzo-calzette* or half-stockings, accused of 'professional' crime such as debt and fraud. This last lot didn't even have the colourful stories of the ordinary criminals: he had had some of them as neighbours in nearby cells, and was struck by how easily they became demoralized. They wept exactly like children, with great loud sobs, invoking Mamma. They were always asking for something, in order to be able to see the guard, exchange a few words and so feel connected with life, proving they still had rights. Individual encounters included a peasant from Salerno who had killed his father-in-law and thereby inherited his property – 'I've killed and I've inherited' was his refrain – and a Calabrian gangster, sixteen years old, to whom Gramsci gave a pair of shoes and a vest and who solemnly promised in return that he would never steal his chickens. A shoemaker from Messina recited all the adventures of Sinbad the Sailor in a Sicilian version he had heard from his grandfathers; he refused to believe, and Gramsci did not insist, that the story came from *A Thousand and One Nights*.

Through 1927 and into 1928, the legal and investigative proceedings against Gramsci and the other communist leaders in prison churned on relentlessly. The problem for the Fascist lawyers was finding credible concrete evidence against him. The regime had not yet cast such considerations completely aside. Police reports on Gramsci consisted of routine observations of his daily life as a communist MP, or vague generalities about him being subversive, a trouble-maker or a threat to public order. One report from the Rome *carabinieri* stated that he had been found in possession of arms and explosives in November 1922, when he'd already been in Moscow for six months and would remain abroad for another year and a half. So the authorities set about gathering evidence through other means. There was a sudden easing of the conditions under which Gramsci was kept at Milan prison, especially his contact with other prisoners. He had to give up his right to those of his periodicals that were classified as political, in case he used them to incite insurrection, but he was bored with what now seemed to pass for everyday political life on the outside, and it seemed a small price to pay for some very welcome company. He and his fellow politicos were even allowed to organize an exhibition of photographs of their children. He wrote in a note to Julia, included in a letter to Tanya, that Delio was greatly admired, hoped that this might make her smile, and added sadly that it was only with great difficulty that he could imagine her smiling.

At this point, Dante Romani reappeared, permitted to approach Signor Gramsci and even to spend whole afternoons in his cell. At first Gramsci was glad to see him, and set aside the doubts he had felt on their previous encounter in Bologna. When he said he thought Romani was being released, Romani replied breezily that he had got into trouble again. Gramsci decided he should just enjoy the company. He described Romani to Tanya as an alert and lively young man from a village near Monza, awaiting trial on a charge of theft and damages to a brothel, part of a self-appointed vice-squad of vigilantes, raiding the place for cocaine. It was all, Gramsci wrote, highly entertaining. They talked freely about their lives and families. Romani had a charming and pretty little girl called Maria Luisa. In accordance with Sardinian custom he and Gramsci decided that Delio should marry Maria Luisa as soon as the two children reached the age of consent. But then Romani started offering to convey messages, letters and orders to the outside. The *PCd'I* was, he said, in a bad way, and needed Gramsci's leadership to put things right. This crude police trick only confirmed Gramsci's previous suspicion that Dante Romani, or whatever was his real name, was an agent provocateur.

When a new warrant against Gramsci was issued in May 1927, accusing him of provoking civil war and destroying life and property, it was clear from the supporting documents he saw that there was still very little hard evidence against him. In October, another prisoner introduced himself as Corrado Melani to

Gramsci in the exercise yard. Melani said he was the lover of the sister-in-law of the secretary of the Milan Fascist federation, Mario Giampaoli. He was being persecuted by Giampaoli because he knew certain things about him. For example, the attempt on Mussolini's life in Bologna was a set-up organized by Giampaoli. One of his sidekicks shot in the air, and Giampaoli jumped on the so-called assassin Anteo Zamboni and slit his throat. Melani claimed to have documents proving Giampaoli's involvement with brothels and gambling, and that a number of Fascist MPs were homosexuals. If any of this got out, Melani confided to Gramsci, the Fascists would surely fall, which was why Giampaoli was out to get him. Melani offered to sell his documents to the *PCd'I*. Gramsci politely but firmly turned him down, and saw no more of Corrado Melani. He wrote a strongly worded complaint to the Ministry of Justice about police attempts to entrap him. His conditions were tightened up again, with the limitations on contact with other prisoners re-imposed and stricter than ever surveillance by the guards.[6]

His worst problem now, he wrote to his sister Teresina, was the boredom of enforced leisure. He spent one whole month whittling away at a stick until it bore some resemblance to a letter-opener, which he conveyed to Julia via Tanya with great pride in his craftsmanship. He became quite adept at constructing papier-mâché balls from old copies of the *Gazzetta dello Sport*, with the vague intention of sending them to his sons to remind them of him. With the onset of winter, the trajectory of the sun – when it deigned to appear at all from behind dull cloudy Northern Italian skies – sank lower and lower, until the daily ration was just a few minutes of pale light on a patch of ceiling just in front of the barred window. For company he was forced back onto the insects and birds that periodically joined him in his cell. The former offered limited possibilities: he failed to find a spider to train, he wrote to Tanya, there weren't any mice and the remaining zoology was not very attractive. The local bird life was more cooperative. He was especially fond of the sparrows that flew in through the *bocca di lupo*, and he even managed to tame a couple of them by clipping their wings. The first sparrow was very proud and extremely lively, resistant to handling, beating its wings and pecking his hand fiercely. If he offered it a dead fly in a matchbox, it never took it until he moved away. Then one morning it came up close and started pecking his shoes for food. After that they were the best of friends, until the bird stopped coming. By contrast, Gramsci's next tame sparrow was very servile and unassuming: it liked to be fed although it could eat perfectly well by itself, hopping onto his shoes and nestling in the turn-ups of his trousers.

In late 1927 Gramsci, well aware of the edginess in his mood, received what he immediately regarded as a strange letter from Ruggiero Grieco, writing from Moscow on behalf of the exiled *PCd'I* leadership.[7] At a time when the communist political prisoners were preparing a legal defence which rested on disavowal of their status as party leaders, Grieco referred to 'the great responsibility assigned to you … as communist leaders'. At one of the preparatory hearings, Gramsci was asked about this apparent contradiction by an examining magistrate, who observed: 'Signor Gramsci, you have friends who seem to want you to stay in prison quite a while.' The letter was probably little more than a routine rallying cry to all the communist prisoners, a rather clumsy attempt at comradely morale-raising, thoughtless rather than malicious. Gramsci conceded to Tanya that perhaps prison life was making him unduly suspicious, but the memory of the strange letter from Grieco would remain with him for the rest of his life, and come to represent his own growing sense of isolation and the insensitivity towards him of those on the outside who were supposed to care for him.

A second letter from Grieco, sent some months later from Moscow with news of the latest situation inside the Russian Communist Party, had a quite different secondary purpose. Grieco meant to reassure the Russian authorities, who he knew would intercept it, of the Italian party's whole-hearted support for the new Stalin–Bukharin majority's crackdown on the Russian opposition. Gramsci recognized another cack-handed political gesture, meant to quell any lingering suspicions amongst the Russians about him and his letter to them via Togliatti in October 1926. But even here he saw something irresponsibly foolish that could be used against him at his trial. Similarly, his relations with Tanya, written and in person, were coming under strain. She had written to him, saying that he seemed different without specifying how. With so much time to brood between visits, he had agonized over what she might have meant, and wrote back saying he wasn't aware of the differences she had mentioned, though he understood that prison life changed people so slowly they may not notice at all. He accepted that he may have grown colder and apologized for causing her any upset, but added in an attempt at light-hearted mitigation that people always torment those they love most. He then went on to chide her for sending him books he hadn't asked for and for letting weeks go by without writing. He concluded on what he thought was a more positive note: 'For a long time I had planned to offer you some flowers grown here in my cell (what prison romanticism!), but the plants dried up and I was unable to keep alive the five or six little flowers that budded.'[8]

In her next letter, Tanya inferred that these closing remarks were some kind of comment on their relationship, at which point Gramsci decided not to write again until he saw her. When she came next, in late September 1927, he was suffering from severe toothache which no amount of Aspirin seemed to touch, and contemplating another brutal bloody extraction by the huge monosyllabic guard who bore the laughable title of Prison Dentist. Gramsci had already lost five teeth to this butcher in the eight months he'd been here. On top of the teeth he'd lost in his years of freedom, it was beginning to feel like his mouth didn't have many left. He and Tanya were having regular altercations over what she chose to send him in prison. He wanted her just to send what he'd asked for, whereas she insisted on sending other things which were simply confiscated because they contravened prison regulations. She offered to procure a new suit for him to wear at his trial, while he pointed out that he had an old suit set aside, that there would be no legal benefit to him dressing like a dandy, and that when sentenced he'd be given a regular prisoner's outfit to wear.

In the New Year, into 1928, Tanya fell ill again with her nervous debility and constitutional weakness, which this time took the form of bronchial pneumonia. For several months she was again confined to hospital and unable to visit Antonio in prison, and had to give up her job at the Soviet trade delegation in Milan. He could not help reflecting that the demands and pressures he had put on her, not to mention the mutual irritations he had tried to pass off in a letter as normal between brother and sister, which was how he now thought of her, had contributed to her relapse. In the meantime he started, to his immense surprise, to receive letters from Julia again. The first was written on 26 December 1927, amended on 24 January and (to Antonio's puzzlement) finally arrived at the end of February 1928. Julia apologized for not writing when she was ill or distressed, and hoped that he would forgive her. The rest of the letter consisted of news of Delio and Giuliano, now aged three-and-a-half and eighteen months, respectively. Delio was drawing ever more graphically organized pictures, and showing an interest in the construction toys now appearing in the Moscow shop windows. Giuliano had taken his first steps and begun to call people by their names and compose simple sentences. He was especially attentive to his big brother, and tried to copy everything Delio did and said. The news brought Gramsci equal parts delight and dismay, proud of his family's development but desperately sad that it did not include him.

He wrote straight back to Julia, via Tanya in hospital, trying hard to stay positive and not communicate his own mixed feelings at her news, while remaining truthful and sincere in what was his first direct contact for over a year. He told her how he was finally adapting to prison life, overcoming the crises of his first year in captivity, which he attributed to his own futile attempts at resistance. Now he was consciously slowing down and allowing himself to succumb to the routine, the privations and necessities, the enormous number of minute events that occur day after day, month after month, year after year, with the same mechanical rhythm of sand in an hourglass. He had initially resisted these external pressures, but to no avail. He had now arrived at the serene decision not to struggle any longer but instead seek to control the process. He would never become a complete brute, since he was ready at any moment to toss off the second skin – half stubborn donkey, half docile sheep – of the long-term prisoner. Striking a lighter note, there was one thing he'd never be able to do, give his own skin the smoky colour it once had. Little Delio, despite Julia's contribution, must be much smokier by now than him. That winter he had gone three months without seeing any more than a few remote reflections of the sun. The light that filtered into his cell was somewhere between that of a cellar and that of an aquarium. It made him feel like one of those monstrous fish that live at the bottom of the very deep sea, so pale that you can see right through them.

In early April 1928, he received via Tanya a lock of Giuliano's hair – a lovely ash blond colour, the same as his own as a baby – and the latest report on the child's developing speech. He was now able to say clearly 'Mamma Julka' and 'Mamma Zhenya'. In reply to Tanya, Antonio noted Delio's upcoming fourth birthday and asked her to purchase and send a Meccano set on his behalf. He wondered whether these mass-produced construction sets were better than the much more primitive materials available to himself as a child, which demanded so much more imagination and creativity. He recalled constructing an entire naval fleet out of sticks and stones and horse-bone glue. At the end of that month he wrote to his mother, enclosing for safekeeping the single photograph he had of Delio, taken nearly two years earlier in June 1926, and which he had displayed in the prisoners' exhibition in November 1927. He said he was eager to hear her impressions, 'particularly whether he looks like us when we were children. You'll see how handsome your grandson is and be really proud of him. I want you to leave the prison stamps on the back. The photograph should remain just as it is, with the signs of its passage through the prison system where I've been held for so long. Far from feeling ashamed of my imprisonment, I consider it an extreme honour. This will certainly be the child's feeling too, when he is of an age to understand these things.'[9]

Antonio Gramsci was taken for trial in Rome on 11 May 1928, one of thirty-two leading Communists, of whom eight exiles were to be tried *in absentia*. From 12 May he was held again in Regina Coeli prison, this time sharing a cell with his close comrades Umberto Terracini and Mauro Scoccimaro, who were due to be tried alongside him. It was becoming clear to him as well as others around him that his health was rapidly deteriorating, not least because he was now denied the special diet prescribed by the prison authorities in Milan, who had been anxious to stop the stories circulating internationally about his ill-treatment and impending demise. In Rome the situation was almost the opposite, he wrote to his mother, with no indication how to gain permission to obtain food – at his own expense – that he could digest. There was a limit of just one official request a week. If this was turned down, there was a further week's wait to make another one, so it was pointless to even bother. All the same he was still trying to reassure his mother and others that his current state of physical and moral health was good, and that he felt serene and satisfied in himself. Life was difficult, and sometimes sons – for the sake of their own honour and dignity – had to make their mothers suffer.

The trial began on 28 May. It was meticulously planned and designed, with strong elements of theatrical production, borrowing freely from church-style liturgy, language and ritual. Security was provided by dozens of Fascist militiamen with black helmets, daggers and rifles with fixed bayonets. Posing in cordons as guards of honour for the judges, they could have passed as sacristans in a cathedral, guns instead of crosses held aloft as at some perverted black mass. The proceedings were conducted according to an entirely new, specially devised court-martial protocol, with a general as President of the Tribunal and a jury of five colonels from the Fascist militia. Gramsci and the others were accused of conspiracy, instigation to civil war, justifying criminal acts and fomenting class hatred. They were further accused of being directly and primarily responsible for the illegal and criminal activities of the Communist organization as sponsored by the organs and general policy of the party itself. Defence lawyers continually asked for more specific charges, supported by new and concrete evidence, but none was forthcoming. The prisoners, they concluded, were being tried for their politics rather than any crime they might have committed.

Gramsci was represented by a lawyer from Milan, Giovanni Ariis. His brother Carlo was there, along with other prisoners' relatives, and the Rome correspondents of the *Manchester Guardian*, *Le Petit Parisien* and the Soviet News Agency *Tass*.

Gramsci was the first to be questioned, on 30 May, and acknowledged that he was a communist MP and journalist. But he denied engaging in any kind of clandestine activities, not least because for years six police agents had followed him about everywhere, supposedly for protection but actually for surveillance. This was now his best possible defence. How could he have done the terrible things he was accused of when he was under constant surveillance? When the President of the Tribunal asked Gramsci what was meant in his writings by 'talk of war and the seizure of power by the proletariat', Gramsci replied, 'all dictatorships end sooner or later by being overthrown in war. Given their intrinsically coercive character, it's the only way it can be done. When that happens, it seems clear to me that the proletariat should replace the ruling class, assume the reins of power, and try to build the nation back up again.'[10]

In summing up the case against him, on 2 June, the Prosecutor Michele Isgro declared 'We must prevent this brain from functioning for twenty years!' On 4 June, Gramsci received a sentence of twenty years, four months and five days. His fellow detainees received similar sentences. An appeal was immediately presented on behalf of all of them, and almost as immediately rejected. At first Gramsci was supposed to be sent to the prison at Portolongone, on the island of Elba ninety kilometres south of Livorno. But with his health still worsening, his sister Teresina wrote to Mussolini requesting a careful medical examination and transfer to a prison hospital where he could receive the proper food and care his weak constitution required, and endure his punishment more humanely. This prompted a medical report of 6 July, which declared that Gramsci had recently lost twelve teeth and was suffering from gingivitis with abscess formation (gum disease), caused by uraemic disturbance (kidney dysfunction) and accompanied by nervous exhaustion. It was decided to send him to Turi di Bari, a penitentiary reserved for sick prisoners, in the south-eastern heel of Italy. Mussolini declared in the press that this demonstrated the humane face of his regime, and contrasted Gramsci's treatment with the expulsions, imprisonments and summary executions dealt out to some of his old comrades in Moscow.

Chapter 17

SETTLING IN AT TURI DI BARI

Antonio Gramsci's journey from Rome to Turi di Bari prison was, he wrote to Tanya some days after his arrival, another taste of hell. He had been granted a medical certificate, meant to alleviate his travelling conditions, but somehow at the moment of his departure it had been mislaid. The journey lasted twelve days, in an ordinary prison transport, manacled and shackled in transit, lurching southwards between holding cells in filthy provincial gaols, the huge worm heading back in the opposite direction from that which had borne him from Ustica to Milan. Gramsci had attributed his illness in Rome to liver trouble on top of his usual ailments, but on departure it flared up and got very much worse. At Caserta, about a third of the way to Turi, a brusque local doctor diagnosed herpes zoster, commonly known as shingles, a viral infection of the nerves causing a painful unsightly rash down one side which can last for months and cause permanent discomfort and nerve damage. This, Gramsci observed sardonically to Tanya, was one of the few complaints he'd not yet suffered. The doctor at Caserta refused to give him the gauze he needed to bandage his sores because at the front soldiers had gone as long as six days without having their wounds bandaged. He then demanded in lieu of payment half the big bag of cherries Tanya had sent from Rome. The illness soon got very much worse: 'At Benevento I went through two absolutely horrible days and nights; I twisted around like a reptile. No matter where I put myself, sitting, standing up or lying down, I just couldn't get any relief.'[1]

But perhaps it wasn't shingles after all. A more sympathetic prison doctor at Benevento diagnosed Erysipelas or (the aptly named) St. Anthony's fire, a subcutaneous bacterial infection which causes rashes, soreness and boils all over the body. He couldn't offer any treatment, but advised that the infection would have to run its course and last weeks rather than months.[2] He didn't ask for payment either, but Gramsci gave him the rest of the cherries in gratitude for a more reassuring diagnosis. Between Benevento and Foggia the pain receded, and the rashes and boils started to fade and dry up. Gramsci stayed at Foggia for five days, and by the third felt somewhat better. The pain was just about bearable when lying down, and he managed to sleep a few hours each night. He finally arrived at Turi di Bari on 19 July, still suffering from skin inflammation, struggling to eat and digest, breathing with great difficulty and unable to walk more than a few steps at a time without leaning on someone. Every movement required careful forward planning and long minutes of heavy-breathing recovery. Altogether, he had barely slept the whole journey. There was some consolation, in the form of a letter from Tanya waiting for him, and another from his brother Carlo enclosing a very welcome 250 lire note.

The special prison at Turi was a traditional, squat, castle-type building with four landings, built from local stone and surrounded by a kind of moat whose high walls deterred escape and contained the exercise yards. The windows of the cells were heavily barred but mercifully large, with shutters against the winter cold and the summer sun. Unlike the prisons in Rome and Milan, they let in plenty of air and light. There would be no fretful calculations of how many minutes and hours of sunlight Gramsci could expect, or how much of his cell it might reach and warm. To begin with, he was held in a kind of quarantine or assessment area, prior to being assigned to a permanent section of the prison. This first cell was a communal dormitory with five other prisoners, strangers from all over Italy, anxious and wary of each other as only imprisoned strangers can be. After a couple of weeks he was transferred to another cell with four others, all political prisoners, but with a variety of bronchial and lung complaints. He managed to sleep a little better, and it was a great relief to be able to share news and opinions with other politicos, even if they belonged to different factions and movements, but he fretted about what illnesses he might catch from them on top of everything else. As soon as he was able, Gramsci asked to see the prison governor, Giuseppe Parmegiani, who told him bluntly that he had received strict instructions from above that the Honourable Deputy Gramsci was to be treated no differently from any other prisoner. The authorities had already demonstrated their compassion by not sending him to a normal prison hell-hole but here to the *Casa Penale Speciale* at Turi, with its specialist experience, expertise and facilities in dealing with prisoners in ill-health. Gramsci had struggled to see any of this. It looked to him like any ordinary prison, apart from the preponderance of frail and elderly prisoners and the added risks of communal contagion. 'Let me remind you,' he replied as civilly as he could manage, 'that I was arrested while still a parliamentary deputy and theoretically protected by my office. You should be treating me like a Cardinal, rather than worse than a humble parish clerk.'[3] The governor simply reiterated that the normal rules would apply, including – and here he picked up the two letters Gramsci had already written to Tanya and his mother – one letter per fortnight. He said that Gramsci was to indicate which of the two he wanted sent now, and which could wait another two weeks. The Governor further pointed out his own underlining of Gramsci's written instruction to Tanya never to send him anything unless he asked her for it.

Gramsci got even shorter shrift from the local doctor, Dr. Cisternino, who was responsible for providing the prison's rudimentary medical service and refused to see him for several days. When he finally did, conducting a cursory examination and simply reading out what the doctor in Benevento had written, he observed that Gramsci appeared to be on the mend, while adding that of course, as a good Fascist he would like nothing better than to see him dead. Gramsci heard later that when Cisternino was called out by the townspeople at night, he would look down from his window and fix the fee – 'Is it a 5,000 lire or a 10,000 lire visit?' – before deigning to descend. In mid-August 1928, Gramsci did at least manage to get a cell on his own on medical grounds. He wrote to Tanya that the Special Tribunal sentenced him to imprisonment but did not specify that this should be aggravated by tuberculosis. But to his great dismay the new cell was located right next to the guardroom, with noisy comings and goings all day and all night. He never again slept a whole night through at Turi. Sleep disturbance and deprivation became his principal torment and bugbear.

From the very start of his imprisonment proper, Gramsci knew that the first weeks and months would be the hardest. Apart from the uncertainty and disruption of the quarantine and assessment period, it was also a matter of getting used to this horrible new place, which largely came down to convincing himself – denying all the evidence of his senses and intellect – that it was not quite so horrible as it seemed. He had never been adept at self-delusion, and now he lived, he wrote to Julia, in continuous fear of being overrun by the prison routine. From his own observations of the other prisoners, he could see that those who had been there for more than a year or so were acclimatized, resigned to their fate, but when he observed men who had been in prison for five, eight or ten years, and how their minds had become warped, he dreaded what would become of him. At least some of them must have been convinced at the start that they would never give in. Instead, without being aware of it, so slow and molecular was the process, they found themselves utterly changed; and this change in them prevented them from realizing exactly what had happened. Of course he intended to resist but he wasn't able to laugh at himself as he used to, and this was a worrying sign. Little more than six months into his sentence, he wrote to Tanya that he found himself falling into the trance-like state of the drowning man, typical of old convicts, who no longer reason by making realistic connections but by magical intuitions.

The longer sentence from the Special Tribunal, the twenty-odd years that now formally superseded the initial five years of *confino*, had a kind of weighty finality about it. It was Mussolini's last word to his fellow *Avanti!* journalist and old Socialist Party comrade. Insofar as any kind of future was conceivable in the new order of Fascist Italy, rapidly beginning to feel like a permanent fixture, this really did feel like a life sentence. Finally, at Turi di Bari, with the journeys between other prisons and the brief stops inside them looking more like a strange interlude, and now settled in a cell of his own, Gramsci realized that he was not going anywhere else any time soon. There was a kind of peace in this gloomy realization. The fight was over; he was now, as he would put it increasingly more firmly as the years of incarceration proceeded, out of active service. But it wasn't simply a matter of his own personal withdrawal from the front. The war he had described so proudly to his mother just a few months ago had been irretrievably lost. The proletarian revolution and the making of socialism was an inglorious failure, at least here in Italy but quite possibly all across Europe too. All that remained was to figure out the reasons for its defeat; to pretend otherwise was another kind of self-delusion. The Honourable Antonio Gramsci, one-time delegate to the Executive Committee of the Communist International, with its abruptly modern acronym of *Ispolcom*, more recently Secretary of the *Partito Comunista d'Italia* and Deputy for the Veneto region in the lower house of the Italian Parliament, was now Gramsci A., Prisoner 7047 at the Turi di Bari State Penitentiary for Sick Prisoners. The stern critic and would-be leader of the Italian state was now amongst its most powerless captives, in body if never wholly in spirit.

As if to underline this transformation, the guards at Turi were very different from the edgy thugs he had encountered in Rome and Milan and all the other prisons along the way. They were calmer, and in some cases kindlier, because they understood that this was the best way for them as well as their charges to get through their working day, and all the working days that made up their careers and sentences. That doesn't mean they made life easy for the prisoners, or for Gramsci in particular, but in most cases their cruelty was inadvertent, insensitive rather than wilfully malicious. The noise from the guardroom next to his cell was more or less constant, day and night, as the guards came and went, talked and joked amongst themselves, spoke on the telephone or handed over to the next shift. This was their workplace, and required the same kind of procedural tasks, menial chores, practical collaboration and orderly communication as any other job. But understanding all this didn't make it any easier to bear.

Like all prisoners with a shred of intelligence and curiosity, Gramsci watched out for accounts of prison life in the books, papers and periodicals he ordered or that came his way, and which might elevate his own miserable existence to the historical tradition of incarceration, and eventually recorded them in his notebooks. The first such account to catch his eye was by Jacques Riviere, a French essayist and editor who had spent some years as a German prisoner during the First World War. Immediately after a search of his cell, during which his matches, some prohibited food, writing paper and a book on Goethe were confiscated, Riviere wrote: 'I think about all that they have stolen from me: I am humiliated, ashamed, naked. I long for my release but I'm no longer sure I can make it till then. This slow misery takes more out of me than any single ordeal. I feel it pressing down on me from all sides, entering my cell, entering me, robbing me of whatever I have left and leaving me discarded in a corner like a piece of trash. I know nothing more depressing than waiting for this evil to possess me, totally powerless to avert it. Every prisoner knows this tightening of the heart, this profound insecurity, this constant sense of helpless vulnerability to whatever might be thrown at you, from the small inconvenience of a few days in solitary confinement right up to death itself. There is nothing you can do but turn your back, to become as small as possible.'[4] To this quotation, Gramsci appended a note of his own, some time in early 1930, based on his own observations of the individual and collective effects of imprisonment:

> Prison Tears: others sense whether the tears are 'mechanical' or 'anguished'. A different reaction when someone screams 'I want to die!': rage and indignation or mere noise. One feels that everyone is anguished when the tears are sincere. In the tears of the younger prisoners the idea of death presents itself for the first time; all of a sudden they grow old.

Gramsci read widely and voraciously throughout this first period at Turi, from the surprisingly well-stocked prison library but also books and journals he was able to order from Sperling and Kupfers in Milan, courtesy of the ever faithful Piero Sraffa, and those he had brought into prison with him. The journals and reviews were drawn from an extensive European literary culture which thrived in the 1920s and '30s, and provided an invaluable guide for the intelligent reader in this first age of mass literacy. Gramsci read as many as he could get his hands on, even those sponsored by the Catholic Church and the Fascist State, and ordered books which looked especially interesting or received favourable reviews. But for now it was all rather random and aimless, a bit too much like reading for leisure and pleasure than for any clear political or even intellectual purpose. He felt, he wrote to Tanya, that he was just devouring books one after another like some kind of literary glutton, and – albeit in a rather more purposeful way than most of his fellow prisoners – killing time.

Chapter 18

FURTHER TORMENTS

In the winter of 1928–29 Gramsci's health deteriorated again, with recurrent kidney infections that made it hard to stand and move around his cell. He had to remain seated during much of the exercise periods, or be helped to stand and walk by other prisoners. In December Tatiana Schucht – still not fully recovered from her own illnesses and neurasthenia – made the long and arduous cross-country journey from Milan to Turi, and took a room for a couple of weeks in an inn near the prison. She was able to visit Antonio almost every day. Now it was his turn to be truculent, and hers to be perplexed. He was plainly ill and immobile, and he had not seen any of his family for many months. This provided some explanation if not excuse, but nonetheless she struggled to cope with his ill temper. This was a side of his personality she had only previously glimpsed in sarcastic remarks or especially aggrieved passages of his letters, or in passing comments from her sisters, but which for now seemed to be entirely dominant. He chided her – in person and by letter – about things he had asked for and not received, such as the American fava beans with which he flavoured his tobacco, or items she had had delivered to the prison, mainly clothes and food, which were simply confiscated under prison regulations before he'd even seen them, and earned him another ticking off from Parmegiani the Prison Director. Tanya could be forgiven for recalling her family's remarks about Antonio being rude and moody, like a goat that has lost an eye and just keeps going round in circles, as Julia Grigor'evna had put it. On another of Tanya's visits he brought up the representations she had been making to the Ministry of Prisons, asking that he be transferred to the *Casa Penale Speciale* for sick prisoners in Soriano near Vitorbo, which would be nearer to Milan and easier for her to visit. She had claimed, and still did, to be acting on his behalf, but she had not consulted him at all. Then there was Julia's continuing silence, which somehow he seemed to think Tanya could account for. Months had gone by without any kind of communication, not even the hastily scribbled notes enclosed or transcribed in Tanya's letters. The very last of these in the summer of 1928 had been especially confusing, a few short sentences full of effusive declarations of closeness, affection and sympathy – 'I feel as if I finally know you!' she wrote, with no obvious cause for this sense of revelation – accompanied by lovely photographs of herself and the children.[1] He wrote back to her, cautiously delighted: 'Now I am really happy once again.' And then nothing.

He wrote to her, as gently as he could manage, about how he longed for contact and for some 'immediate, direct, living impression' of her and the children's lives.[2] Without it, he felt that 'my life is frozen up and paralysed'. He had sent her, via Tanya, the wooden paper knife he had whittled away at for over a month, 'and at the end of it my fingers were half worn away too. Have you made use of it?' He asked her how Delio was getting on with the Meccano set he had sent for his fourth birthday and what her father Apollon, with his extensive studies of Rousseau and other classical pedagogues, made of the child's development. In conclusion he pleaded, 'My darling, write me a long letter.' Still no response. He convinced himself that there was something he was not being told. He was furious again when he discovered that Delio had not been told that he was in prison, and berated Tanya about it, with obvious reference to his own childhood experience. Had no one considered that Delio might find out about it indirectly? That was the worst way to learn something like that, because the child mistrusted everything he was told and withdrew into himself. He started making things up for himself, on the basis of his worst fears and fantasies. Children were rational creatures, and they could understand even the most serious matters. In fact it made them stronger, because they felt trusted and respected rather than disregarded and abandoned.

In February 1929, about seven months after his arrival at Turi, and nearly two years after his first, unsuccessful application, Gramsci finally received permission to write in his cell. This meant he could take notes on his reading, and impose a structure, order and purpose onto his reflections they had so far lacked. What had been a diverting pastime could become a programme of study and research, with some kind of written product as outcome. This was, for him, a moment of profound release, a massive improvement in his conditions of existence. His brother Carlo had again helped out by engaging a lawyer to petition the prison authorities. With distinct improvements in his health as winter turned to spring, Gramsci faced the future with fresh vigour and enthusiasm. He wrote to Tanya on 24 February that: 'The tonics I have been taking have helped me enormously. The weather here has been better than elsewhere. I've suffered much less this winter than in Milan, let alone the winter 1926/7, which I spent travelling lightly clad in prison vans that had stood the whole night in the snow.'[3] These early months of 1929 found him in much better spirits, he assured her. He might just be able to wring something worthwhile out of all this miserable time in confined isolation. 'Do you realize? I am actually writing in my cell. For the time being I am only doing translations to get back into practice; meanwhile I am putting my thoughts into order.'

He even received a note – relatively long and expansive by her standards – from Julia in May, with news of the children, their development and daily routines. Delio was now nearly five and going to school. He was over a metre tall, and weighed twenty-five kilos. Apollon had observed that the boy was very outgoing and expressive, like an engineer or an aviator, destined to survey the world and make his mark upon it, and serve the great cause of socialist construction like his father and grandfather. Giuliano, who would be three in August, seemed much more introspective by comparison, deep in his own thoughts and sensations, and taking unusual care over his responses to other people and things. Perhaps he had a more artistic bent, like his mother and maternal great grandfather. Antonio wrote back to Julia, thanking her for her news and her father's evocative descriptions of the children. He had pondered on them for several days, like a naturalist who finds a tooth or a small tail bone in some prehistoric cave and from it tries to reconstruct an extinct animal the size of a whale.

He described his own current state of mind as passive and apathetic. This might seem paradoxical to her, especially in the light of his improved physical health and the permission to write in his cell, but he considered it a good sign of his adjustment to prison life and his overcoming the fear of death which was at the root of all the psychological phenomena he observed around him. Prisoners were terrified that they would die before release. For most of them imprisonment itself was a kind of slow, inexorable death, and they were deeply degraded by the realization that they were caught in the vice and couldn't get away. Or they could reconcile themselves to their fate and draw quiet strength – as he felt he was now doing – from this reconciliation. He was becoming a real fakir; soon he'd be able to swallow swords and stroll barefoot over Gillette razor blades. For now he was absolutely calm, and not even the prolonged lack of news could cause him anxiety, although he knew this could be avoided with a modicum of good will on her part. 'But I don't mean to reproach you!' he reassured her, 'During the last few days I've reread all the notes you've sent me over the years, and felt your love all over again. When I write to you, I sometimes feel I'm too dry and dour, while you write to me so freely and naturally, as if it was just part of your busy daily life. It makes me feel like I did those few times when I made you cry, especially that first time (do you remember? In our room at the Lux?) when I was really bad with you, and on purpose too, just to get a reaction.'[4]

In his first separate letter to Delio, enclosed with this letter to Julia, Gramsci asked his son to write him letters of his own as soon as he could, even if he had to dictate them to the grown-ups. 'I know that you like making aeroplanes and trains, and that you're taking an active part in the industrialisation of the country. But do these aeroplanes really fly, and do the trains really run? If I were there with you, I'd put my cigarette in the funnel, so that at any rate we'd have a bit of smoke!'[5] Then in late June and early July there was another flurry of letters and photographs from Julia; 'Two in a fortnight!' he told Tanya exultantly. Julia told him of an altercation between the boys, when Giuliano had damaged a paper hat made from folded newspaper Delio had brought home from school. Delio had set to fixing it with great determination, and a practical streak which she couldn't imagine came from either her or him, their father, with what she called his literary and philosophical tendencies. Antonio wrote back that:

On the contrary, as a child I was an intrepid and deeply practical pioneer. I never left the house without grains of wheat in my pocket and matches wrapped in little scraps of oil cloth, just in case I was cast away on a desert island. I was also a gallant builder of ships and handcarts, and knew all the names and types of naval vessels from A to Z and back again. My greatest success was when a village character asked me to make a paper model of a double-decker schooner so he could reproduce it in tin![6]

Julia's next letter, which reached him just a week or so later, included a new photograph of the children. He wrote back that it made him very happy. Apart from anything else, it pleased him to see that they had bodies and legs. For three years he'd seen nothing but their heads, and was beginning to suspect they'd turned into cherubs, minus the little wings behind their ears. Delio looked like he understood the need to pose for the camera, took himself very seriously but was impatient to get on with something else. Giuliano, on the other hand, was staring at that mysterious object, not at all sure there wasn't some nasty surprise behind it. An angry cat might spring out at any moment, or a magnificent peacock. Why else would they have asked him to look in that direction and not move? He asked for more photos of her, at least once a year. Otherwise all sorts of daft ideas entered his head. He started imagining that she had grown much older and weaker, with lots of white hair and wrinkles. He also asked for a group photo with the children, because a group gave a more vivid picture, with some idea of relationships between people, which can be elaborated into other groupings and episodes of real life, leaving the photographer and his carefully aimed camera behind, with his cats and peacocks.

He fretted that he had never clearly expressed his appreciation of her, of how strong she had had to be in bearing the heaviest burdens of their marriage, in both their brief periods together and their much longer separations. Part of the explanation for his reticence was her deference towards him, he wrote, which made him feel like a farmer appraising livestock. They were still struggling, nearly thirty years into this new century, with traditional notions of how men and women should treat each other. He was supposed to be strong and authoritative, which in all honesty he rarely felt, while she was supposed to be weak and submissive, which he knew her not to be. But they could not simply shrug off the burdens of history and social convention. The fully conscious, autonomous and liberated new man and new woman of Socialism would be a long time coming yet. What's more – he had acknowledged to himself for some time, but was only now confident enough in Julia's understanding to share – he was foolishly jealous of her intimacy with the children and deeply resentful that he could play no active part in their upbringing. On every level – emotional, intellectual, even pedagogical – he would have loved to be intimately involved in caring for them and helping them to develop. Apart from anything else, he would have been able to counter the influence of Rousseau which the Schuchts had picked up on their travels around cosmopolitan Europe, all that hopelessly Bohemian nonsense about letting a child grow up naturally and spontaneously and without direction. 'But perhaps I'm annoying you with the mention of Rousseau which once before (do you remember? In the apartment on Via Vesalio?) made you so angry.'[7] Or that time a couple of years before when he had the temerity to recommend via Tanya that Julia read *The Constant Nymph* by Margaret Kennedy, a rather silly but immensely popular English novel about a musical family headed by a wayward patriarch, 'children of nature' wandering the 'deserts of Bohemia' in a most peculiar ideological atmosphere, and where to cap it all the pubescent heroine appeared to die of growing pains.[8]

Then it all went quiet again. In the whole year from July 1929 to July 1930, Gramsci received just one letter from Julia, in late December. It was brief and cursory, a few random jottings about the children between other obviously more important tasks. Delio had got lost in the apartment block; Giuliano liked to help with the washing up; both had been out playing in the snow. Her previous letters had felt like engaging communiqués from within her daily life; this came over as a burdensome duty, a reluctant chore on a par with peeling potatoes or mopping the floor. He wrote back to her about another worsening in his health and mood over the winter, caused in part by her lack of communication and the growing sense that he was losing touch with his family, the children in particular. He professed to know almost nothing of their development, but from what she said Delio seemed very backward for his age. At five and a half he could not find his own way around the apartment block. At less than five, Gramsci wrote, he could freely move around his village and the surrounding area. Without ever having travelled more than a couple of kilometres in either direction, he could point out where he lived on a map, as well as the big cities of Italy. He didn't think he was that unusual. A very young child absorbed an amazing amount of information which guided him in that initial period of logical thought as he learnt to speak.

At the risk of making her angry, he had to bring up Rousseau again. The problem was that her own conception of child development (and that of other members of her family) was too metaphysical. It presupposed that the whole person was already latent in the child, and that it just had to be helped to emerge, letting the spontaneous forces of nature do their work. Rather, a child had to be consciously formed and directed by the norms and standards of his own social circumstances and historical era. Otherwise he was not equipped to play a full and useful part in them. He would pick up bad habits and his personality would develop quite haphazardly. The idea of education as unwinding a pre-existing thread had been useful in countering the harmful indoctrination of the Jesuits, and the oppressive effects of rote-learning, but it was now quite out of date itself. Education could be systematic and rigorous without suppressing natural curiosity and love of learning, assisting the child to engage with the world around him rather than leaving him to his own devices while he was buffeted with extraneous sensation. Strangely, Freudian psychoanalysis seemed to be reviving the idea of the noble savage, corrupted by society and history, in some new and even more insidious form.

Gramsci conceded in conclusion that he may be extrapolating far too much from the very little information he had to work with from Julia's sporadic notes and Tanya's second-hand reports. Recalling his naturalist analogy, he recognized the danger of starting with a piece of a mouse's tail and ending up with a sea-serpent. He wrote to Tanya about Julia's almost total silence on 13 January 1930: she mustn't think he was angry; he was actually past caring. He didn't want to feel sour with rage again or go through more weeks of migraine, agonizing and punishing himself for something – he knew not what – he might have said to cause this stand-off. He asked her not to mention this subject again when she visited or wrote to him. She should share whatever news she received, but wasn't to exhort or preach at him. He went on to tell her about a collection of letters and writings he had been reading by Silvio Spaventa, an Italian patriot imprisoned for his involvement in the Neapolitan Parliament in 1848.⁹ Gramsci was struck by the similarity in Spaventa's account, 'in the somewhat romantic language of his day', of his time in prison to 'certain states of mind I frequently experience'. Spaventa wrote to his father in 1853: 'It is two months since I have had news from you; four months or more since I heard from my sisters ... Don't you believe that for a person like me, who is finely attuned to his feelings, this privation is bound to be extremely painful? I do not believe that I am loved less by my family than I always was, but misfortune tends to have a dual effect. People cease to care for the unfortunate, and he ceases to care for them. I'm less worried about the former than the latter. Cut off as I am from every human and loving exchange, beset by the intense boredom of long imprisonment and the fear of being forgotten, my heart is slowly becoming bitter and sterile.'

What Gramsci had not foreseen about his own imprisonment was the other prison added to the first, which consisted of being cut off not only from other people in general but also from his own family. He anticipated the blows of his enemies, but not from his loved ones. Finally, he acknowledged Tanya's efforts on his behalf, and the sacrifices they required of her: 'But there's always you, you're bound to say. It's true, you are very good, and I love you greatly. Only there are some things for which one person can never take another's place.' For that other person, his wife Julia, he still felt 'a great upsurge of tenderness which would be best expressed in a loving embrace, but only clumsily in words'. In August 1930, Palmiro Togliatti wrote from Paris in an internal memorandum for the *PCd'I* leadership in exile that Antonio must be demoralized about certain family matters, whose substance could not be easily grasped. Attempts might be made in Moscow to see Antonio's wife and clear things up. 'It seems incredible to me,' Togliatti wrote, 'that there should be people around him who create so much muddle. Apparently his wife sends her letters to him via some office, which then has to forward the letters. This office had held the letters for six months! Couldn't someone teach this blessed woman that in modern cities (and in villages too) there are rectangular boxes with a slit at the top and that when letters are put in them one can be sure that they reach their destination with reasonable speed?'¹⁰

Chapter 19

FÜR EWIG: A NEW SENSE OF PURPOSE

For all his despondency and isolation at Turi di Bari, and perhaps not coincidentally, this was the period in which Gramsci was most intensively, creatively and productively immersed in his research, reading and note-taking. The notebooks he filled over the following four years between 1929 and 1933 – the duration of an undergraduate degree course or a doctorate – would nearly half a century later form the philosophical and historical framework for which he would become renowned around the world. He wrote his notes, excerpts and translations in ruled school-type exercise books ordered from *Laterza e Figli*, the booksellers and stationers in Bari. The first notebooks contained fifty sheets, one hundred pages with twenty-two lines on each side. They had red and black marbled covers made of stiff card. On the front was an oblong space where the Prison Director Parmegiani wrote Gramsci's prison number and his own signature of authorization. Upon completion each sheet was examined to ensure that no prison regulations had been violated, and stamped with the prison seal in the top right-hand corner. In the same spirit of petty bureaucratic scrutiny, he was not allowed all his notebooks to hand in his cell. As he filled them up, they were deposited in a storeroom, and he could only take out a few at a time.

Gramsci wrote in a small, precise, right-leaning copperplate, with the headings singly or doubly underlined according to their function and importance. Notes which had been revised and rewritten elsewhere were crossed out (but still legible) with neatly ruled, cross-hatched lines. If they were meant to be disregarded altogether, they were crossed through (but again still legible) with a single horizontal line. Each letter was written clearly and precisely, with capitals – especially A-s, T-s, S-s and F-s – stately and almost ornate, betraying long hours of calligraphy practice in childhood and a lingering commitment to appearance and legibility. His very first prison writings were translations, mostly from German and Russian, with the aim of improving his facility in those languages but also just getting used to studying systematically again. His first translation was Franz Nicolaus Finck's *Die Sprachstamme des Erdkreises*, a short but authoritative catalogue of world languages published in 1923, which reminded Gramsci of his student love of linguistics and philology. He also understood and wrote in French, which was customary among Italian intellectuals of the time, and some of the later notes were written in or translated from French. At this early, preparatory stage, he even tried his hand at English translation. He did not understand much of the language, so his exercises were simply isolated phrases such as 'last not least', 'Hard Times' (the Dickens classic) or (one he especially enjoyed disentangling, not least for its resonance with the prison mentality) 'I can find fantasies where none is.'

When soon afterwards he began making notes of his own, they were mostly short fragments, quotations or commentary on other writers he was reading or could remember from the last twenty years. They were thrown together scatter-gun style as he recalled an event or an observation, or was reminded of something else altogether. At this stage, they were little more than references, pointers and *aides-memoires*. He was looking for a way into history, along quite definite lines of enquiry: the formation of intellectuals, the influence of religion, the practice and theory of politics, the latest developments in philosophy and ideology, the interests of social classes and how parties sought to represent them, the overriding importance in Italy of the north–south split and the limitations of national unification. Some of these Gramsci set out on the very first page of the first notebook, dated 8 February 1929, in the sixteen-point programme of study he would pursue tenaciously over the next few years. The only one of those sixteen points he did not undertake or even begin was the only vaguely autobiographical one, number 8, 'Experiences of Prison Life', though piecemeal observations on this theme would recur throughout the notebooks as well as the letters.

Gramsci's early prison studies were focussed around a single overriding theme, dictated by his own recent experiences of political defeat and imprisonment, agitating his mind like a grain of sand inside the shell of an oyster: the mystery of Italy, and why it had taken its fatal turn towards Fascism. Day after day, week after week, month after month, through the last year of the 1920s and into the fretful, uncertain 1930s, he sat – or more often stood and paced around his cell, reflecting on his last note and composing the next one – wondering how on earth had it come to this? How had he ended up here, imprisoned for the crime of political persuasion in the cause of social progress, with that cause trashed in the name of a half-baked ideology of reaction which itself claimed to be 'progressive' or even 'revolutionary'? That question was gradually honed into more political, impersonal, historical shape. At the heart of this enquiry was an even simpler question: why was the country he had been born and grown up in, albeit on its outermost periphery, with its proud antecedence in classical civilization, and later the cradle of the Renaissance, so fundamentally silly and half-formed? How could he explain the paradox of a country that was simultaneously very young and very old, puerile *and* senile?

How could it throw up such philosophical peculiarities as *Lorianismo*, named after the influential writer and prestigious academic Achille Loria (1857–1943), a self-professed historical economist who claimed to have surpassed Marx? When he wasn't composing overblown poetry along the lines of his *Ode to my Walking Stick*, Loria specialized in such absurd predictions as a solution to world hunger and class exploitation involving huge aeroplanes with glue on their wings and fuselages which would catch birds for food as they flew around the world. He foresaw the decline of the occupation of doorman and other ground-level servants because of the danger of death by binoculars dropped from the high-rise buildings where everyone would be living. This would soon be followed by social revolution instigated by these unemployed servants. Juvenile delinquents could be effectively rehabilitated in prisons on high mountains or even on yet more immense aeroplanes, because there was a direct, scientifically established correlation between morality and altitude. According to Loria, people behaved better in thin air. Pain could be overcome by sleeping outdoors because it thickened the skin. War could be overcome through the curing of syphilis, the cause of the widespread intemperance and despotism found amongst the ruling classes. Italy could level its troublesome, obstructive mountains and transport the soil to its Libyan colony to fertilize the desert.

How could such arrant nonsense, even if dignified with the labels 'futurology' or 'science fiction', find a hearing in any self-respecting national culture? Part of the answer was Italy's failure to create its own national intellectuals. Instead, they were formed either by the progressive currents of French and German culture or the reactionary perspectives of the Roman Catholic Church. They were thus either free-floating pan-Europeans or agents of the Vatican, but never primarily Italian. Either way, they were cosmopolitan not national, and left space for all sorts of local oddities in between. Italy had no settled, constructive, mature intellectual life of its own, which meant that preening charlatans like Loria or more recently the posturing, self-styled 'idealists' clustered around Mussolini could rise to the top and gain great prestige and influence. Public life was characterized by bluster and gesture, with a tradition of 'say one thing, do another' government. Reality was obscured by rhetoric; rank careerism and opportunism by supposedly grand principle. A seam of prolix oratory ran deep through Italian politics, from the ineffectual unifiers and scheming cliques of the *Risorgimento*, through the windy demagogy of the maximalist Socialists, to the stupid gladiatorial posing, martial pomp and fawning philosophy of 'pure action' of the Fascists. This latest outburst was all the more ridiculous for its glorification of the innate genius of the Italian race and other pieces of populist flattery that had no basis in the historical record. The single most notable feature of Italian politics was the weakness of the central state and its remoteness from most people's everyday lives out in the provinces, cities, towns and villages.

This lack of a mature national politics and an effective state accounted for successive Italian governments' misadventures in what Gramsci called half-arsed, castle-in-the-air imperialism, based on the mirage of exploitable colonial lands and the vacuous slogan 'Italy goes it alone'. This was backed up and enforced by incompetent and frequently disastrous military campaigns against native populations usually armed with little more than sticks. What this meant in practice was grabbing a few dusty scraps of land no one else much wanted, dumping on them those mostly Southern surplus peasants who didn't want to emigrate to the United States or South America, and by and large leaving them to get on with it. Or not, because the Italian colonies amounted to very little without the investment capital, technology, resources and skilled labour the country could not (unlike other more successful empires) afford to export. This was why Italy was never taken entirely seriously abroad, and why the menace and the brutality of its own local version of paramilitary reaction were so often underestimated and so rarely understood. Foreigners saw only the comic opera of Italian Fascism, with its beautifully tailored uniforms, its highly choreographed ceremonies and posturing, its overblown oratory; all easily mimicked and, from a safe distance, enjoyed. They did not see its very real and threatened violence and its systematic reorganization of politics and the state. Italian Fascism was an iron fist inside a velvet glove puppet, and foreigners were amused or even charmed by it. They fawned and swooned, this endless parade of holidaying dignitaries, political grand tourists, personalities and literati come to marvel at 'the glory of Rome' and the delights of Mussolini's patronage.

Beneath all of this was the curious childishness of the Italian people, most purely represented in its petty bourgeoisie, and a determined refusal to grow up. You could see it in any gathering of Italians away from home, Gramsci observed, which soon forms into giggling, nudging, fearful cliques, worried about contagion and abandonment, and what these foreigners might be talking about in their strange guttural barking languages. Then they start looking round for some figure of authority who might tell them what to do and where to go. It was like some strange folk-memory of the latter days of the Roman Empire, when most of its citizens were still living well and peaceably but increasingly fretful about the encroachments of the barbarian hordes. The modern Italian popular masses were just too comfortable – with their tasty food and light entertainments, their mostly temperate climate and their just about adequate housing – in their craven subordination to the prevailing order of the ruling elite. Upon these silly people Gramsci turned his harsh 'social moralism', which he contrasted to the populist indulgence of the Fascists and the unsympathetic paternalism of the northern industrialists and their pseudo-scientific apologists.

The Italian petty bourgeoisie were like the Bandar Log 'monkey people' in Kipling's *Jungle Book*, Gramsci wrote, 'who sing every minute of every hour … but do not act, who claim to be the wisest, cleverest, most clear-sighted people on earth; you'll see just what we're capable of … tomorrow.'[1] Or they took after the seventeenth-century popular-theatrical character Stentorello, 'talkative, vain, hollow … howling, bawling and preening like smug academics. They eulogize the virtues of their race and the wisdom of their ancestors, while they themselves do no work or produce anything of any note or value.' They are 'pensioners of economic history … absolutely parasitic classes, living off their ancestral patrimony … leftover people in their cities of silence', all those beautiful but pointless mediaeval centres, urban clusters without industry but with centuries of accumulated wealth and prestige to swaddle them against the upheavals of global capitalism. The Fascists had flattered these people by calling them 'producers of savings', when all they ever produced were rents on land and property they were largely absent from. Around these small-town *signori* and provincial gentry were ranged various grumbling sub-types: the primitive share cropper who pays his rent with a portion of his harvest, owns some tools and a yoke of oxen and a small house he has built himself with extra earnings in the mines or the *carabinieri*, 'in other words by "contriving" and saving ... He hates "the bureaucrats" because they impose taxes for state services he does not personally receive or understand'; then, agricultural day-labourers, who are 'drunkards and spendthrifts, incapable of sustained work, physically deficient because of chronic malnutrition or simple stupidity ... semi-beggars with a makeshift life on the margins of the rural underworld'; finally, the 'petty intellectual starvelings ... a famished threadbare rabble hoping for minor municipal postings as clerks and messengers, jostling for political favours and merging with the career criminal underworld'.[2] All of these types see themselves as subversive of the established order, but with no clear political purpose or social identity, they are available to the highest bidder but always finally on the side of reaction.

Not surprisingly, when it came to the way in which the country was governed, 'between the normal political poles of consent and coercion stands corruption and fraud ... there has never existed a "rule of law" but only a politics of arbitrary power and personal cliques'. The most recent example of this was the latest change in electoral law, adopted in parliament in May 1928 and approved in a plebiscite (Mussolini was very fond of referendums) in March 1929. This stipulated that a single list of four hundred candidates, selected by the Fascist Grand Council from a thousand names submitted by the state employers' and workers' confederations, would be presented for approval to the electorate. At the same time, three million people in places and social groups with a tradition of anti-Fascist politics were removed from the electoral roll. At a stroke, parliamentary democracy – for which Mussolini had an abiding contempt, as 'totally unsuited to the character, education and mentality of the Italian people' (a judgment uncomfortably close to Gramsci's own, albeit from the opposite political perspective) – was absorbed within the Fascist state.[3]

This also meant, beneath the veneer of 'order' and 'discipline', deep and persistent contempt for legality and morality in public affairs, widespread tax evasion and opportunistic criminality. This in turn engendered public fascination with violent crime, reflected in the popularity of serial novels and lurid press coverage at one extreme and at the other the explosion in the academic subject of criminology. In its most positivist guises this new 'science' explained criminality by national or regional stereotypes. This was a step forward from the Inquisition – its new, more humane methods of incarceration and rehabilitation, an improvement on torture and summary execution – but it still rested on a notion of innate good and evil, albeit geographically rather than morally distributed. Certain settings produced bad people, supposedly, especially in the South. This line of thinking removed whole social subgroups from their cultures and their histories, from their real places of work and residence, from their own accounts of themselves, and imposed upon them an authorized, sanitized 'identity'. They were excused for their wrongdoing – with just as much condescension as the absolution of the Catholic confessional – but in the process rendered subhuman, almost animalistic. More than once Gramsci had heard Sardinians like himself referred to as 'monkeys' by northern mainlanders, of a lower order than even the 'monkey people', giving the otherwise respectable, condescending game away.

This antiquated, fragmented Italy, whose classical culture lay at the foundation of Western civilization, was little more now than a collection of squabbling, self-interested, petty-fogging cliques, gathered around the fountains and statues in the archetypal village square, arguing the relative merits of their own local wine or cheese or *Signor* Big Man. Nothing was definitively wrong or right, because there was no common law, just a stream of declarations and instructions from the centre which were met with indifference or contempt in the localities. A weak central state went hand in hand with the mythology of the outlaw, whose forms and secondary expressions Gramsci could see daily all around him, even in this obscure provincial penitentiary for sick prisoners. Most of them, even some of the politicos, carried about them a kind of subversive glamour, as though their petty thefts and gestures of defiance automatically possessed some larger political purpose, a noble fight between some ill-defined 'us' against an even vaguer 'them'. It was utterly pathetic, but always worthy of close study, because within it lay the historically specific source of their abiding subalternity, throwing around a weight in here they lacked on the outside.

As the months and years passed, Gramsci spent more time alone in his cell, and frequently turned down the chance to exercise. He had to figure it all out, and he only had so much time before release or – the more likely outcome, he already suspected – death. He preferred to continue reading and writing on his own, rather than mill about with the same old deadbeats and losers, playground bullies and self-styled 'kings of the wing'. Life in company killed him, he wrote to Tanya, irritating his nervous system to the point of convulsions. Even his own personal pursuits and interests became more confined to his cell, more focused and organized as he put it, as his studies went ever deeper. Tanya had brought him a small rose cutting and some herbs and flower seeds on the last of her visits in December 1928. He set about cultivating them in his designated patch of the prison courtyard, a square metre beside the wall, as far as the limited sunlight and fluctuating temperatures allowed. In late April he reported to her that the rose had gone down with terrible sunstroke; all its leaves were burnt and blackened. It looked desolate but amazingly it was putting out fresh buds. The sunstroke was inevitable, because all he could shade it with was a piece of paper, which the wind blew away. In any case it was still alive, and the prognosis was favourable. On the other hand, 'the seeds have been very slow to emerge; most of them seem to want to remain in hiding! They were rather old and moth-eaten; perhaps the gardener who sold them to you as good seeds meant they were good to eat. What has come up looks more like parsley and onions than flowers. Every day I'm tempted to pull them up gently to help them grow, but I can't decide whether to follow Rousseau and let nature take its course or intervene with an "authoritarian" hand. The two ideologies are fighting it out in my head! The six chicory plants are doing well enough by themselves, and should provide seeds for my next crop, but there's no sign of the dahlias and the bamboo.'[4]

In early June, he was able to draw up a final balance sheet on the flower situation. All the seeds had failed except one. He wasn't sure what it was, except that it was probably a flower and not a weed. The chicory was blooming away, and the bamboo had put out a leaf as large as a hand, with another on the way. The rose was budding well, and recovered from its sunstroke; but would it cope with the summer heat ahead? He suspected it was too weak and sickly to come to much, but time would tell. In fact, by early July the rose had completely recovered. From 3 to 15 June it started putting out leaves till it was green again. Its branches were now fifteen centimetres long. It had even tried to put out a tiny bud, but this withered and turned yellow. Anyway it had taken root; perhaps this tiny timid rose would flower the next year. It would not have the chance to, because new prison regulations forbade such recreation. The flowerbeds were ripped up and their contents destroyed.

Chapter 20

VISITATIONS AND VOCATIONS

On 16 June 1930, Gramsci received a visit from his older brother Gennaro, the only person from outside Italy who could legally get to see him. The visit was entirely unexpected and unannounced. Gramsci was simply summoned from his cell at the appointed time in the early afternoon and told he had a visitor. It couldn't be Tanya, because she had been just a couple of days before and did not plan to come again till the following week. She was again unwell, so even that was uncertain. The only other visitor he ever had at Turi was his younger brother Carlo, who had to make prior arrangements to travel from Sardinia and wouldn't just turn up like this. Piero Sraffa had promised to come during one of his trips to Italy from England, but so far had not received permission because he was not an immediate family member. Antonio had last seen his older brother some time before he left for Moscow in May 1922. Gennaro then left for Paris in December of that same momentous year. They were both still living in Turin then, both working on the communist press but not having much to do with each other outside work. They had always been closer to each other than to other members of the Gramsci family, mainly in their shared political outlook and engagement, but there was still ill feeling between them from their forced, impoverished years together in Cagliari and Turin, not to mention the irritability of siblings some years apart in age. Then there was the beating and mutilation Gennaro had received when the Fascists mistook him for Antonio, and the issue of Gennaro drawing his brother's salary while he was away. Gennaro was now forty-seven, eight years older than Antonio, apparently comfortable in prosperous middle age. Perhaps, Antonio might have reflected, Nannaro really did have some of that talent for business his father and other brothers had always gone on about.

The purpose of this unusual visit was a rather different kind of business. Gennaro had been approached by 'Ercoli' (Palmiro Togliatti's party codename) in Paris. The party wanted Gennaro to visit Antonio in order to determine his attitude towards the latest developments in the movement. The fierce struggles at the top of the Russian Communist Party, and hence in the Comintern, had finally come to a head, with Stalin installed as the undisputed successor to Lenin. Having vanquished Trotsky and the Left opposition in 1927, he had then taken on the Right opposition around Bukharin, Rykov and Tomsky. They had all been removed from their posts in the party and the Comintern, and finally expelled.

Antonio was familiar with this part of the story – indeed, he had anticipated just such damaging splits in his letter to the Comintern in 1926, which had been intercepted and suppressed by Togliatti – but more recent developments surprised and shocked him. Stalin's latest factional manoeuvres necessitated the left turn of 1929, when the Bolsheviks had renounced all aspects of bourgeois democracy and political collaboration with the social democrats of the mass Socialist Parties. They were now vilifying these former comrades and allies as 'social fascists' or the 'left wing of the bourgeoisie'.

Gennaro, who never joined the *PCd'I*, and whose own politics and circle of friends were closer to the left-wing social democrats, would have had some difficulty conveying these not so finer points of ideological schism. The Comintern leadership were even retrospectively blaming the social democrats for the failure of the botched German revolution of October 1923, perhaps the single most disastrous and largely self-inflicted setback the movement had ever suffered. The Comintern's own immediate, measured and self-critical reflections on the catastrophe, under Lenin's clear-eyed if faltering guidance, seemed now to have been entirely forgotten. More broadly the communists had decided that the final crisis of capitalism, long ago hopefully predicted by Marx as the global economic system tottered under the weight of its own internal contradictions, was not just inevitable but imminent. Communists should agitate and prepare for the international dictatorship of the proletariat, led by the vanguard parties of the Communist International, without any kind of transition through parliamentary democracy and political legality, or even as in Italy cooperation with other anti-Fascists to overthrow Mussolini's regime.

Any opposition within the Communist International was being condemned as 'opportunism' and 'deviationism'. Resistance or even doubt was being dealt with by large-scale expulsions, as the new hard line was driven through every national Communist Party. Angelo Tasca had been expelled in late 1928, and at the opposite political extreme Amadeo Bordiga soon after. Neither had come as any great surprise to Gramsci – he never regarded Tasca as a fully committed communist, and Bordiga was an indefatigable oppositionist – but the latest expulsions, of Alfonso Leonetti, Paolo Ravazzoli and Pietro Tresso, were a different matter. Gramsci regarded them all as good loyal comrades. Leonetti had joined the Socialist Party branch in Turin during the war, and helped found the *Pcd'I*. Tresso was a protégé of Gramsci, intellectually limited but thoroughly sound. Ravazzoli was never any kind of threat, just a bit too inclined towards Tasca's collaboration with the trade unions. Gramsci understood that this new line was imposed by the Comintern, with the full weight of its global authority, but his initial response to Gennaro (only disclosed many years later, long after the issue had ceased to matter) was that Togliatti had agreed to it too readily. Gennaro left it with him to mull over before reporting anything back. He would return later in the month, after his own visit to the family home in Ghilarza, so Antonio could tell him then what to say.

The atmosphere at that next visit, a fortnight later, was very different. In the meantime Gennaro had been under heavy surveillance because the police had realized he was up to something, and sent a whole detachment of plain-clothes men to follow him around the country. When he met Tanya for dinner, prior to visiting Antonio at the prison, she told him she had got quite used to being watched, even when she was back up north. She was regularly called in for questioning, and her rooms searched. Every time it felt like a violation, and necessitated frequent moves. Here in Turi, they were aware of being watched from every corner of the restaurant, and overheard by one particular fellow who insisted on being seated at the very next table and even moving with them when they asked to be seated somewhere else. At the prison Gennaro was met and accompanied by the Prison Secretary, who had been expressly instructed by Signor Parmegiani the Prison Director to enforce the prohibition on political discussion during visits to Special Tribunal prisoners. In the visiting room itself, this fussy little man insisted on sitting at the table with Antonio and Gennaro, indicating disapproval whenever their discussion strayed anywhere near the real purpose of the visit. 'What about the three?' was the nearest Gennaro could get to it. Antonio, exasperated on a number of fronts, was unable – or perhaps disinclined – to give a clear answer. Otherwise their conversation was confined to family matters. Their mother Signora Peppina had been ill earlier in the year, but seemed to be on the mend. Nannaro's daughter Edmea was growing into a fine girl, pretty and intelligent. Everyone else seemed well enough. On his return to Paris, Gennaro reportedly told the *PCd'I* that his brother had no clear view on the latest developments in the party and the Comintern, and this reticence was taken as tacit approval of the left turn and the associated purges. Indeed, his letters and notes of the time reveal no explicit interest in the twists and turns of Comintern policy. What they do indicate is a period of intense, dedicated study of the history, structure and global strategy of the Roman Catholic Church.

When Antonio Gramsci was eleven and just finishing at elementary school, he would have been asked by the parish priest – like any intelligent Catholic boy, especially from his straitened family background – if he had 'a vocation' to be a priest. Several times in his childhood, teachers (and rather more sardonically, his brothers and sisters) had said he would make a good little Jesuit, with his enquiring mind and way with words and his serious demeanour. Nino always had something of the cleric about him. He approached his Catechism classes, in preparation for his confirmation at the age of eight, with the same earnest devotion and appetite for learning that he brought to *Robinson Crusoe* or observation of foraging hedgehogs. Antonio ceased to believe in God as soon as he could properly think it through for himself. In a world explained and governed by science and reason, and a new century offering endless giddy mechanized human progress, there was no place for some distant, immaterial supreme being who demanded total obedience and blind faith, and in return offered little more than consolation for suffering and loneliness. With his father in prison, and Sardinia in deep and persistent economic depression, both God and humanity seemed to have given up on each other, at least out there on the edge of the modern world. At best, he would later write to Julia, 'God was only a metaphor for an ensemble of men organised for mutual assistance', always a subject of ignorance and illusion, and at worst a cover for repression and exploitation.[1]

But he remained fascinated by religion and its institutions, and the hold they seemed to have over the thoughts and feelings of otherwise rational, practical people, not to mention their global reach and power. He witnessed the solace it gave his mother and other family members during times of trial and hardship, and the sense of purpose it endowed on otherwise mundane lives. It offered a badge of belonging to these people of the periphery which no other agency – the state, the ruling or opposition parties, the monarchy and the nobility, the press, public culture and the arts – could be bothered with. Their lives had religious if not civic meaning and purpose. These were the building blocks of mass faith, cemented by a subtly mixed mortar of coercion and consent, and forming a secure and durable pyramid, with the community of the faithful on the lower levels, the several upper layers of the clergy in their own strict hierarchy and the Pope at the very top. Above all, Gramsci appreciated the historic, universal standing of the Roman Catholic Church. All across the Western world an eleven-year-old boy could confess the same sins and receive the same penance, and be asked the same question about a vocation by a more or less kindly parish priest. There was a set script and moral calculus fixed in Rome and rigorously enforced everywhere, with interesting but superficial local variations. This was the most effective and durable global movement there had ever been, at least until the emergence of communism. It touched the everyday lives and deepest thoughts of half of humanity, and in some way conditioned the existence of all the rest. Without armed forces of its own or much by way of economic power, at least since the late middle ages, the Church was still able to dictate the policies and actions of states and governments all over the world.

The Lateran Pact of 1929 between the Pope and Mussolini was the latest example, securing the operational autonomy and moral sway of the Vatican within Italy while consolidating – literally blessing – the Fascists' grip on secular power, not least by reining in the church-sponsored and previously oppositional Popular Party and other Catholic social movements. It also had a massive economic impact on the country by transferring huge funds from the state to the church, to compensate for the surrender of any claim to temporal, territorial sovereignty over the country beyond the Vatican City itself. This in itself had boosted the real local power of the church and the attractiveness of the priesthood, which had been suffering a collapse in recruitment for at least the previous fifty years. All of a sudden, a vocation to the priesthood had become a much more attractive proposition, especially in a period of persistent high unemployment. The Pact – approved by yet another of Mussolini's referendums – might be derided in the left wing press as a concordat of tinpot dictatorships, but this was to underestimate its historical significance, its economic and political benefits to both Church and State and its negative impact on any prospect of a revival in progressive politics.

Even at moments of steep decline, under the combined assaults of industrial capitalism and positivist science, and the shallow materialism and popular scepticism they jointly engendered, the Church was capable of adapting and renewing itself, and maintaining its influence alongside the global empires of the great nation-states. Just how did this organization, based ultimately on obscure mythology and doctrinal nit-picking, retain its pre-eminence? How to explain the subtlety of its morality and the complexity of its theology, alongside the mumbo-jumbo of its liturgy and the hollow ritual of its ceremony? Or the glaring contrast between its magnificent buildings and ornaments and vestments and the grinding poverty of most of its adherents, its aptly known 'flock'? Or the depth of popular faith in a religion which conducted its proceedings in an obscure classical language unspoken elsewhere for centuries, so that (as Gramsci observed) the people watch religious rites and hear exhortatory sermons, but have no real idea what's going on. They cannot follow discussions and ideological developments, which are the monopoly of the clerical elite. This was a religion, a body of belief, which seemed to allow its believers to take from it an infinite variety of influences. How could this tradition simultaneously inspire Dante's *Inferno* and a cult based on a relic reputed to be the penis of an angel? How, Gramsci wondered in one of his earliest prison notes, could a popular and reputable Catholic novelist produce a book – plucked off the shelves of the Turi di Bari prison library in a well-thumbed, yellowing edition – which 'seeks to enlist our pity for a priest who has raped over thirty young girls, because he is bound by the vow of chastity?'[2]

Part of the answer lay in the social origin and location of the clergy, all those clever and talented sons of respectable but impecunious families like his own. They were drawn from real communities all across Italy, unlike the cliques and castes who dominated the political parties, cultural and intellectual life, and public administration. Once ordained, literally 'indoctrinated', their deployment closely corresponded to the organization and structure of the Italian state, and in many places far surpassed it. They respected and adapted to the prevailing mores of different parts of the country, sometimes in flagrant defiance of official church policy, acquiescing for example in the distinctly flexible sexual moralities of agrarian communities. These relatively educated individuals had a presence in the smallest habitations, usually benign and occasionally disciplinary, representing both God and their congregations to each other, interceding between the divine and the lay. When Gramsci thought again of his own family in distant Ghilarza, they and all their neighbours would always approach the parish priest for help and advice before any public official. These were the organic intellectuals of the Universal Church, drawn from the key intermediary classes of feudal and then bourgeois society, with suitable local adaptations. So, in the north they were drawn from among the artisans and peasants, whereas in the south they tended to come from the land-owning gentry. There they often owned land and extracted rents on their own and also the Church's behalf, and constituted a subsection of the feudal ruling class. Some even took a wife, stretching the tolerance of the church's moral code and the community of the faithful to its very limits. But as long as they came from the town or area where they preached and prayed, and performed the ceremonial and pastoral functions of the priesthood reasonably competently, they were accepted by the locals as one of their own. This contrasted sharply with schoolteachers who, with the rapid expansion of elementary schooling in the later nineteenth and early twentieth centuries as a key instrument of the fledgling liberal state, were dispatched from training colleges in the big cities to the outlying towns and villages where most of the people still lived. Even if they stayed at their posts, which many didn't as soon as they saw where they'd been sent, they were regarded as alien invaders, bringing a very young and shallow civilization to the natives. Popular literature was full of stories where some upstart young teacher was seen off or tamed by a wise old priest.

The accommodation between church and people worked both ways. At least in the rural South and for usually good practical reasons, the supposedly strict moral codes of Roman Catholicism were surprisingly adaptable in their application, and not just for the convenience of priests. Childless marriages could be dissolved for a fee, and in other cases matrimony took place only after conception, once its fruitfulness had been tested and proven, a practice widely known in country lore as 'testing the heifer'. In the era of widening, ultimately universal suffrage, the Church had also developed its own political capacity and organization, through such agencies as Catholic Action and the Popular Party, with a socially progressive or even left wing veneer over a conservative or downright reactionary politics. The Church had organized and sponsored a whole host of popular cultural initiatives, including novels and plays by writers Gramsci called 'Father Bresciani's progeny', after a nineteenth-century Catholic novelist who specialized in sentimental homilies.[3] They had very little literary merit, but they sold in vast quantities, and plainly touched a common chord. This was a kind of literary Lorianism, peculiar to Italy, which said as much about its audience as its creators. In an era of growing literacy, within strictly defined intellectual and political limits, it kept the Church deep inside people's hearts and minds.

But at the same time, the Church was losing whatever grip it ever really had on the faith of lay intellectuals, who were drawn towards the new sciences of positivism and materialism, in the process becoming ever more detached from the popular masses who persisted in their religious convictions. Part of the explanation for the failure of Italian Socialism was its rabid and shallow anti-clericalism, which Gramsci had described in a 1918 newspaper article as 'nothing more than the peevishness of a child who believes that his mother gives larger bowls of soup to his eldest brother.'[4] Even his own *PCd'I* had failed to appreciate the deep historical roots of this new social Catholicism and its popular agencies. Hundreds of thousands of peasants were drawn towards these semi-detached subsections of the Church and had even organized strikes and cooperatives through them. They had been amongst the first targets of the Fascist upsurge in the countryside, because Mussolini at least understood the challenge they posed to his 'revolution'. One of the key provisions of the Lateran Pact of 1929 was to bring Catholic Action within the political orbit of the state, thereby neutralizing its progressive potential.

From the top down, successive Popes had tried hard to modernize the Church, particularly Leo XIII with his encyclical *Rerum Novarum*, which recognized the plight and interests of the emerging, late-nineteenth-century industrial working class. Leo had promoted a scholastic Thomist philosophy (Gramsci noted) 'not as a narrow, static and exclusive frame of knowledge but as an organism of living thought.'[5] This helped to disguise the fact that at least since the French Revolution, the Church had grown increasingly out of touch with the emergent creeds of economic liberalism, moral individualism and political democracy. There remained within it deep currents of resistance to any form of modernity. In those countries which had embraced the Reformation, and which not coincidentally played key roles in the industrial revolution, Roman Catholics had become a marginal, persecuted sect. Across the world, the reassertion of the authority of the clergy had suppressed the community of the faithful and delimited lay involvement in church affairs. The Church was slowly losing the historical initiative, the hegemony of mass faith, reacting to rather than shaping social development. Its internal politics had always been complicated. 'It is noteworthy,' Gramsci wrote in December 1931:

> That all the innovations within the church, unless they come from the leadership, contain something heretical. These heretical elements become more explicit and strident until the centre reacts forcefully, throws the innovators into disarray, reabsorbs the waverers and casts out the recalcitrants. The church has never gone in for self-criticism, despite its self-proclaimed attachment to the masses of the faithful … The historical development of the church has come about through faction-fighting; the various religious congregations are really factions that have been absorbed and regulated in the form of religious orders. Ultimately, innovations have always been imposed rather than proposed, and accepted only by compulsion.[6]

The Church sought to impose its own institutional prerogatives on life, rather than emerging organically from within it. At least since the Counter-reformation, it had been dangerous to think, write and speak openly and honestly within the Church. Being a Catholic had become simultaneously very easy for most people and very difficult for some. It was easy to believe in general terms and to have respect for the Church, its personnel and institutions; there was very little in practical terms to distinguish this popular faith from Protestantism or Orthodoxy. But it was very difficult to be an active Catholic intellectual, Gramsci observed, because they were expected to embrace a whole slew of notions in encyclicals, counter-encyclicals, papal briefs, apostolic letters, etc. The historical deviations from the Church's line had been so numerous and so subtle that it was extremely easy to fall into heresy or semi-heresy or a quarter-heresy. Sincere religious sentiment had been desiccated; one must be a doctrinaire to write in an orthodox way.

These were for the moment jottings and isolated fragments, to be worked up into fuller accounts at some later stage. But Gramsci applied himself to his studies of Catholicism with a dedication he admitted to Tanya bordered on obsession. It was becoming, with reference to the young Torinese worker he recalled who looked at everything through the prism of 'What will Japan do?', his very own personal Japan. He would already have been acutely aware of the parallels between the Catholic faith he had been born into and the Socialist one he had adopted in his youth, their similar trajectories of rise and decline and patchy attempted renewal, the waves of change and reaction which buffeted millions of people around in their sealed chambers, drowning many and raising select others to the surface. In particular, there were glaring parallels between the reactionary Catholicism and the Stalinized

Bolshevism of the early 1930s, both seeking to impose their prerogatives from above, impatient of dissent or deviation, ruthless towards organized opposition, indulgent towards obedience and loyalty. 'Perhaps', he wrote, 'there is an analogy between political parties and religious sects and monastic orders'.[7] What was Stalin if not the newly anointed Pope of world communism, surrounded by fawning, nodding courtiers and dogma-spouting, heresy-hunting cardinals, proclaiming his infallibility while watching out for the slightest shift in emphasis so they could translate it into official policy? The seminary-trained Josif Vissiaronovitch even adopted the *faux*-humility of St. Peter's successors, simultaneously fostering and disowning his own personality cult, an ordinary man who just happened to have extraordinary skills and powers. What was the emergent creed of Stalinism if not a kind of Counter-Reformation within the historical dialectic of Socialism?

And while it was becoming easier to be an ordinary communist – with millions accepted into party membership on significant anniversaries and subject to minimal political education beyond the mouthing of a few basic dogmas and obligations, the catechism of codified, authorized Marxism-Leninism – it was becoming ever harder to be an active communist intellectual. Indeed, if the latest reports and rumours from Russia were to be believed, it was becoming positively dangerous. But for the moment, in his own deepening isolation, Antonio Gramsci kept his doubts to himself and shied away from their dispiriting conclusions. Under the keen eye of the prison censor, not to mention the ones in Moscow and inside his own head, these glaring parallels between Communism and Catholicism – with their opposing yet matching missions of global hegemony – could not yet be made explicit. Instead they served as the intellectual backdrop for Antonio Gramsci's growing personal isolation and what he himself called withdrawal from the trenches of active political service or anything much by way of human contact.

Tanya Schucht's visit in July 1930 would be her last for two-and-a-half years. She had been staying at Turi for six months, in a small rented room above a pharmacy on the edge of town, in order to be able to visit Antonio more frequently, supply him with books and provisions, and support him during his bouts of illness and low spirits. But her own fragile health had taken another turn for the worse. She had, Antonio wrote to his brother Carlo, been leading a monk's life, isolated from the entire world; even more so than himself, if that was possible. She suffered a prolonged and very painful bout of phlebitis that came on in the spring. It confined her to bed for whole days at a time and otherwise left her hobbling around like an old cripple. She had expected it to ease with the onset of summer and the warmer and drier weather, but if anything it had got worse. She was still wearing the tight bandages that contained the swelling on her legs. Her savings, built up over many years of working as a nurse, a teacher and more recently as a clerk, were now pretty much exhausted. She had come to rely on a small monthly remittance sent to her by her father Apollon in Russia, but he was increasingly inclined to impose conditions and restrictions in return, even hinting that his own funds were now dangerously depleted. He was constantly reminding her in the postcards he enclosed with the rest of the family's letters that he was now feeling the pinch. He was trying to sell off various scattered family assets, including a small farm near Geneva which had stood empty and unused for so long it was no longer clear who legally owned it. In his letters to her, Apollon had begun to question the value and purpose of Tanya's way of life and choice of residence, and to suggest that she might rejoin the rest of the family in Russia for the sake of her own health, to resume paid employment and care for her blood relations.

She did not want to go to Russia, not least because it would mean abandoning Antonio. But without Apollon's financial support, which he had signalled would shortly be withdrawn, she would at the very least have to return to Rome and seek paid work. Tanya had also gathered that their father's standing in the Communist Party as a founder member, respected intellectual and old Bolshevik was also in some jeopardy. If anything, in this new post-Lenin era in Soviet Russia – when the Party's priorities were rapid industrialization and the collectivization of agriculture, and the rising stars of its first Five Year plan were compliant technocrats and untainted proletarians – Apollon's aristocratic manner and background and the substantial legacy it had conferred would constitute a positive handicap. His post of Librarian at the Electronic Institute, which he had held since 1924 and which conferred a small honorarium, had recently been given to a younger man deemed more in tune with the latest scientific and technological developments. More than once, Apollon had been challenged in party meetings on his own record of paid work, which amounted to little more than a few terms teaching Russian to army officers in Rome before the war.

Such high-born Bolsheviks were denounced for their 'Europeanism' in a prominent magazine article, which argued that Russia was more Asiatic than Western, and that the value of Bolshevism was in stirring up the Russian people and enhancing the international prestige and power of the country. In contrast, the cosmopolitan intelligentsia of old Europe had corrupted the soul of Mother Russia. There were not so subtle hints of anti-Semitism in references to elements of the old order who had swapped one set of Talmudic tablets for another, or (as in Apollon's case) married into alien traditions. The people who produced the magazine were outright nationalists, who even expressed sympathy for Fascism. One or two had proclaimed themselves Russian Fascists. But the most worrying thing of all was that they and their vile publication were being tolerated by the Soviet authorities, while old Bolsheviks and lifelong revolutionaries were being rounded up and sent to Siberia or abroad. In these circumstances, anyone who wished to protect themselves and their families would take great care to avoid any suspicion of disloyalty. For the Russian Schuchts, this would at the very least have caused them to question their association with Antonio Gramsci, whose reliability was under close scrutiny by the Soviet and Comintern authorities. And after all, none of them – not even Julia – had spent much time with Antonio or ever really got to know him. He remained, to all intents and purposes, a distant stranger in a faraway land; even the two boys had very little real idea who their father was. For his part, Antonio understood all this. He wrote to Tanya that as far as the children were concerned, he might as well be the Flying Dutchman or the man in the moon. He responded furiously when he discovered that Delio had heard about his imprisonment from another child at school and asked his teacher what prison was. He was even angrier when he found out that his 'mothers', Julia and Evgenia, managed to persuade the child that it wasn't true. Apollon eventually declared that Delio might as well be told anyway, because Antonio would be imprisoned far away for the foreseeable future, quite incapable of contributing to the family's affairs and fortunes. They hadn't actually got round to it yet, Tanya indicated, because they were concerned not to upset the child's nervous disposition.

At around this time, Antonio also finally discovered from Tanya the full extent of Julia's illness. The diagnosis of epilepsy which she had received in 1927 was only part of it. She had been seriously disturbed for at least three years now, on occasions quite deranged. She had given up her job with the NKVD some time ago, and they had just recently got round to stopping her salary, which added to the strain on the family finances. She was largely confined to bed at home, with periods of hospitalization along the way. For her husband, this would at least explain the silences and the scribbled notes and their strange dissociated tone, but he deeply resented having to wait three whole years to discover the truth, all the while conscious that something was seriously wrong without any clear idea what it might be, and subject to the speculations of his lonely worries and worst fears. Yet again, his family had kept him in the dark over a crucial personal matter.

He relayed to Tanya a story from his childhood. He had been a tireless hunter of lizards and snakes, which he fed to a beautiful hawk he had tamed and kept on a long leash. On three or four of his expeditions into the countryside around Ghilarza he came across a creature very similar to the common grass snake, except that it had four small feet, two at the front near the head and two at the back near the tail. It was sixty to seventy centimetres long, very wide and fat, with the girth of a grass snake but half the length. It slid or rather waddled along very slowly and clumsily in short abrupt jerks, without much assistance from its pathetic little legs, which just flapped about and got in the way. In his village this reptile was called a *scurzone*, a Sardinian dialect word which means 'stunted'. Back at school he asked the teacher, who was actually a retired engineer and not a qualified teacher at all, what the *scurzone* was called in Italian. The teacher laughed at the description and told Antonio it was an imaginary animal, usually referred to in mythology as an asp or basilisk, and that he knew of no real creature like the one described. Even when the boys from another village chipped in and said they called it a *coloru*, he insisted that these were all country superstitions and that there was no such thing as grass snakes with feet.

This teacher wasn't stupid – he had done a lot of research into natural history, and built up quite a collection of fossils and rocks – but he couldn't believe that the *scurzone* or *coloru* could be real and not have poisonous breath and burning eyes. 'I can still remember my anger at being told I was wrong when I knew I was right,' wrote Gramsci, 'and at being laughed at for being superstitious. I have always reacted badly against authority based on smugness and stupidity. It is in my experience typical of minor patriarchs used to lording it over people around them who are smaller and weaker than they are.'[8] In fact, he went on, he had looked it up just recently in the *Larousse* table of reptiles, and found a grass snake-type animal with four feet called the *seps* in Spain and southern France, so it was entirely plausible that there should be a variety on Sardinia. 'The beautiful *Larousse* illustration didn't look much like the *scurzone*, which was an ugly thing, with a large head and a conical tail. The front legs are too close to the head, and its feet are white and stunted and of very little practical use. It's quite unlike other lizards and snakes, which may be frightening but are basically elegant and graceful. But I have to say I am strangely fond of the *scurzone*, this ugly deformed Sardinian creature which is not supposed to exist and spends most of its life hidden under rocks, but which I have seen with my own eyes at least half a dozen times.'

Chapter 21

SINKING DEEPER

In late 1930, a new group of Communist prisoners arrived at Turi. They had all exhibited various types and levels of ill-health, and were brought together from prisons across the country to this special penitentiary for sick prisoners. Gramsci had already been holding informal political discussions in the exercise yard, and with this influx of new comrades proposed a more structured programme of study and discussion. They would talk about some of the themes he had been pursuing in his own studies, such as the role of intellectuals in Italian history or developments in popular culture, but also the issues facing the Communist Party in the struggle against Fascism and for proletarian revolution. If it went well it would animate and enrich his own studies, just as dialogue and debate had always done when he was a free man, as well as improving the political understanding and judgement of his incarcerated comrades. From the beginning the discussions did not proceed smoothly or well. This was, Gramsci soon realized, a new generation of communists, somehow harder and more impatient with each other than the thoughtful, open-minded, curious and collaborative comrades he had lived and worked with through the later days of the war, the Factory Councils and the occupations of the red years in Turin, then the breakaway from the Socialist Party and the formation of the *PCd'I*, or even the first years of Fascism. Back then workers, intellectuals and even peasants had mucked along together in the great cause of socialist revolution, largely oblivious to their personal, regional or even class differences, or at least prepared to work together to overcome them. In meetings and less formal gatherings, and on long walks around the night-time streets of Turin and Rome, the talk would roam freely over any topic anyone cared to mention. They could argue ferociously, and disagree profoundly, but they never lost their sense of a common bond and a unitary purpose, and their determination to act together to make a better world.

These newcomers were nothing like that. They were tetchy and unpleasant with each other, bridling at the slightest insult just like ordinary prisoners, disinclined to listen but all too inclined to hector. They didn't seem able to concentrate or pay attention to anyone else for longer than five minutes, and while Gramsci introduced the classes they would talk amongst themselves or even stand up and wander off. They would interrupt his introductions, and challenge the relevance of the topics he had chosen. He was told 'Less of the bloody Croce, Comrade Gramsci, and more of Comrade Stalin!' and 'It's not books we need. It's weapons training!' Gramsci wrote in a note in December 1930, with the latest bruising exercise yard encounter fresh in his mind, that this kind of intelligence, also often called 'talent', revelled in superficial polemic. It aimed to appear independent, challenge every authority and pick away at fundamental truths with objections to minor details. It was in fact a kind of facetiousness, trying to keep a straight face but always inclined to smirk, in reality based on intellectual clumsiness and narrow-minded provincialism.

For his part, Gramsci realized that all this time in isolation and quiet contemplation had rendered him remote and cool. Perhaps his studies had taken him too deep inside himself and into territory which did not actually interest anyone else. He just could not seem to engage or charm people the way he used to, and get them to perceive the remarkable brain at work atop his stunted, ungainly body. He found it hard to deal with the new comrades' interruptions, or any kind of deviation from the notes he had prepared, other than by asserting his authority or simply shouting them down, whereas in the old days he would have welcomed and used them to develop another line of argument; the creative whirr and buzz of the dialectic. He was, he feared above all else, turning into the kind of pedantic, flustered old fool he had sneered at as a university student and young activist. He was just as incapable of reaching these mostly younger hotheads as the most obscurantist professor or pompous party official had been of reaching him and his friends in Turin. They would parrot dogmas and formulas without any clear idea what lay behind them or even what they meant, but simply to declare their allegiance to the cause or to whoever happened to be in charge at the moment. Most of them had joined the party since the 1926 crackdown or just before, and been arrested for clandestine agitation in the streets and factories. They had very little experience of open mass politics or the daily lives of the ordinary people they claimed to represent and (even more absurdly) lead. None of them had ever met or worked with Gramsci before. They showed little deference or even respect for this funny little Sardinian hunchback, who used to be something in the old days but by his own admission had been out of the struggle for some years now and unable or unwilling to say anything very useful about it. They had all embraced the *svolta* or 'turn' to the new hard line imposed by the Comintern, and whatever local consequences it might have for Italy or any other national territory. One was heard to declare, 'Starving peasants have no option but to throw in their lot with the workers! And if we need to starve a few more to get them to see sense, so what?'[1]

Gramsci tried chipping away at their blind certainties – misery and hunger can provoke uprisings and revolts, which may even shatter the prevailing social order, but that does not equate to a revolutionary strategy for building socialism or in itself destroy capitalism – but even this simple restatement of the basic tenets of historical materialism was met with scoffs and sneers. He'd try another tack: Fascism has profoundly disorientated the popular masses. They need a restoration of democracy to recover their balance and their sense of historic mission. Hadn't Marx himself said that political democracy was a prerequisite for the social and economic democracy of socialism? One of the cockiest, a young printer from Bologna, pointed out that this was not what *PCd'I* General Secretary Comrade

Palmiro Togliatti had told the Comintern Sixth Congress the previous year: 'We are now in the period of preparation for the proletarian revolution, not the restoration of bourgeois democracy. There will be no so-called transitional phase.'[2] He dared Gramsci to disagree with the current leadership of the party and the Comintern line. Another older comrade, who had been here as long as Gramsci but had dutifully adapted to the Comintern line and thrown in his lot with the new arrivals, said he was confused. Had he not heard Gramsci himself describe the social democrats in 1926 as the left wing of the bourgeoisie? What's more, he had heard though the clandestine party network that Gramsci had communicated his assent to the *svolta*, and the inevitable and very necessary expulsions of Tasca and the other oppositionists, yet here he was disagreeing with it. How could this be?

To the one or two sympathetic comrades he would complain privately that the party had been infected by maximalism. There was a fear of any and every idea that couldn't be found in the old maximalist dictionary of clichés. Any tactic which did not correspond to this dream world was considered an error and a deviation. You ended up unable to adapt to changing historical circumstances, preferring words to political action or confusing one with the other, and capable of nothing but abstract schemes and fixes. Instead, he would lay out how he saw the basic facts of the situation. Even under the most favourable conditions, the party could not count on more than a few thousand activists in Italy. The working classes were demoralized and disorganized, and Fascism was stronger than ever. The communists needed allies, not sectarian isolation, and that required compromise and concessions to other social classes, mainly the peasantry and the lower middle classes who resented the destruction of their freedoms by Fascism. A popular, broad-based anti-Fascist movement was the only way forward. At best, his audience would respond with sullen acquiescence, but more often disperse around the prison in muttering huddles.

Gramsci's educational programme lasted just a few weeks of November and December 1930. He proposed a fortnight's break to mull things over, and hopefully take the heat out of the situation. But if anything this just made things worse. Opinions hardened into factional differences and sectarian outbursts, and criticism became more personal. Gramsci had become a social democrat, they were saying, a gradualist not a revolutionary, and was no longer even a communist. Hadn't his old *L'Ordine Nuovo* comrade and friend Angelo Tasca been expelled in 1928 for just such right-wing deviationism? His admiration for Croce and other bourgeois intellectuals indicated opportunism and disloyalty, while his line on Fascism and bourgeois democracy flew in the face of the Comintern and *PCd'I* strategy, and recklessly flouted the properly Leninist 'democratic centralism' its implementation required. Hadn't 'the three' been thrown out more recently for just such heresy? There was even talk of writing to the party leadership in exile to denounce Gramsci's disruptive influence, of excluding him from the communist group at Turi and refusing him their company in the exercise yard. One day, after a heavy snowfall, the prisoners threw snowballs at each other. Standing alone in the corner of the yard to avoid being hit, Gramsci felt a snowball whistle past his ear and hit the wall. A large stone fell to the ground.

Finally, when Gramsci tried to resolve a confrontation between some of the new comrades and the prison warders he was accused of excessive regard for legality, and of being afraid to lose the privileges of writing in his cell and receiving books and special food from outside. He tried to explain that he had fought hard for these concessions, with letters and petitions to every level of the prison service right up to Mussolini, but this only seemed to increase the suspicion and animosity. Gramsci didn't disclose the subject of his latest appeal to Mussolini, which 'His Excellency' had been good enough to approve in November after it was rejected all the way up the prison system: to be allowed to read the autobiography of the disgraced Leon Davidovitch Trotsky, with whom he had been in regular contact in the early 1920s. Nor did he point out that his so-called privileges did not seem to include the right to a decent night's sleep, because repeated requests to be moved from his cell, the very first on the first corridor, had been turned down. There was constant coming and going past his cell to the infirmary and other parts of the prison, and the more brutal guards were not averse to banging on his door in the middle of the night just for the sheer hell of it, he wrote to Tanya.

In March 1931 Gramsci wrote to his brother Carlo: 'In order to stick rigidly to my absolutely correct behaviour in accordance with the necessities of prison life, I've come into conflict with some other prisoners and been forced to break off personal relationships.'[3] When the *PCd'I* held its Fourth Congress in Germany in April/May 1931, and repeated the call for immediate insurrection and proletarian revolution, it was duly relayed back to the imprisoned politicos. Gramsci reiterated his private view that Italy would first have to pass through a democratic phase, focussed on the struggle for some kind of constituent assembly. This brought further grumbles and suspicious looks around the exercise yard. Painfully aware of his isolation, he withdrew into his cell and his studies, effectively ostracized. He took comfort in new intellectual insights and skills, including a greater facility at reading English, which he found much easier than German, he wrote to Tanya. He had read an extract from *The Economist* on the Five Year Plan in two or three days, and didn't think a single word escaped him. Meanwhile, rumours continued to circulate among the party networks in Italy and in exile about his dissent from the new line. No attempts were made to seek clarification from him directly, and for the time being his name disappeared completely from the party press.

In the absence of much company inside the prison or visits from outside, the closest Antonio Gramsci came to everyday ordinary human contact over the next two-and-a-half years – from the summer of 1930 to the beginning of 1933 – were the photographs he had collected of his family and loved ones, augmented by the new, latest ones he regularly pleaded for in his letters to them. The various children were especially fascinating, not just for their endearing looks and rapid development, but also for their similarities to each other and their echoes of previous generations. They offered proof of his own place in family history, reminders of his own childhood and, in their expressions of determined optimism, of his own sterling efforts to imbue the squalor of his circumstances with purpose, honour and dignity. To his sister Teresina he wrote that her kids were lovely looking, and strong and healthy; he was really amazed to see how much more robust her son Franco seemed. Some time ago she had sent him a photograph of Franco looking thin and delicate, but this one showed as clear as day that the boy was not only strong but sunny and lively too. He asked if she would send a copy of the same photo to Tanya, who would send it on to Julia. He had sent her a few of the other photographs himself, though from a technical point of view they were rather poor; the Russians would notice these things. Julia had written back that Delio and Giuliano were very interested in them and were asking lots of questions about their Italian cousins.

To his mother he wrote rather more frankly, with a touch of mischief, that he didn't think Franco and Delio, roughly the same age, were like one another in the least, though Delio was very like Nannaro's child Edmea. Franco's hair wasn't curly, and looked dark brown. Delio was certainly much more handsome. Teresina's daughter Mimi was very like Edmea when she was a baby. For the most part, it was marvellous how all these children had the Gramsci family features. So did Delio and Giuliano, very much so. They made him think of faces seen long ago, faces which suddenly surfaced in his memory after so many years of oblivion. The last picture of Delio was like seeing Mario when he was eight years old. Giuliano's features made him think of Nannaro, and even more of Uncle Alfredo. To his mother Gramsci wrote again, about two small blurred photos of her that Gennaro had brought him: 'It seems to me that in spite of your years, and all you have put up with, you've kept youthful and strong. You can't have more than a few white hairs, probably a lot fewer than me. And unlike me, I'm sure you've still got at least some of your teeth! Your expression is very lively, even though it's – how shall I put it, mamma? – a little matronly. I'll bet that you'll live to see your great grandchildren, and see them growing up too! One day in the years to come we'll get a big family photograph taken. All the generations will be in it, and yourself in the middle to keep us all in order!'[4]

Naturally, he took the closest interest in the photos of his own two small sons, and tried hard to construct from them some sense of how they might be living and growing up. Each new photograph would add a detail or a development to the story, some new cause for delight or concern. But towards the end of 1930, it was a group photograph of Julia, Delio and Giuliano that made the deepest impression. The boys looked well enough – Delio as usual a little dreamy, Giuliano slightly annoyed and anxious to be off and doing something else – but Julia's expression was vacant and distracted, inclined to anger, almost warlike he observed. It compared poorly to the earliest picture of her he'd seen, in a group photo taken in Ivanovo in July 1922, in those far off days a couple of months before they met. Somehow the photographer back then seemed to have drawn her out of herself and presented her confident public face, the young music teacher and esteemed member of the Ivanovo Arts Education Committee. The contrast with this latest photo was stark. Her hair was unkempt and falling over her face. She was trying to smile for the camera, or rather for the photographer slightly off to the right. But her thin stretched lips just made her look ill, and their forced smile conflicted with the sad, mirthless look in her eyes.

If Antonio Gramsci's relationship with his two small children was conducted through photographs on his side and scraps of overheard adult conversation on theirs, his relationship with his wife now consisted of garbled hints about her from others, and worried or exasperated outbursts from him. All of it was conducted in writing via second or third parties over great distances, with several layers of possible or actual censorship to pass through. Julia now hardly ever wrote directly to him herself. Her news was more often transmitted through letters from Tanya, who was settled back in Rome, unable or unwilling to travel to Turi. She enclosed the odd scribbled note from Julia or postcard from Apollon, almost as supporting evidence for her own vague allusions to things going wrong. Tanya regularly apologized for not feeling able to tell him more. His own responses to the scraps from Moscow came in increasingly reluctant and terse messages relayed via Tanya in Rome, which he admitted to her were becoming dishevelled. He complained to Julia on 6 October 1930 that when he looked back on their correspondence, such as it was, and the hopes he had when arrested that she, his wife, would be his primary point of contact with the outside world; he could not help but feel bitter disappointment. She wrote to him, her husband, as she would a stranger. They had never succeeded in getting a dialogue going, only ever a series of monologues. He spent many hours wondering why this might be, what had gone wrong or never been right in the first place, and what his own part in the failure of their marriage might have been. Were there any extenuating circumstances, as a lawyer might put it, some excuse or at least explanation in their personal backgrounds, social place and historical setting? Was there still, against all the odds and from the depths of their mutual isolation and misery, something they could actually do to save themselves and each other? Was there even any point in trying?

Without any clear statement from Julia or hard information from anyone else, he lost himself in speculation, clutching at straws, turning every little molehill of fact into a mountain of supposition. He lurched between anguished self-pity in his letters at one extreme and the disinterested chill of his notebooks at the other, from *für mich* to *für ewig*. A fortnight later in October he observed in a letter to Tanya that, from what little he could gather of the real situation, Julia was gradually approaching the state that Zhenya reached in 1919, in that she refused to adopt a regular rhythm of living. What had been understandable in 1919, with all that everyone had recently gone through, was nothing but absurd romanticism in the more settled conditions of 1930. Conscious that Tanya forwarded all his letters to Julia, even personal ones addressed to Tanya, he shared a hypothesis derived from his recent reading and reflection, in the sincere hope that it might be of some practical help in illuminating the way ahead. All mental disturbance had its basis in history, he argued, and varied over time according to the change in historical developments and circumstances. Every epoch generated its own form of madness, a complex interplay of social stresses and personal confusions. The complexity of each era's favoured or even fashionable mental illness directly reflected the complexity of the society and political economy in which it arose. Whereas the post-war epidemic of neurasthenia was a direct result of famine, disease, revolution, injury and death on a mass scale, and the simple exhaustion of living through such turbulent times – as such, an easily understandable human response to social catastrophe and upheaval, a kind of mental counterpart to the post-war influenza epidemic, which had infected many millions including Julia – personal breakdown now had much less obvious causes in the organization of everyday life at work and in the home. Nervous debility had been domesticated or privatized by the turn from war to peace, from severe privation to relative plenty, from social conflict to social stability. To make matters worse, it doubled back on itself in the form of personal shame and social disgrace at having survived what had destroyed so many others. Previously, 'society' was to blame; now, it was the fault of the 'individual', a graphic example of the restoration of bourgeois hegemony over the way in which people saw themselves and each other.

These psychological disorders seemed to be increasingly common across the industrialized world, exacerbated by the push towards 'modernity'. Julia's disturbance was no isolated phenomenon, as evident in the scientific publications concerning the new industrial work systems introduced from America. In the regulation of every aspect of their workforces' lives, Ford and his cohorts were putting their workers' physical and mental health under enormous strain. 'Unless we are able to make the necessary adjustments in mentality and way of life, mechanisation crushes us. And I'm taking mechanisation in the broad sense, to include the scientific organization of brain work, such as you (Julia) and I have been professionally engaged in. Its disciplines and demands are unyielding, relentless, occasionally overwhelming.'[5] This was the psychological or spiritual manifestation of what Gramsci referred to in his notebooks as Americanism, the basis for any modern form of planned economy. At least in America – but also in economies as diverse as Italy and the Soviet Union if its 'scientific' advocates had their way (most notably Trotsky, who in 1924 had called for an Americanized Bolshevism) – it meant relatively high wages in return for strictly regulated performance on automated production lines.[6] Each task was separated and allocated to a specialist worker, who was required to repeat it consistently and endlessly. Every moment of the working day was subject to Taylorist methods of time and motion study, efficiency and quality improvement. Outside work, if there was really any such place under this new managerial regime, Ford employed inspectors who supervised the private life of his employees, their food, their beds, the size of their rooms, their rest hours, their physical and mental health, even their sex lives. If the workers didn't conform they were dismissed. Europeans might bridle at such methods, but this was because of those aspects of Americanism that subverted the stagnant European society; 'We think we can live as we please ... We're absurdly romantic, and in our efforts not to be bourgeois we fall into Bohemianism, which is in fact the most typical form of bourgeois behaviour.'[7]

His hypothesis on the socio-economic basis of Julia's psychological disturbance, and his somewhat muddled suggestion that it was a consequence of both American-style 'mechanisation' *and* European 'romantic Bohemianism', unsurprisingly elicited no direct response from her or anyone else. His own curt summary of her condition – as 'an inferiority complex' in which she 'suffers from unreal problems' – was similarly ignored. In his own deepening isolation, he took stock. After three years of silence or deception following his arrest, he had learnt the full extent of Julia's illness; or so he had been led to believe. He realized now that he had still not actually got from anyone a coherent account of what was wrong, just scattered and inconsistent signals from her of her mental illness and reports from others – all transmitted through Tanya – of the various vague diagnoses and cures she was being subjected to. These latter ranged from full-blown Freudian psychoanalysis to a rest-cure with the children in the Crimean resort town of Sochi; this last, one of the final, hard-won fruits of Apollon's dwindling prestige. None of them seemed to do much good. A manically cheerful and resolute note from Julia about her latest self-discovery or treatment – enabling her to 'rebuild my psyche … and attain a development of my personality that I did not have when we were together, when I always felt like your little girl' – would be followed by months of aching silence, then a message from Tanya that things were back to square one.[8]

His own letters back to Julia, by turns chiding and tender, began to seem to him as confused and contradictory as hers. And in their confusion, there was the ever-present risk that some throwaway remark or hypothesis would come over as clumsy and seriously hurtful. It was like walking on eggshells. How could it be otherwise, given how little he knew of the real situation, and how unused he was becoming to dealing with other people in normal circumstances? How could he, in the publicly imposed isolation of imprisonment, hope to understand what Julia was going through in the private isolation of mental illness? His words to her really were shots in the dark, casting his love into a void, expressing nothing so much as fear or contempt towards his own feelings. He was hiding in his mind from his heart; or rather behind his heart, where the ancients located the soul, observing his own feelings clinically and dispassionately but quite unable to do anything about or with them. More and more, he fell back into what he himself described to Tanya and Julia as pedantic lectures, apologizing frequently and profusely for his seeming inability to strike any more human or sympathetic note.

After one of Tanya's most downbeat accounts of Julia's condition, he declared to his wife in November 1930 that 'all is revealed'.[9] She was undergoing, he suggested, a psychological crisis which was bound to have a physiological basis in her many years of irregular hours and habits and inadequate diet. When Tanya had told him that Julia was undergoing psychoanalysis, this had prompted him to reread her letters from a psychoanalytical point of view. He could now detect in them ruptures between form and content, for the purposes of disguise and distraction. Perhaps this reflected something permanent in her personality which had now surfaced against the background of a social environment which constantly demanded an extremely strong tension of the will. He understood and accepted her recourse to psychoanalysis as a response to the growing moral pressure exerted on individuals by the apparatus of State and society and the mental illnesses this pressure produced. This was, he had gleaned from his reading, the basis of the latest and most advanced 'scientific' approaches to psychiatry, though one should be as wary of it as of any formulas for living which promised much but at best translated half-formulated desires into conscious aims. Freudism was a useful tool in the passage from the old economic individualism to the planned economy. It could help you find your own way through life, so long as you set aside such eccentricities as its apparent advocacy of sexual relations between fathers and children and its overriding preoccupation with the feminine personality. But perhaps a properly historicist psychoanalysis could best be done alone, 'dialectically and with intellectual objectivity … You can thereby become your own doctor.'

He wondered whether she might not be better served by hard and purposeful work. In other words, in this most intimate and interior form of medicine, she should seek to 'heal thyself'. To this end he set her the task of researching for him a debate recently conducted at Oxford University between Benedetto Croce and the Russian intellectual and Soviet official Anatoly Lunacharsky on the tenets and veracity of historical materialism. The wily old Italian liberal philosopher's intimate knowledge of Marxism had clearly taken the Bolshevik luminary and recently displaced Soviet Minister of Education by surprise, and revealed in the latter a surprising ignorance of the main currents of Italian cultural and intellectual life. In particular, Lunacharsky had struggled to refute Croce's critique of the hidden God in the economic base posited by Marxism, the notion that economics determined every other aspect of life. Against this, Croce set his own master concept of 'ethico-political action', conscious planning and strategic intervention by real live human beings, as the primary factor in the course of history. Antonio – placing himself between these two intellectual currents of materialism and idealism – wrote to Julia that he would be interested in any special essay Croce had composed after the debate. In the same spirit of occupational therapy, he further suggested that she might propose a Russian translation of a new edition of *Ancient Capitalism: A History of the Roman Economy* by Giuseppe Salvioli, which he had been reading and was much impressed by. It required a Russian translator with a very good knowledge of Italian, who could understand and correct the distortions of syntax and the rather clumsy grammar in the Moscow edition published after the author's death. He understood that the Soviet state publishing house paid for proposals for translations which were published, and suggested this might help the Schuchts' straitened finances. They were, according to Tanya, worse off than him here in prison, with his daily allowance and the money sent to him via Carlo from the *PCd'I* in exile, which sustained a prison 'account' of several hundred lire. Even the Gramscis were probably better off back in Ghilarza, where several working-age adults now enabled the family to employ a maid again. This had been beyond the Schuchts for some years.

There is no record of Julia's responses to any of these rather desperate suggestions, beyond hints in the correspondence that they were merely adding to the strains she was subjected to. Whatever Julia felt or decided to do, Antonio pleaded with her to write to him with utter frankness and – as tactfully as he could manage, in the light of the scatter-brained nature of much of her previous correspondence – with a greater love of system. In response, in one of her sporadic, pained attempts at an ordinary letter, on 9 January 1931, she confessed that 'when I think of writing – which I do every day – I think of what makes me remain silent. I remember that my weakness is new to you'.[10] He duly responded a month later, in a similarly clumsy, halting attempt at endearment and sympathy, that he had always known that she was weak, in other words that she 'my darling Julka' was a living, breathing woman. In the circumstances it was hardly surprising that she was a little harassed mentally, and that he felt powerless to do anything about it.

> When I think about our life, I cannot but conclude that we never really had a chance. We were together too briefly, always in abnormal circumstances, and cut off from the concrete reality of everyday life … All we can do now is try to salvage the little joy we had and that lives on in our children. I want to be a real father to them, and not just a memory in an ever-receding past. Who are you? What is this family I am supposed to be a part of? Who is Julka + Delio + Giuliano?[11]

The matter of the children's upbringing and education continued to provoke distant conflict. Antonio had been forbidden to write directly to them, having written once to Delio and had the letter returned unopened and unread, because of fears that it might upset the child's sensitive nervous system. He had cause to wonder whether the Schuchts were still keeping his imprisonment a secret, or at least a family taboo, and were worried that the child might ask awkward questions about the prison stamp on the letter and the envelope. It turned out that Delio had not yet learnt to read and write, because (Tanya wrote) the doctors didn't want him to go in for brain work too early. In April 1931, Tanya forwarded two photos and a sheet of paper with Delio's scrawled attempts at handwriting. Antonio wrote back to her that he couldn't make head nor tail of it, or of why he should start writing right to left, and not left to right. He was however glad the child wrote with his hands; that was something anyway, better than writing with his feet. Since the Arabs, Persians and the Turks who'd not yet accepted Westernization, and perhaps other people too, wrote from right to left, it didn't seem terribly serious or dangerous. Once Delio had learnt Persian, Turkish and Arabic, writing from right to left would be of great advantage. But why not take this logic further? Wouldn't it have been better to leave his personality free to develop on its own in other ways too? Why was he forced to dress like other people? Why not leave his clothes scattered around the room and let him choose spontaneously: socks on his head, shoes on his hands, gloves on his feet?

Tanya chose, perhaps wisely, not to share this letter with her Russian relatives. She had recently met with Antonio's brother Carlo, who had visited Moscow to discuss Antonio's situation with officials in the Comintern, and taken the opportunity of meeting his in-laws. They were, he reported to Tanya when he returned, turning the children against Antonio because they believed he was not a dutiful father. They were even considering making a complaint to the authorities about his failure to support his wife and children financially, apparently oblivious of his repeated attempts to get Julia to accept gifts and money, because they had been advised that this would entitle them to state support. In turn, Tanya chose not to tell Antonio what Carlo had told her, but forwarded a message from Apollon that Julia did not refuse to write because she was sick, but because she found it very painful under the conditions she was obliged to do it in. These conditions were not specified. Julia wrote again to Antonio in early May 1931, in an apparently upbeat mood. She was feeling very much better, conveyed news of the children and her own wishes for the future, even some observations on the spectacular achievements of the first Five Year Plan. Was this permanent, or another false dawn? He wrote to Tanya that Julia seemed to have recovered a certain confidence in herself and her own strength. Perhaps, he speculated, she had escaped from the deep sea to the shore. Her recovery owed a lot, she had said, to the new scientific methods being pioneered in the Soviet Union for the treatment of mental disorder. This was, Antonio wrote to Tanya with more than a hint of his customary irony, 'a touching example of the Soviets' great faith in science, of an almost religious character, in stark contrast to the corresponding loss of faith in science in the West'.[12] And what did this latest wonder treatment amount to? Apparently, someone had suggested to Julia that she should 'unravel herself', whatever that might mean, and as if she had not already embarked on that process of her own volition.

On 1 June 1931 Antonio finally received a properly legible letter, or rather what he described to Tanya as an 'epistle', from Delio, in which the child expressed his 'love of Pushkin's stories'.[13] Antonio wrote back to Julia, asking was the sentiment genuine? Had the letter been composed or even written by the child? In response, he transcribed a folk tale from Sardinia which he asked Julia to recite to the children: A child is sleeping. Nearby there's a big cup of milk ready for when he wakes up. A rat drinks the milk. The child, waking to find the milk gone, screams. The mother screams too. The rat bangs his head on the wall in desperation, but realizes that won't achieve anything, so he rushes to a goat for some milk. The goat says she'll give him some milk if he gets her some grass to eat. The rat goes to the country for grass, but the parched land begs for water. The rat goes to the fountain, but the fountain has been ruined in a war and needs stones to plug the holes. The rat goes to the mountain for stones, but it has been so devastated by logging that all the stones have rolled down and broken into dust. The rat tells the mountain the whole story so far, and promises that when the child grows up he will replant the trees on the mountain. In return, the mountain tells the rat where he can find stones still intact. The rat takes the stones to the fountain, the water to the land, the grass to the goat and the milk to the child, who has so much he can even bathe in it! He grows up strong and tall, and plants the trees which attract new soil and regular rain to the mountain, which prevents flooding in the plains. 'In other words,' Gramsci concluded this charming piece of popular ecology, 'the rat conceives and executes nothing less than a *piatilietka*, a proper Five Year Plan (especially welcome in Sardinia, where coal mining has caused almost total deforestation)! And even the smallest creatures are capable of the greatest acts!'[14]

In July 1931, Gramsci received permission to write weekly rather than fortnightly letters, an easing of conditions following on from a slight reduction in his sentence by one year, four months and five days the previous year. These were, everyone understood, small acts of government mercy that actually meant the Fascists were feeling even more secure. As for the increased entitlement to letters, he confessed to Tanya that he was surprisingly unmoved by this substantial increase in what had been his most enjoyable and purposeful activity. Now he found it increasingly onerous and disruptive of his personal routines, and a distraction from his research and note-taking. He frequently forgot things he'd previously been informed of or even written himself, which created regular misunderstandings with his correspondents. Awaiting their responses became a fresh trial, especially when they were delayed by tardiness, mishap or the censors. He felt less desire to write than ever, and this in turn exacerbated his isolation; every day another thread tying him to the past broke. When Tanya wrote back asking him to elaborate, he replied that from their silence and the lack of visits he could only conclude that the people he loved had grown used to the idea of his being in prison. Previously, he had been glad to leave the past behind. These broken threads had been a mark of his independence and personal progress: 'I was almost proud to be isolated. But today I realise the squalor and sterility of a life directed solely by one's own will ... I no longer have a real programme of study and work. I'm no longer curious about anything, daunted by the scale of the tasks I set myself and the limits of my own resources.'[15]

When he finally brought himself to write directly to Julia again, he reiterated that when he was arrested he believed that she would help him keep in touch with the outside world, or at least her and the children's lives. It seemed to him now that she had done just the opposite, only aggravated his isolation. He knew next to nothing about her, not even if she had gone back to work. Her letters were extremely vague. He couldn't imagine any of her life. He had tried so many times to start a real dialogue, asked her so many questions and indicated the kinds of things he'd like to know. All this had produced nothing, so he had fallen back into a crab-like state of mind, which made it very hard and painful for him to write to her at all. Try as he might, and though he hated himself for it, he just could not summon the sympathy and understanding to reach out to her and offer the support she undoubtedly needed. He was simply too cut off, too deep down inside himself. In these circumstances, expecting him to have anything truly worthwhile to say about her own depression was like asking a drowning man to show someone how to walk.

At the very end of July, with the approach of the children's birthdays, he wrote to her again. In a few days Delio would be seven years old, and at the end of the month Giuliano would be five. This birthday was especially important for Delio, because the age of seven was widely considered an important point in the development of a personality. The Catholic Church, undoubtedly the global institution with the greatest body of organizational and propaganda experience, had fairly recently set the first communion at seven. This represented a solemn entry into the community of the faith, and endowed upon the young child an ideological formation that should stay with them for life. He didn't know whether Julia was planning to celebrate this birthday in any special way. Perhaps this was the moment to explain to Delio that his father was in prison and what for, though she may still want to keep it from Giuliano. Such an explanation, together with the sense of trust and respect it conveyed, especially if he was required for the time being to keep it from his younger brother, would make a great impression upon him and mark an important point in his development.

In early August 1931, Antonio Gramsci suffered his most serious medical crisis yet. On the morning of Monday 3rd, he suddenly started coughing up blood. In response to his cries for help, the guards sauntered along from the guardroom next door. When they saw the blood on his bed and his clothes, and in large splashes on the stone floor, they panicked and sent out for the prison doctor. Doctor Cisternino was, they were told and they told Gramsci, out at lunch and would then be attending to other patients in the town. But he would come to the prison as soon as he had finished with them. In the meantime, he had told them to keep an eye on him. Gramsci's coughing fit went on till four in the afternoon, by which time he had brought up – by his own reckoning – over half a pint of blood. It wasn't anything like a continuous haemorrhage, he later wrote to Tanya, more like a gurgle in his breathing to begin with, like you get from catarrh. An abrupt cough followed, and his mouth filled with blood. The coughing wasn't especially violent, or even pronounced. It was exactly the sort of coughing you get when you've got something in your throat, just isolated bursts.

When Cisternino finally showed up, he conducted a cursory examination and prescribed calcium chloride with a trace of adrenalin. He did not say what this was supposed to achieve or alleviate, or what he thought the basic problem might be, and Gramsci did not feel inclined to ask. Cisternino returned two days later on 5 August, and made a more thorough examination with a stethoscope. He was at least able to rule out any bronchial infection, and suggested that the blood had come from the intestines. Given Gramsci's medical history of digestive problems, this would not be entirely surprising. In the meantime, he might also consider smoking rather less. Gramsci did try to reduce his smoking, as much for reasons of thrift as health, by making three small cigarettes with the tobacco that would previously have made one. But the effects on his concentration made him reluctant to give up altogether. Instead he tried to eke out his tobacco, getting through one packet every five days.

The coughing eased over the next few days, and there was no more blood in the catarrh. But in the meantime, Gramsci's left side was covered in a rash of red spots. It had been unusually hot recently, even for August, and he had been sweating profusely on many nights in recent weeks. But he had also been feverish, especially in the couple of nights before and after the blood-coughing fit. He chose not to call Cisternino back to examine the rash or consider the fever. The initial examinations and prescriptions had cost enough, a large chunk out of his prison account, and he was loathe to give Cisternino any more business than was strictly necessary. Besides, he would not want the doctor to think he was weak, or malingering. In the meantime he made frequent, sometimes obsessive, use of a thermometer he had had Tanya purchase and send him, noting the slightest variation in his temperature, especially before and after eating. He wrote to her, trying to reassure her that there was nothing very worrying about it. In response to her concerns about his meagre diet, he told her he bought whatever he could to supplement the prison rations; the problem was there was not much to buy. Fruit had been on sale just a few times recently, and fresh cheese even less frequently. The canteen sold only stuff he couldn't eat; even ham had been forbidden by the doctor, not least because of the state of his teeth, so he ate nothing much but eggs, milk and rice cooked with butter. Various dietary 'cures' – going for days on nothing but milk, or grapes, or even lemonade – might briefly calm his stomach, but mainly because they passed right through him without troubling his digestive system.

Medicine didn't seem to make much difference either. The stuff Cisternino prescribed just made Gramsci feel drowsy and constipated, and the various remedies Tanya sent or ordered from the local pharmacy did little lasting good. He made meticulous notes of their ingredients and their effects on his temperature, weight and well-being, and duly reported them to Tanya for her to consult with her medical friends; all to little effect. Rather, he thought prison conditions were much more significant. Frequent disturbances and wakefulness in the night made his condition noticeably worse, whereas sound sleep made it much better. To that end he wrote several letters to the Prison Director Parmegiani to protest against the continuing noisiness around his cell at night, without result beyond official acknowledgement of the receipt of his complaints. If anything, his complaint that the application of regulations became an object of trafficking between the guards and prisoners – packets of tobacco and quarter litres of wine exchanged for special consideration during inspections – made the nightly rackets even worse. He spent his days in a dull torpor, and his nights tossing and turning. The best use of his time at any hour was to read or write in his notebooks, his own preferred therapeutic work. It did not require physical health. If anything, deep thought offered a way to rise above illness, spurred on by the sense of urgency induced by failing powers.

Chapter 22

HEALING THROUGH WORK

Throughout 1931 and 1932, Gramsci continued to study intensively and for long hours, to consult and order a wide range of books and periodicals, which were sent to him by Tanya, his brother Carlo or direct from the bookshop in Milan where Piero Sraffa kept an open account for him. They were, he observed to guards or fellow prisoners who noticed the piles of well-thumbed journals and rows of heavily annotated books in every spare corner of his cell, his lifeblood or more frivolously his menagerie. He was especially proud of the books and periodicals he had to fight to read, like his treasured volumes of Marx, and which he knew were now lifetime companions. Through these years he was translating a small anthology of Marx's writings from German into Italian, to help him through those periods when he didn't feel capable of original thought. He also undertook a highly original study of *Canto X* of Dante's *Inferno*, which offered some light relief, taking up where he had left off as a student before the war. But even this had a serious aim: to demolish more conventional interpretations such as one he had just come across by a certain 'Rastignac', and to demonstrate that the representatives of a subaltern social group can give short shrift to intellectual pimps like Rastignac in matters of science and artistic taste. Gramsci's reading of Dante had an added but unstated personal purpose, to focus attention on the anguish of the character Cavalcante over the fate of his son Guido; it was a beautiful and moving portrayal of a worried, grieving father. When he had finished with books and periodicals, he sent them to Tanya or Carlo for safe-keeping or disposal, or donated them to the prison library. He was quite meticulous in their cataloguing and storage, with lists of publication and location details worthy of any library, and in overseeing their further usage. He instructed Carlo not to lend them to people outside the family circle. He didn't see why his books should help entertain people who were indirectly responsible for his being in prison. Rather, he hoped they might form the basis of a family library for his brothers and sisters and nephews and nieces, and perhaps one day his own children.

Alongside his reading he made new notes, revised and rearranged old ones, gradually filling up the marbled exercise books with his spidery writing, and bringing his reflections on history, philosophy and political economy into focus. For months at a time, he went back over his several years' collection of journals and reviews, sorting out what he wanted to keep from what he would dispatch for storage or disposal. It took so long because he couldn't resist using select quotations or responses of his own as a stepping-off point into original reflections. Some of these – monographs as he called them – were beginning to take on the shape of fully formed outlines of what were becoming his central themes, the role of intellectuals in Italian and European history in particular, which he allowed himself to imagine being published somewhere, some day. His only problem, he wrote to Tanya, was that he was too often plagued by serious headaches that did not permit the necessary concentration. For most of this time he was entirely alone, cut off from his family in Russia and Sardinia and from his party in exile and in Italy, and even from most of his fellow prisoners at Turi di Bari. They might glimpse him through the bars of his cell, standing in his customary position at a high desk covered in books and papers, pacing around and in between the stacks on the floor as he cleared his thoughts, or sitting in the sun when he ventured out into the yard during exercise periods, usually with a lit Macedonian cigarette in his hand or his mouth. By and large he kept himself to himself, politely but cursorily answering enquiries into his health and welfare, or exchanging comments on the weather. He showed little interest in the frequently loud and feverish disputes on topics of the day among the other political prisoners.

His own mood was a kind of serene fatalism, a sardonic peace with himself, a settled melancholy, chiding himself only (he wrote to Tanya) for the weakness of not having dared to remain alone, of allowing himself ties of love, obligations and close relationships. Those he had formed in his years of freedom, he now felt, had brought him nothing but trouble. If only he could insulate himself altogether from other people and the outside world, he might convince himself not to ponder any more, to resist any external stimulus, and to put aside any letters he may receive without reading them. This was, he argued, a highly desirable and productive kind of emotional continence which was decidedly out of fashion, but in his circumstances – stuck in prison but hard at work – represented by far the most psychologically healthy and intellectually productive mode. He sought to allay Tanya's continuing anxiety about his physical health, which had prompted her to write to his brother Carlo and even the prison doctor Cisternino, by insisting that he had made a fair recovery from the blood-coughing episode in August. He was as sceptical of medicine as any sensible person should be of any science which makes such grand claims for itself, but he did respect and listen to doctors, even Doctor Cisternino. He had even greater respect for vets, because animals couldn't describe their own symptoms, which meant vets had to be accurate in their diagnoses. After all, animals cost money, whereas most of humanity was a dead loss.

Antonio was now making systematic if sometimes perfunctory use of his new entitlement to one letter out per week, spreading them roughly equally between his birth family in Sardinia and, via Tanya, his new family in Russia. But their responses were still sporadic. Whole weeks or even months would go by without a word, which left him feeling irritable and resentful at their apparent failure to understand the importance correspondence assumes in prison. As he wrote soon after his illness to his mother, who had been strangely quiet: 'It fills up the blank days, and gives some savour to life.'[1] Even his brother Carlo, previously so diligent in his communications and representations, had made only sporadic recent contact through Tanya, despite having moved to Milan with Piero Sraffa's help to be within easier reach of his brother. There were hints that Carlo was in some unspecified difficulty over the money he received from the *PCd'I* in exile; with the Italian authorities, the party or the Comintern, or even with his own personal expenditure and accounting, Antonio knew not what, though he was aware that Carlo had been in and out of work. The job Sraffa had helped him get, with the Milanese textile company Snia Viscosa, had not lasted more than a few months.

Antonio found the long silences from Sardinia as hard to bear as Julia's, especially when his brother and sisters' most recent letters had made much of their mother's worsening health. Signora Peppina was now in her seventies, and feeling the effects of a lifetime of hardship and personal sacrifice. Because of pains in her hands she was unable to write, and only able to communicate with Antonio by dictating letters to others. He detected in this a certain historical justice, because she had taught all her seven children to read and write, and could now make use of them to ease the strain on her own hand. All of them, he assured her, remembered her strength, kindness and tenderness towards them when they were young. She was now and always had been in the only real paradise that exists, which for a mother must be in the hearts of her own children. It turned out that Signora Gramsci and the family, and much of their village of Ghilarza, had been struck down with malaria in the summer of 1931. With the onset of autumn and cooler weather, they were all now feeling much better. Antonio responded in some relief to the news by recommending that they petition the local council for the construction of sewers, just as their predecessors had the foresight to construct an aqueduct. An aqueduct minus sewers meant malaria as sure as night follows day. 'The women of Ghilarza used to be fat and ugly because of the bad water; nowadays it must be because of the malaria! The village men no doubt will be going in for an intensive wine cure.'[2] He gathered from the renewed correspondence that his nieces and nephews had been asking about him, and complaining that their Uncle Nino never wrote or sent gifts to them. He asked that someone explain to them that not being able to do what you want when you want is precisely what being in prison involves. 'Tell them I've got a very big cell, bigger even than any of the rooms in their houses. The only trouble is that I can't leave it.' To his mother he concluded: 'I am more serene than ever, though I'm getting older in prison. I've lost all my teeth and can't chew, which is especially annoying because soon there'll be lamb for sale in the canteen.'

In contrast there was no better news from Moscow. From what he could glean from Julia's scribbled notes enclosed with Tanya's fuller letters, his wife's psychological condition was now worse than ever. From his great distance, Antonio struggled to understand and to help, all too obviously (at least in his own mind) failing, not least because he was discouraged from communicating directly, but had to address his wife through Tanya, the other Schuchts or whoever else might be reading these letters. His tone was by turns hectoring, pedantic or simply exasperated. He routinely interspersed his lectures with apologies for them, then proceeded with another one, apologizing again for his intellectual formation and inadequacy in matters of the mind and heart. Julia was now placing inordinate faith in psychoanalysis, it seemed to him, with all its phantasmagorical and witch-doctorish elements, harking back through dreams and fantasies to some kind of innate 'human nature' which actually derived from previous and entirely different historical epochs. By taking her deeper inside herself, it was simply taking her further away from her own real life in the present day and the outside world. If it had any value, it was as a means of understanding and treating what Dostoyevsky called 'the insulted and the injured', unfortunate and unusually vulnerable individuals who find themselves trapped between the iron contrasts of modern life.[3] They were quite incapable of reconciling their own internal desires with the external demands of work, family and community, and all those other social forces which bind people together but at the same time can tear them apart, including the love of those around them. The resulting conflict was disastrous for exceptionally refined and sensitive temperaments like Julia's, but psychoanalysis offered only limited insight and very little practical help. She had to seek her own resolution to her personal crisis rather than some kind of ready-made formula from elsewhere. It did no good, for example, for her to disown her artistic and musical skills and wish she could do something more useful, as she had recently taken to doing. This metaphysical error simply cut off an important source of personal pleasure and expression, and a crucial outlet for her personality, not to mention one of her few remaining occupational options. Julia had to find a way of reconciling herself to the world around her, but could not hope to achieve this by simply denying herself, her personal background and formation and family history.

This latest lecture went down especially badly with the Schuchts. Julia communicated via Tanya her displeasure at being called injured and insulted, which she (and, she might have pointed out, Dostoyevsky) took to mean the most decadent members of the lower social orders. Another possible translation of the original Russian into Italian was 'humiliated and offended', which conveyed much more accurately the way Antonio's insinuations had left Julia feeling. In one of her most recent outbursts, with an added undertow of suspicion and jealousy, Julia had even urged Tanya to break off her relationship with Gramsci and return to the family in Russia. Tanya also transcribed the brief, gruff postcards Apollon enclosed with the latest correspondence from Moscow, expressing his paternal displeasure at the upset Gramsci continued to cause his family and asking Tanya to pass it on. It was especially hard, he pointed out, on his wife, mother Julia Grigor'evna, who was herself in failing health and felt the slights against her family acutely. Antonio tried to explain himself more clearly, with reference to the debilitating contrasts between the ideal and the real, the personal and the public, the individual and the collective, especially at historical moments of crisis and stress. All human beings, including himself, were subject to social forces and cultural leftovers that they could not individually control. Various personal responses were available: vulgar scepticism, social hypocrisy, absolute conformism, or (and this is what he would advocate, and attempted to apply to his own troubles) thinking historically, dialectically, and identifying one's own problems and solutions – what Freud called the 'work' of psychoanalysis – with intellectual dispassion. Again, one must be one's own doctor. He sent off this further clarification, more in hope than expectation, and more aware than ever of his limitations as a husband and the fragility of his bond with his faraway wife.

His reading, especially the lighter popular fiction he used to wind down towards attempted sleep, began to resonate with his personal preoccupations. Whole paragraphs or even chapters would leap out at him and illuminate his own miserable predicament. So, in December 1931, he read *Villa Beatrice: Storia di una donna* by the Florentine Catholic writer Bruno Cicognani, in which the personality of its protagonist was laid bare like some natural phenomenon, as Gramsci wrote in his latest notebook. 'Beatrice is the personification and typification of emotional coldness, incapable of loving anyone else, in part because of a heart ailment … Naturally Beatrice is unaware that her psychic existence is determined by her physiological condition.'[4] Cicognani's account was 'hackneyed' and 'inconsistent' and 'lacking in artistic representation', but Gramsci could not ignore the parallels with Julia's personality and his own increasingly detached attitude towards her, 'an anatomical specimen not a woman'. In another note that same dark month, he recalled the play *La Morte Civile* by the popular nineteenth-century playwright Paolo Giacometti, about 'a man serving a life sentence in prison who manages to escape, and discovers that his wife and daughter have been able to rebuild their lives successfully in his absence. Rather than disturb their happiness, he kills himself.'[5]

There was also in this period growing discord in Antonio's communications with Tanya. What started out as mild teasing and mock scolding – with jokey threats to break off correspondence – began to turn serious. She made careless mistakes in ordering books for him. Instead of a German grammar for Italians, she sent an Italian grammar for Germans. She sent him some new glasses, which he acknowledged went some way towards alleviating his headaches, but she had spent at least four times more than necessary by choosing such fancy frames. More seriously, she had taken it upon herself to write letters on his behalf to the lawyers who had been involved in his trial and subsequent fruitless appeals, or to the prison authorities, the government and even Mussolini about his conditions and his sentence; all without consulting him. They entered into a long convoluted dispute over whether they should seek an independent medical examination to get to the bottom of his various ailments. Tanya, with her own medical knowledge and connections, thought the prison medical service wholly inadequate. Antonio could not see the point of going to the considerable expense of an examination by a doctor of their own choice to tell him what he already knew. Could she not see how it undermined what little power and dignity he had left, he wrote to her, this wilful interference in the only areas of his life he felt he had some control over? Such special pleading to the authorities represented for him a form of suicide. He wrote in his notebook at around the same time about the nineteenth-century anti-Austrian rebel Count Confalonieri, who had written to the emperor 'like a broken man, pleading for mercy and compassion … His imploring words betray a violation of the spirit a hundred times more humiliating than a death sentence; they are the groan of defeat by a shattered will.'[6]

Tanya continued to send things to him that were denied under prison regulations: items of food which did not meet his dietary restrictions; a Thermos flask for coffee which was deemed a potential security risk; live yoghurt which went off in the post; books he hadn't ordered, and which would in any case only be allowed in the prison if they had been sent by the bookshop in Milan. These were all useless gestures, especially the clothes she sent. He had enough jumpers to last several years, four or five, and two of them he hadn't even touched yet. It wouldn't be so bad if she was able to care properly for herself, since he needed above all for her to be well and strong: 'I had to laugh at your remark that you are "always hungry" as if this was an illness and not a sign of good health. It reminded me of the Neapolitan comic figure Monsignor Perrelli who tried to cure his horses of the disease of hunger by starving them to death. But at least,' he added in a dig at Tanya's self-neglect, 'he didn't apply his strictures to himself!'[7]

During Tanya's six-month stay in Turi, Antonio grew even tetchier with her at visits or in letters. Just as frequently, he apologized. He was not used to such intimate personal contact, he reasoned. Her proximity reminded him of the family life he was missing and his effective estrangement from her sister, his wife. Her meekness, combined with the obvious effects of her own fragile health, just made him more irritable and impatient, then guilty for the way he had treated her. Reporting sardonically that his mother called her a saintly creature, he began to openly question her motives in caring for him, and coming all this way to be near him. He wondered whether she had lost the desire to live for herself, and could live only for others. He noted her poor health and inadequate diet, which confined her to bed in her small room in Turi for days on end. Might she be better off back in Rome or Milan, or even – as Apollon was now openly urging – back in Moscow with her own family? Antonio accused her of living in an intellectual miasma when she told him she quite enjoyed the feeling of not knowing what to do with her life, and of wishful thinking and childish daydreams about travelling around Italy. The 'Grand Tour' was as outmoded as the Romantic poetry and idealized landscape painting it gave rise to. He repeated his earlier accusations that really she had no clear understanding of his life in prison, which was utterly devoid of any kind of heroism or nobility. In her eyes he was a kind of new Gandhi. She still thought of prison as a boarding school for little aristocratic orphan girls under the patronage of queen mothers. And as for the central issue of Julia's illness, Tanya had shown merciless cruelty in concealing it for more than three years. Again, in subsequent letters and visits he apologized profusely and tried to explain why he sometimes seemed to provoke conflict for the sake of it, in order to create a dialogue. His whole temperament, not just his political outlook and principles, was governed by the dialectic. What she took to be ill temper on his part was just his own personal manifestation of the 'passionate sarcasm' inherent in Marxism. Or so he said. The tone of their correspondence improved markedly when Tanya moved back to Rome. She regularly wrote that she was making plans to visit him soon. When they came to nothing, he was saddened and exasperated, but once his irritation had died down, relieved. She should spare herself the expense and the strain on her health of the long and arduous journey across half the country.

As he had done before, he used his personal troubles and worries as a spur to work. His master-concept of hegemony was coming into plain view, the essential ingredient of the most modern philosophy of praxis, as he wrote to Tanya, eliminating the mechanistic, fatalistic conceptions of economic determinism which had dominated Marxism in the plodding social democracy of the Second International, but also superseding the later historical idealism of Benedetto Croce. It took the best of Lenin's conception of political action, and broadened it out into a theoretical exposition of how any society is governed.[8] Though Gramsci (and other Marxists) had made regular use of the term previously, in its conventional sense of national superiority or domination by force, it began now to take on much richer, deeper meaning and broader explanatory power, mainly in answer to two questions. First, why do popular masses consent to their own subordination and exploitation, when it is so plainly not in their own historical, material or moral interests? There is an element of coercion in the process, with any half-competent state not hesitating to deploy its own police and security forces against the population for the purposes of repression, but brute force is only half the answer. For the most part state force is held in reserve, always visible as a deterrent but rarely used, for the simple reason that no state could resist a concerted or permanent internal siege. Instead, popular consent is continuously won through a complex process of political persuasion, economic negotiation and cultural influence. A common sense of ordinary daily life emerges, a kind of subaltern mentality which the vast majority readily espouse because it enables them and their families to lead their lives in relative comfort, conformity and peace, getting by and making do, making the best of a bad job in the hope of some small amelioration. With a bit of luck, the standing and wealth of their families and communities will improve over generations, with each set of sons and daughters slightly better off than their parents. In the meantime, subaltern classes are subject to the initiatives of the dominant class. Even when they rebel against them, they are in what Gramsci called a state of anxious defence.

There is a kind of infantilization at work in the exercise of hegemony in a class society. The subaltern classes surrender their dignity and autonomy in return for relief from the burdens of power and responsibility, which are retained and exercised over every aspect of public life by the dominant class. In this condition of lifelong childhood, ordinary people never get to run anything much beyond their own personal lives and immediate families – private spheres which are themselves subject to increasing restriction and control under the 'Fordist' disciplines of industrial society, not to mention the commodification by capital of functions of personal and private care and consumption previously performed within and by families and communities – so they lack the experience, skills and self-confidence to take control of broader society. They routinely defer to their superiors. These subaltern classes form a kind of shield, or 'historical bloc' to use the old French syndicalist George Sorel's term, around the ruling group, protecting, dignifying and disguising the raw corporate self-interest of their rule. Alliances of social classes and subgroups are negotiated through manoeuvre, exhortation and concession, and come to identify their own subaltern corporate self-interests with the status quo. At its simplest this is represented by the acceptance of the terms and conditions of waged labour; at its most complex it takes the form of compliance with the precepts of parliamentary democracy. In broader, contemporary terms, they support the dynamics and hierarchies of capitalism because firstly they can't see any better alternative, and secondly because it seems to offer individuals a chance of betterment, even though most of them – given the rigidities of class rule – stand little chance of substantial, lasting success.

In this process the role of intellectuals, by which Gramsci meant so much more than 'great thinkers' or academics, is absolutely crucial. Traditional intellectuals – teachers, clerics, lawyers, etc. – sustain the established order through the institutions of civil and political society and the state which employ them. But they are not much good at promoting change, in part because they have their own corporate interest in the established order, but mainly because of the lack of a close organic relationship or connectedness with the masses of ordinary people or general public, from whom they maintain a fastidious distance and sense of superiority. In this situation of social stasis, he wrote in a beautiful summation of what we might call the cognitive landscape of hegemony, the people feel but do not understand or know, while the intellectuals know but do not understand or above all feel. Their function is purely bureaucratic or formal, and they remain a caste or a priesthood within the settled hegemony, flattering themselves with an assumption of personal and group autonomy they do not in fact enjoy. Organic intellectuals have very different roles and characteristics. They emerge from within specific social classes to organize any necessary adaptations to the established order through the political parties, civil and spiritual associations, the arts and the media. These adaptations could be relatively minor, with the aim of absorbing critical ideas or oppositional groups into the historical bloc around the ruling elite. This kind of piecemeal change or accommodation is typical of the process of transformism, whereby opposition elites are bought off, or of periods of passive revolution when radical change is imposed from above. In certain exceptional situations and historical moments, the organic intellectuals of a formerly subaltern social group can be truly revolutionary, aiming to overthrow the ruling elite and construct a new historical bloc around a new leadership drawn from a rising social class.

This gave rise to Gramsci's second central question: how are those intellectual strata formed in any specific historical period and situation? And more to the point, how can some new potentially hegemonic social class like the industrial proletariat cultivate its own organic intellectuals to assist in the revolutionary process and the construction of socialism?[9] This was already happening as a consequence of industrial development, the expansion of civil society and the widening of the vote – all those 'autodidacts' and popular library subscribers, hungry for enlightenment and some measure of culture and political power – but they still had to be forged into a coherent, constructive force. This is never easy: 'The revolutionary class is always intellectually weak. It struggles to give itself a culture and to give force to a conscious and responsible cultured cadre of its own. What's more, all the malcontent and redundant members of other classes throw themselves on its side in order to regain a position for themselves.'[10] What all too often you end up with, passing themselves off as 'opinion formers', 'influencers' or the 'cultured elite', is a shifting rabble of coteries and cliques adding a bit of spice and flavour to the bland stale stew of bourgeois society. This was evident in the mainstream intellectual and cultural life of most advanced industrial countries, especially in the 1930s.

There was a further complicating distinction among the organic intellectuals, between the cultural intellectuals who form artistic avant-gardes and assist in the winning of hegemony but are cast aside by the newly hegemonic class, and the technical intellectuals who are then favoured and brought forward to consolidate the new hegemony. This process was evident in the history of bourgeois revolutions, which were always presaged through art and ideas but solidified through science and technology, but it was nothing like as clear how proletarian revolution would manage it. This was clearly an undercurrent within the continuing struggle in the Soviet Union between Stalin and the various strains of old Bolshevik opposition, whose cultural formation had been mainly literary and artistic, ill-suited for the technical tasks of industrial development and national planning. Though Stalin himself was by no means devoid of culture, and notoriously took a close interest in the latest literature, film and theatre, he calculated (like Julia, with her disavowal of her musical career and determination to do something supposedly more useful) that the Russia of the 1930s had more need of technicians than poets. Accordingly, the political conflict in Russia was represented in the intellectual sphere by the engineers and planners of economic and technological development on one side, the foot soldiers of the Five Year Plan, and the constructivists and futurists in art and literature on the other, all those wild-eyed and paint-spattered, plainly doomed geniuses building giant flowers and declaiming blank verse in the salons and market squares of Moscow and Leningrad.

For the moment Gramsci did not feel able to spell it out in those terms, not least because of the risks of direct political intervention at a time of crisis and high tension in the communist movement. Besides, in the very early 1930s the outcome of this conflict – technology or art? – was not at all clear. But he had at least glimpsed the process whereby the organic intellectuals of the revolutionary proletariat came forward, learnt their craft and helped to mount a serious challenge to the prevailing hegemony, in the constructive resistance of the Turin Factory Councils and the early years of the Soviet Union. These hegemonic projects had contested the dominant ways of doing and thinking in almost every aspect of human experience. This in turn held out some prospect of an effective revolutionary party for the circumstances of contemporary, developed, liberal-democratic capitalism. This new kind of party would form, in an updating of Niccolò Machiavelli's exquisite study of the art of government in the sixteenth century, a Modern Prince for the twentieth century.

But what of the greater cause of international proletarian revolution Gramsci had devoted his pre-prison life to? For all his professed disinterest and protestations that he was out of action he would surely have observed, alone or with one or two confidantes among his prison comrades, how it was degenerating into a maelstrom of terror and purge; a 'Thermidor' far worse than anything the first revolution of the modern era in France had thrown up. The defeats in Europe and Asia, and the failure to make much headway in the Americas or the African and Asian colonies, helped to explain the retreat at Stalin's insistence towards the doctrine of socialism in one country and the arrant subordination of revolutionary prospects across the world to the Russians' *raisons d'état* and foreign policies. The Bolsheviks had a country to run, as Gramsci had heard Lenin himself say to the Fourth Comintern Congress all those years ago, admonishing the rabble of left oppositionists who could not even run their own tiny marginal parties and factions with any semblance of unity, purpose or efficiency, including the young *PCd'I* led by Amadeo Bordiga. But this did not justify it, or offer any real insight into why Soviet Bolshevism had turned out so brutal and crude, and so utterly unsuited for export to other more advanced societies.

To answer that conundrum, you had to look deeper into history. In particular, you had to tease out the historical differences between the societies and economies of the east, with their cultural and social simplicities and the brutal uncompromising state machines which had made them relatively easy to run but also topple, and the much more sophisticated, malleable, established and popularly accepted, deeply hegemonic ruling orders of the West. The revolutionary strategies they called forth were also profoundly different. In military terms, the struggle in the East had been a war of manoeuvre, with mobile forces making sudden assaults on easily identifiable points of weakness in the enemy's defences. That was how the Bolsheviks were able to take over the Russian state in October 1917. The weak Provisional Government of Oleg Kerensky could simply be pushed aside by a small organized band of *putschisti*, arrested over their soup and pheasant at a marble table in the Winter Palace. But that was when the real revolution began, with the civil war and the struggle against bourgeois subversion and foreign intervention that was not decisively won for a further decade or so. The Socialist Eden of liberty, equality and fraternity remained a very distant prospect, for all Stalin's outlandish claims. The worry was, as 'the Frenchman' Victor Serge had argued years before, that one autocracy had simply been exchanged for another.

Revolution in the West was a very different matter, a war of position, of gradual attrition across a wide front against an enemy that was well dug in and could call upon several layers of defence all along the line. The new emergent power, the industrial proletariat guided by the Modern Prince of the revolutionary party, had to engage the old enemy in every sphere of modern life – popular culture and the arts, the press and public opinion, the organization of the economy, industry and agriculture, education and social services, the endless battle of ideas alongside the fine detail of daily routine – with the aim of assuming responsibility and control in every one of them, not as some single bold and decisive, one-off event or balance-tipping intervention but in the process of taking more formal political control. By that stage, the class war for state power would be largely won, and the aftermath of revolution would thankfully be far less destructive than it had necessarily been in the East. Any other political strategy, such as the call for immediate insurrection that Stalin continued to foist on the Communist International, and that Gramsci would have heard loud and clear whenever he ventured into the Turi prison exercise yard, was just a dangerous, counter-productive dream, inviting public backlash and state reaction.

In the meantime, Gramsci wrote in his notes, with a clear eye on Italian Fascism and the emerging National Socialism in Germany and Austria, but with the implication that this might also apply to the ruthlessly re-stabilized, decidedly post-revolutionary Soviet Union under Stalin, the global class war had reached a precarious stalemate. 'The so-called crisis of authority consists precisely in the fact that the old is dying and the new cannot be born. In this interregnum, morbid phenomena of the most varied kind can emerge.'[11] If the ruling class has lost consensus, or failed to achieve it in the first place – that is, if it no longer leads but only rules through sheer coercive power, or in some cases appears to have left the stage altogether – this actually means that the great masses have become detached from traditional ideologies. They no longer believe what they used to; instead, apathy and cynicism prevail. The most important lesson for Marxists, or any self-styled 'progressives' for that matter, is that there are no guarantees of historical progress. The motor that had driven social and economic development for the last hundred years of industrial, commercial and imperial expansion had stalled. It could even appear to go backwards, and only get going forward again by concerted, broad-based political and cultural action. Or – and this was clearly what was happening in Italy and Germany and arguably Russia – a 'strong man' could impose authority and order without regard for democracy, legality or justice, or genuine consensus and unity; a Caesar or Bonaparte figure prepared to sweep aside all internal opposition for the sake of a semblance of security and stability. Caesarism could be relatively progressive or reactionary, but its achievements would always be precarious, short-term and top-down, because its hegemony did not rest on political and cultural consensus. It consisted of coercive domination not educative direction, and would become the typical mode of government of the 1930s, against a background of unresolved crisis and nascent military conflict.

Chapter 23

FINAL YEARS

In early 1932, Gramsci found out about a programme of prisoner exchange between the Soviet government and the Vatican, now constituted as an independent state under the terms of the 1929 Lateran Pact. The Pope had been able to secure the release of communist prisoners in Italy in return for a Russian archbishop who had been condemned to death. Ever since, both sides had kept lists of prisoners they might swap, and Gramsci's name had been included in the latest discussions. The Deputy Foreign Minister of the Vatican even visited Turi prison. He was unable to see Gramsci but left him a card, signed 'Mons. Giuseppe Pizzardo, Deputy to the Secretary of State to His Holiness, Regards.' In the meantime, Tanya Schucht had heard from someone in the Soviet Embassy in Rome that their Foreign Secretary Litvinov had made contact with the Italian ambassador in Moscow about the possibility of Gramsci's release. She relayed the information to Carlo Gramsci, who in turn (during one of the very few visits Antonio received at Turi in this entire period) excitedly told his brother. Nothing came of any of it, even if it had any truth or mileage in the first place. Soviet foreign policy at that moment was directed towards good relations with Italy, with the aim of pre-empting an alliance between Italian Fascism and German National Socialism. This went as far as a pact of friendship in 1933, on top of burgeoning trade in armaments and oil, which led Mussolini to hope 'that Stalin might be moving towards corporativism and "state capitalism" and possibly might be becoming something akin to a fascist'.[1] For their part, the Soviets were keen to avoid even the suspicion of interference in Italian internal affairs, which would include whom the state chose to imprison. Besides, what real value was there in this ex-leader of one of the smallest parties in the Comintern, notoriously truculent and non-collaborative, out of action for over five years now and rotting away in an obscure provincial jail in the remote Italian south? If the stories from within the *PCd'I* itself were to be believed, there was some doubt over whether this fellow was still or ever really had been a loyal communist anyhow.

Antonio Gramsci now felt entirely abandoned by everyone and everything he had ever belonged to: the *PCd'I* and the international movement it was a minor part of; his family in Sardinia, who corresponded fitfully and half-heartedly, and (Carlo aside) never even thought of visiting him; his family in Moscow, who sent him the occasional scribbled note or message translated by Tanya from the Russian and attached to one of her letters, but otherwise showed dwindling interest. Even Tanya for one reason or another – distance, ill-health, inconvenience, work obligations, Gramsci's own concerns that a return to Turi would simply end with her in the local hospital again, some vague inhibition that was never clearly spelt out but which most likely came from Apollon Alexandrovich or a rather more direct injunction from Evgenia – stayed away from Turi for the two-and-a-half years between June 1930 and January 1933. She maintained her end of their correspondence dully and dutifully, with long and painful periods of silence explained by other, obviously more important matters to attend to, in letters largely devoted to general reflections on the state of the world, the daily news and her latest reading. Misunderstandings and personal disagreements proliferated, requiring long and tortuous clarifications. In the autumn of 1931 Tanya and Antonio got involved in a strange protracted exchange, prompted by a popular film she had seen, about the notion that Jews and Gentiles lived in two worlds, quite separate, different and self-contained. He pointed out in response that this was historically wrong, essentially anti-Semitic and very odd coming from her with her partly Jewish ancestry. In lending this idea of *due mondi* credence, Tanya was subscribing to a way of thinking worthy of the Black Hundreds, the Ku Klux Klan or the Nazis. Perhaps she was revealing her Russian heritage: 'Many Cossacks used to believe as an article of faith that Jews had tails!'[2]

For her part, Tanya resented his implication that she was anti-Semitic and might, as she put it, take part in a pogrom. All she had done was make a passing reference to a film she'd seen. He had seized upon it to try to back her into a corner and play word games like the journalist he once was. He wrote back that he too found her remarks positively offensive. He had never been the kind of jobbing journalist who sells his pen to the highest bidder, and for whom an ability to lie is an occupational necessity. He had always stuck to his principles, told the truth as he saw it, and never been anybody's yes-man. As for this two worlds nonsense, he regretted ever taking the matter seriously in the first place. He should have shrugged it off with some joke about cultural stereotypes of English reserve, French pomposity, German organization, Spanish arrogance, Italian flair and finally Slav mysticism, all the caricatures used by popular novelists and scriptwriters.

She responded that racial differences were real, and could be acknowledged without blame or prejudice. She cited a number of historical and contemporary examples, including her own family, where her parents' differences in temperament, due in turn to their difference in race, had caused unhappiness which had undoubtedly and adversely affected the condition of their children. At this point Piero Sraffa felt moved to intervene, by referring to various recent changes in the law and in public opinion which revealed the growing force of anti-Semitism, prompting real fear amongst Italy's small and previously integrated and secularized Jewish population. Antonio, secluded in prison and working with the universalist attitudes of a much earlier era, could not be expected to have kept up with these developments. Sraffa was also embroiled in further discord between Antonio and Tanya when he asked her to seek Antonio's advice for his own work on Croce. Tanya passed it off in her letters as help with a book review she herself was writing, but Antonio's long and detailed responses over the course of six letters were interpreted by the censor as an attempt to get his own writings published abroad. He was interrogated and his cell was searched, and new restrictions placed on the subjects he could write about and the publications he could consult.

More productively, Antonio's own letters to Tanya outlined his latest reading and writing – on literature, religion, intellectuals in Italian history, developments in Marxist philosophy – interspersed with bulletins on his health and moods. He was working hard on getting his notes in order and conducting fresh research. Though he never said so, and she never pointed it out, it was clear that his studies – systematic, fruitful and profound as they were – were both driven by and a diversion from his personal troubles. His own deepest conscious thoughts began to feel like a safe haven from both a cold uncaring outside world and the dull, debilitating routine of prison life, not to mention the ghosts and demons of his own mental undergrowth. He fought hard and with mixed results against the personal feelings his sense of abandonment provoked: self-pity, resentment, vindictive ill-temper, exacerbated by continuing illness and insomnia. His irritability towards anyone and everyone, he noted, even raised eyebrows among the prison guards. For all his efforts to maintain a calm and cheerful demeanour, the best he could achieve was a kind of emotional neutrality or numbness. Try as he might, he could not prevent his worst feelings surfacing in the opening or final paragraphs of his letters; or more to the point, souring them. The 'two worlds' business was the least of it. He chastized both Tanya and Carlo for their small part in the abortive prisoner exchange, mainly for not keeping him adequately informed or enabling him to contribute to the process. Tanya continued to write to the authorities – all the way up the 'Head of Government' himself – about Antonio's declining health, and to ask for outside medical examination and treatment, but without telling him much about it. Worried as he was by his own deteriorating physical condition, he deeply resented her undermining his position as master of his own life. The customary concluding 'tender embrace' in his letters often jarred violently with the preceding tirade.

Spurred on by the thought that he might never leave prison alive, he made endless complex calculations of how long he had left to serve under the permutations of various amnesties and appeals. This prompted further rancour with Tanya over the slightest deviation from his instructions. Carlo's interventions were similarly well intentioned but often clumsy and counter-productive. When the government announced a limited amnesty for political prisoners on the tenth anniversary of the March on Rome in October 1932, Carlo sent Antonio a telegram intimating that he might soon be released, and looking forward to coming to Turi to embrace him as a free man. For some hours Antonio dared to believe it, before being disabused by a curt remark from the Prison Director passing his cell. It subsequently turned out that his mother, sick and frail herself, had actually been told that he'd been set free. He thought back to his own few hours of delusion, and the gut-wrenching disappointment that brought it crashing to an end, and multiplied it a hundred times to imagine the effect on her. He wrote furiously to Tanya and his sister Teresina about the muddle and what he saw as their part in it, and declared that after the fiasco with the telegram he wanted nothing more to do with his brother. He regretted and resented his dependence on Carlo as the conduit for funds, when he had proved so immature and unmanly. To them all, he tried desperately to convey a clearer sense of the state of mind that prison had reduced him to: 'I've grown insensitive to other people's feelings, yet sometimes I have the impression that I am being skinned alive. The weeks, the hours, even minutes weigh on me; it's as if someone were filing away my nerves. Ideally, I would wish to be left alone, to forget the world and live like a beast in a den.'[3] In December 1932 he wrote to Tanya that, after the first phase of his arrest and conviction, and the second of his most tolerable and productive time at Turi, a much more difficult 'third phase of my life as a prisoner has begun'.[4]

In the same spirit of what he called 'sharp cleavage', he proposed through Tanya that he and Julia should consider themselves formally separated and free of their obligations to each other. It was ridiculous, after all these years apart and with no prospect of reuniting, that they should maintain the pretence and keep their lives on hold; especially Julia, who might not enjoy the best of health but still had her freedom and much of her life left to live. He had long ago accepted that he no longer (if ever he did) embodied any kind of romantic dream she might have of a 'Prince Charming' figure. But it may be that he made her condition worse. Someone else, nearer and stronger and physically available to her, might make it better. However, in the summer of 1932 Julia's mental health actually seemed to be on the mend, enough for her to write directly and coherently to him. She was now saying she hadn't much use for her doctors, and that she was determined – as Antonio had been urging all along – to stand on her own two feet. She was even considering going back to work, and pursuing his suggestion that she might propose or even attempt Russian/Italian translations. In response he expressed his delight. Why should they let themselves be crushed by the lives they'd led up to now? He was especially pleased that she had got over her fixation with a psychoanalytical cure, thoroughly steeped in charlatanry. As for her plan to go back to work, it would make him extremely happy to see her apply herself systematically and reach a high level of specialization in technical translation. This would surely make her feel practically useful to the great Soviet cause of constructing Socialism. He also urged her to dedicate part of her time to music, which she had given up in an act of spiritual self-harm because she considered it incompatible with her immediate practical responsibilities; he had always believed that only artistic activity brought her fully to life.

From Tanya he received the first photographs of Julia in some time, which he found delightful, though it was clear that she had suffered a great deal. Nonetheless, he wrote back that she was clearly through the worst of it and beginning a new life. For a while longer, he and Julia corresponded freely and openly. He asked for more photos of her and the boys, and added as a joke a reference to his time on Ustica: she didn't want him thinking of her as the Bedouin's wife, did she? He even felt able, in the light of her apparent recovery, to give a full and frank account of his life in prison, 'terribly and depressingly empty … I barely live at all, but hang on grimly to the outskirts of animal, or rather vegetable existence.'[5] The tedium was only relieved by her letters, which 'I read and re-read constantly; they give me a few hours of serenity and happiness'. He even dared to suggest that Julia and the children might come to Italy to see him. But again nothing came of it. Julia went quiet again. Perhaps she had decided to accept his earlier offer of formal separation, but hadn't got round to telling him. Without any word for months on end, how would he know? Perhaps his own encouragements, chastisements and suggestions for therapeutic work had provoked some new crisis. Even if it was not literally true, he began to think of his wife as one of the judges who had determined his fate, albeit unconsciously, and condemned him to imprisonment for what was beginning to feel like the rest of his life. He felt a desperate need for clarity and order, a settling of accounts, and offered again via Tanya to end the marriage. It was simply too late for him and Julia; there was now no realistic chance of making anything of their relationship.

Perhaps the life of a full-time communist militant was in any case incompatible with personal intimacy and family responsibilities. Was there any such thing as a happy marriage in Jacobinism or Bolshevism? In this he saw a terrible and destructive egotism, where one's own philosophy of life and political ambitions prevent real attachment to the people around you. You're so busy trying to save the world, you can't save yourself or the individuals you love. He was now too old, ill and isolated to change, and stuck in prison for the foreseeable future. But Julia was only thirty-six, and hopefully returning to full health. She still had it in her to make a new life for herself. Why should a living being remain tied to someone as good as dead? His gesture may appear romantic, a kind of emotional blackmail – she'd be so overwhelmed by his magnanimity that she'd feel compelled to refuse – but he was quite serious and resolute. He didn't doubt that it would be difficult and painful for everyone, but he was convinced that it would ultimately be for the best. All of this was conveyed to Tanya in Rome, in the hope that she might find an appropriate way to communicate it directly to Julia, reflecting coolly and calmly on what he had been saying and thinking primarily of Julia's life and future. Tanya understandably prevaricated, and the matter became – towards the end of 1932 – yet another issue of distant altercation between her and Antonio. He wrote in exasperation: 'Just answer me one thing: are you willing to act as go-between with Julia or not? A yes or no, that's all I want. I will be very annoyed by any further evasions, which will simply prolong the agony. It has to be like a surgical operation or decapitation, and can only be justified if done firmly with one clean cut.'[6] Unbeknown to him, Piero Sraffa urged Julia via Tanya to visit Nino as soon as possible in order to save the marriage, but received no direct response.

In the round of amnesties that commemorated ten years of Fascist rule in October 1932, Gramsci's sentence was reduced to twelve years and four months, which meant that he had a further eight years to serve. Piero Sraffa petitioned the government, through his uncle who was a senior judge in the Italian Appeal Court, for conditional release for Gramsci in the light of his worsening health. This would, they argued, prevent him from undertaking any kind of political activity or even normal daily life, so he couldn't possibly pose any kind of threat. The government did not dismiss the petition but made clear that they required a formal plea for clemency from Gramsci himself. He refused, on the basis that this would represent an admission of guilt and as such a kind of suicide for a political prisoner like himself. In his notebooks he made several further references to Confalonieri and his grovelling pleas to the Austrian emperor. For some weeks afterwards, Gramsci and the other politicos at Turi were placed in strict solitary confinement to absorb this latest demonstration of Fascist power and their own weakness.

Later that month, on 30 December 1932, Gramsci's mother died in Ghilarza. His family decided not to tell him, because they feared the effects of the shock on his own ill-health. Carlo, the only brother in regular contact with Antonio, was also still feeling some remorse over his role in the telegram fiasco a couple of months before, and the upset this had caused their mother. For several years after Signora Peppina's death, Antonio was still writing to the family expressing his concern over her health and asking for news. He even wrote directly to her, wishing her all the best for Easter and her birthday. He was dismayed but not entirely surprised to receive no reply, and surely had some inkling of what had happened; yet another Gramsci family secret. 1932 had been, Gramsci wrote to Tanya on the second day of the new year: 'the worst of my years in prison. Nor does the new one look particularly enticing. If '32 was bad, '33 is almost bound to be worse. I'm very run down and the load I have to drag along gets heavier all the time. The balance between my personal resources and the efforts I have to make gets more and more unfavourable. I am not demoralised though. On the contrary, I gain strength from realistic analysis of my situation and my determination to resist.'[7]

Tanya Schucht returned to live in Turi in January 1933, and resumed regular visits to Antonio at the prison. With her own health for the moment restored, she felt able to come back south. Her savings had been replenished by her earned income and the very favourable terms on which she had been renting a room from Nilde Perilli in Rome. And though she never spelt it out to Antonio, an ailing Apollon was confined to a sanatorium and unable or disinclined to impose his will on the family (he would die in May, and be buried at Novodevic cemetery; again, this was kept from his son-in-law in Italy for several years). Evgenia was now putting it about that Gramsci was a Trotskyite and would bring further catastrophe upon the family. She had raised predictable objections to Tanya rejoining Antonio, but without the authorization of their invalid father, Tanya could disregard them (in the interests of family harmony she chose not to tell Gramsci about them either). She could take up again what she was beginning to think and speak of quite openly, if sometimes ruefully, as her life's work of caring for her brother-in-law. As if to underline her own growing confidence and their renewed intimacy, she began to refer to him in person and in writing as 'Nino', which she'd not done before. In February, now back in residence in Turi, she wrote to Piero Sraffa her impressions of his condition and appearance after their two-and-a-half years of separation. Nino looked like a little child, a baby, he had lost so much weight. He was very pale and drawn. He had described to her a bout of several weeks of true neurasthenic frenzy, of continued and spasmodic obsession that did not give him a moment's peace.

On 7 March 1933, Antonio Gramsci suffered a further bout of acute illness and partial paralysis. As he was getting out of bed he fell to the ground and couldn't get up again. He was helped back to bed, where he remained for several days, weak and feverish. At times he was delirious and hallucinating. He found out later that for hours on end he had held forth quite lucidly on the futility of religion, interspersed with long tirades in Sardinian dialect. He reasoned in a letter to Tanya that he must have thought he was going to die, and did not want to be attended to by a priest. He recalled with horror the experience of Jean Barois, the central character in a popular pre-war French novel, who received the religious sacraments before dying. His wife later discovered his will, which stipulated that he did not believe in a substantial and immortal soul, that his personality was a mass of atoms, and that there should be no religious ceremony at his death. In the novel, the will is thrown into the fire. 'At least I did not suffer that indignity,' Gramsci wrote to Tanya afterwards, 'so my ranting and raving about religion must have had some effect! My audience was a worker from Grossetto, nodding off in exhaustion, who I'm quite sure thought I was going round the bend … '[8] In his delirium, the windows and walls of the cell were covered in figures and faces, not frightening but benign and smiling, in all sorts of poses. These weren't people he knew, or at least could remember, but they didn't wish him ill. Every so often he would struggle to sit upright, only for the air to crush him back onto the bed with a thud. New images were superimposed on top of old ones, a tumble of faces and bodies and buildings and fields. He kept hearing things too, voices saying very clearly 'Are you there?' or 'Are you asleep?' or other odd words. Again, he had no idea who these voices belonged to, but they were not hostile. It was as if he was watching a film.

Doctor Cisternino was called, and eventually arrived, to offer a diagnosis of cerebral anaemia, a disruption of the flow of blood to the brain, which might account for the blackout but not for its severity and duration. On 18 March, Tanya wrote to Piero Sraffa that Antonio's condition seemed hopeless. Two weeks later, Gramsci was visited by another doctor from outside, in long delayed response to Tanya's letter to Mussolini the previous autumn. Professor Umberto Arcangeli, a colleague and friend of hers from Rome, diagnosed 'Pott's disease, a form of tuberculosis of the spine; he also has tubercular lesions in the upper lobe of the right lung which have caused two discharges of blood; one of these discharges was copious, and accompanied by fever lasting several days. He is also suffering from arterio-sclerosis, with hypertension of the arteries. He has suffered collapses, with loss of consciousness and partial aphasia lasting several days. Since October 1932, he has lost seven kilos in weight. He suffers from amnesia, and is unable to write as he used to.' Professor Arcangeli concluded that 'Gramsci cannot survive long under present conditions. I consider his transfer to a hospital or clinic to be necessary; that is, if it is not considered possible to grant him conditional liberty.'[9]

There was no immediate response from the prison authorities. Gramsci remained in his cell for the next few months, into the summer of 1933. He was largely confined to bed, sometimes feeling better, sometimes worse, usually drifting along on a tide of semi-conscious memories and speculations. The veins in his feet swelled up, which made it extremely uncomfortable to wear shoes or even socks.

He now had eleven teeth left, most of them loose, which made eating well nigh impossible. One week he complained in a note to Tanya: 'I have nothing to say to you or anyone else. I'm completely finished.'[10] The following week he wrote to apologize for having hurt her feelings. He'd become half-mad from the pain in his head, and the spasms in his hands were getting worse. He was hoping for a transfer to a modern prison infirmary. All that mattered was to get out of the hellhole where he was slowly dying. He was at least transferred to another cell in the basement of the prison, well away from the noisy guardroom. It was damp and dark, normally used for punishment, but much quieter. He was also allocated a permanent cell mate to keep an eye on him, Gustavo Trombetti, the worker from Grossetto who had attended to him in March. As Gramsci's symptoms eased, he began reading and writing again, only to have permission temporarily revoked while the prison authorities pored over his notebooks to see if they might provide the basis for some kind of forbidden communications or conspiracy between Gramsci, Trombetti and the other communist prisoners at Turi. This prohibition caused him as much pain and annoyance as his physical ailments, desperate as he was to get his scattered notes in proper order while he still could. His correspondence began to prepare people for some kind of end. To Tanya he wrote that he was emptied out, and to his sister Teresina that she shouldn't be surprised if he didn't write much from now on.

In the summer of 1933, an international campaign was established in Paris for the liberation of victims of Fascism, including Antonio Gramsci and other prominent Italian communists and socialists. The writer Romain Rolland, from whom Gramsci had taken the motto 'Pessimism of the Intellect, optimism of the will', published a pamphlet *Ceux Qui Meurent Dans Les Prisons de Mussolini* with Gramsci's face prominent on the cover looming over a posturing *Duce*. The propaganda bulletin *Azione Antifascista* devoted most of its June issue to Gramsci, as part of a campaign for political prisoners of all persuasions. It was an overture by the Comintern to other political forces, and signalled some easing of the sectarianism and dogmatism of its 'Third Period' and a move towards the Popular Front strategy that would bear considerable fruit in the mid-1930s. It was also belated recognition of the counter-productiveness of its denunciations of bourgeois democracy and 'social fascism', which had plainly assisted the rise of actual Fascism, most notably in Germany, where Hitler and the National Socialists had just come to power and proceeded to quash the divided communist and social democrat opposition. Now the watchword was 'left unity'. One of the earliest responses to this new more open Comintern line came from the French Trotskyists, who launched their own appeal for Gramsci's release. After almost two years of silence, the *PCd'I* underground and émigré press began referring to Gramsci again in his official capacity of General Secretary, and urging action to 'Save Our Leader!' Illegal leaflets appeared in Italy referring to 'Gramsci, the greatest Italian of the age, leader of the Italian workers'. Professor Arcangeli's medical report was published by the French Communist daily *L'Humanité* in May and elsewhere in succeeding months. This time the headlines 'Gramsci is dying!' did not seem far-fetched, though the accompanying allegations of torture and assassination might have been. There was a report in the French press that Gramsci had actually died, which was quickly corrected, and further talk of high-level contacts between the Soviet and Italian governments, but nothing concrete.

The international campaign did at least cause the Italian government some diplomatic discomfort. They rejected the claim that the amnesty of November 1932 entitled Gramsci to immediate freedom, but in the face of the medical evidence began to relent on whether Turi was a suitable place of confinement. In October 1933 authorization was granted for Gramsci to leave Turi prison and an official request circulated around local authorities across the country for a clinic suitable for an important political prisoner suffering from tuberculosis and other serious diseases needing special treatment, who could be easily watched and guarded. A clinic was identified in Formia, a small town near Gaeta (where Gramsci's father came from and had himself been imprisoned), half-way between Rome and Naples. Antonio Gramsci left Turi di Bari Penitentiary for Sick Prisoners on 19 November 1933, aged forty-two, after almost five years there. During that time he had lost his health, all his teeth and most of his contacts and reputation in the outside world, and composed the bulk of the notes and letters which would establish his posthumous fame. Before Gramsci left Turi, Gustavo Trombetti managed to hide the notebooks among the personal possessions in Gramsci's trunk, while Antonio kept the guard talking in the prison storeroom. He stopped for eighteen days in the prison infirmary at Civitavecchia, while his new room in Formia was fitted with iron bars at the windows and transformed into a cell. On the way to Civitavecchia, he saw himself in a mirror for the first time in five years, and returned in shock and haste to his police escort. During his stay there, he recognized a number of former comrades in the prison halls and corridors, but they chose not to make contact.

Gramsci finally arrived at the clinic in Formia run by Professor Giuseppe Cusumano on 7 December 1933. He was still a prisoner, formally in a state of detention, with a round-the-clock police guard on his room and regular police patrols of the clinic gardens and surrounding area. Tatiana Schucht visited him regularly from Rome where she had relocated, back in her room at Nilde Perilli's. She now routinely called him 'Nino'. On several occasions he mistook her for Julia as she entered his room or gently shook him awake. He was also visited by his brother Carlo and by Piero Sraffa. All three were followed by the police and routinely reported on. In Formia, Gramsci felt well enough to resume light work on his notebooks, revising and reordering old notes and composing some new ones. In the summer of 1934 he was examined by another independent doctor and friend of Tanya's, Professor Vittorio Puccinelli from the Quisisana Clinic in Rome. Puccinelli was not impressed with the conditions and standards of care at the Cusumano Clinic, which charged 120 lire a day for prisoners like Gramsci. This money had to be raised by his relatives in Sardinia and Russia, and topped up by clandestine funds from the *PCd'I* in exile. Puccinelli relayed his concerns to Tanya, who reported to Piero Sraffa a lack of edible bread and of hot water for bathing, and medical care that was desultory and often incompetent.

In early October 1934 Gramsci submitted his own petition for conditional freedom, based on clauses in the penal code on the rights of sick prisoners. On 25 October his conditional freedom was granted, in return for an assurance that he would not use this new provision to make propaganda in Italy or abroad. He was even allowed a few brief outings with Tanya, Carlo or Piero Sraffa in the gardens of the clinic and nearby streets, on foot or by carriage. But he remained under close surveillance by the police, who suspected an escape plan hatched by anti-Fascist elements in New York. Gramsci's name continued to feature in anti-Fascist propaganda, but the escape plan had no basis in reality. Tanya visited him at least weekly, talking or sitting quietly in his room while he rested or slept. For the next eighteen months he wrote hardly any personal letters. The only substantial one was to his dead mother on her name-day in March 1934. Tanya wrote to his sister Teresina in April that he lacked the strength to write, which she said caused much suffering to Julia, who had not had any direct news from Nino in more than a year.

In June 1935 Gramsci suffered another breakdown and asked to leave the Cusumano clinic, which was ill-equipped to deal with his mounting health problems. This included, he said in his application to the Inspector General of the Formia police, an attack of gout due to medical negligence. For more than a month he had been complaining of muscular pains and swollen ankles, and the beginnings of a hernia caused in part by an inappropriate diet and poor hygiene, flies and ants in the food, and fingermarks on the dishes; all to no avail. It was also noisy, not least because the small building housed the living quarters of the large Cusumano family, which meant continuous disturbance overhead from five in the morning till midnight. His request to move was granted and on 24 August Gramsci travelled with Professor Puccinelli to the Quisisana Clinic in Rome. There was some irony in the name of the clinic, which was 'Here Heal Yourself' in Latin, his own clumsy prescription for his wife's psychological troubles.

At the Quisisana, Tanya visited almost every day, work permitting, and frequently stayed into the evening. Carlo and Piero Sraffa also continued visiting when they could, still with a police escort at a not so discreet distance and twelve armed guards stationed around the clinic. According to Tanya, writing to Sraffa in September 1935, Antonio never left his room, except to stand out on the balcony. This was not entirely accurate. A fellow patient, Lina Corigliano, later recalled that she was the only patient with a radio in her room, and when Mussolini was due to give an important speech announcing the foundation of the African empire, everyone at the clinic crowded in to listen. She knew that in the next room there was an important personality under constant guard, and sent him a message asking if he too wanted to listen to *Il Duce*. The invitation was politely declined. Instead, he came the next day to listen to a broadcast of Bizet's *Carmen*.

Into 1936, Gramsci began corresponding again with Julia and his sons in Moscow, after a silence of some years. Addressing her once again as Julka, he reassured her that he was still waiting for her, and that she had always been one of the essential elements of his life. He commended her on her apparently improved mood – on one occasion he said he couldn't remember when she last wrote so gaily, and with so few mistakes – and several times suggested in vain that she might come to see him. This was not so much a reconciliation with Julia/Julka as with his own steady decline. For all of that year and into the next, he was largely confined to bed, growing weaker, still able to read but unable to write without enormous effort. His letters were now mostly short missives to his sons, wishing them well on birthdays and other special occasions, telling them to behave themselves and work hard at school, commending or criticizing their own letters and enclosed drawings, and recalling childhood experiences of his own. He proposed that at a set time every day they and mother Julka should observe Papa's five minutes when they should think and talk about him, while he did the same in Italy. For their twelfth and tenth birthdays in August 1936, he sent them both watches as gifts, procured for him by Tanya at a watchmaker's in Rome.

He understood all too well that he knew next to nothing about his sons. What he did find out – about Delio's flights of fancy or Giuliano's slow development and the concerns of their teachers, above all the false, cloying, artificial atmosphere in which they were growing up with Julia and their 'little mother' Evgenia – continued to displease and sometimes disturb him. He made frequent unfavourable comparisons with his own childhood capabilities and interests, surprisingly oblivious to the massive historical, geographical and social differences between growing up in remote rural Sardinia in the late nineteenth century and in a major industrial metropolis in the mid-twentieth, or indeed to the fact that to these Young Pioneers he was himself a distant stranger. To Delio he begged for longer letters, and chided him gently for the oddly formal tone the boy tended to adopt: 'You've written me four lines which sound like they're from a phrasebook for foreigners. "The parrot is well." Give him my heartiest congratulations and best wishes! "What's the weather like? We're having good weather here" etc … ' When Julia wrote that this gentle rebuke had annoyed the boy, Gramsci wrote back to him: 'Why didn't you tell me yourself? If you don't like anything in my letters, you really should say so. I love you so much, and the last thing I want to do is hurt you. I'm so very far away, and I can't take you in my arms and kiss you, but I so wish I could.'[11]

To Giuliano he wrote: 'I know you only from your letters', which were few and far between.[12] The boy's interest perked up when he saw an enormous picture of his father in a display of prominent communist political prisoners in Gorky Park in Moscow. He found out from a neighbour that his father had been in prison for some years, and wanted to know all about him. With Delio and Evgenia he met Romain Rolland, and got a taste of impending political celebrity, with stirring speeches, photographs taken for the anti-fascist press, pats on the cheek and ruffled hair. Antonio was touched and amused. He made tentative and sometimes clumsy attempts to communicate with this child he had never met, about trips to the country and the seaside, or how he was getting on at the special school the Schuchts had decided to send him to, a boarding school near Sochi for children of a nervous disposition. The boy would otherwise, Tanya told him, have been kept behind for at least a year at the school he had been attending in Moscow. He wasn't happy at this new school either, she intimated, and kept getting into trouble. It brought back to Gramsci his own feelings when he had been sent away to complete his elementary schooling. He encouraged the boy to face events with courage and calm.

He continued to berate Tanya about her poor diet and its effects on her health. It was nothing to do with her appetite – he'd seen her eat a whole boiled chicken for lunch, followed by lamb and potatoes for dinner – so it must be something to do with her lack of routine. Carlo would chime in on joint visits, and Antonio or Tanya would report on the latest set-to with Julia or Evgenia, or worries about the boys' education. It was something like family normality. In late 1936 they finally acknowledged openly that Signora Peppina Gramsci and Apollon Alexandrovich Schucht had died some years before. Antonio must have suspected as much all along, but chose not to make a fuss about yet more bad news being kept from him, supposedly for his own protection. As for his general outlook on life, he achieved a certain intellectual serenity bordering on political resignation. Accusing Julia yet again of 'a certain superficial and bohemian slackness', he said he preferred the humdrum rigours of 'a *Corporal's Manual* (an Italian military handbook) to Valles' *Resisters*' (the record of glorious defeat of the 1871 Paris Commune) and confessed to a burgeoning gradualism in his personal manner and perspective.[13]

On 21 April 1937 his sentence formally expired, but he was not well enough to leave the Quisisana. Before any plans for his release could be finalized or implemented, he suffered a cerebral haemorrhage on the evening of 25 April, lay unconscious throughout the next day, and died early the next morning, 27 April 1937, aged 46. On hearing of Gramsci's death, a close comrade and protégé from Turin Mario Montagnana wrote to Palmiro Togliatti:

Few can fully comprehend the loss the party and therefore the country have suffered. Antonio only ever revealed his true greatness, his enormous political, intellectual and moral gifts in conversation, in the course of ordinary everyday life. Still, I was struck when a young comrade who did not even know Antonio told me that the biggest tragedy is that his genius went largely unused and unknown.[14]

POSTSCRIPT: THE AFTERLIVES
OF ANTONIO GRAMSCI

In the ten-and-a-half years between Antonio Gramsci's arrest in 1926 and his death in 1937 the world changed dramatically, mostly (from his perspective) for the worse. The international revolutionary ferment of the 1920s had given way, after the crash of 1929 and subsequent crises, to revived capitalist competition across the restabilized nation-states of Western Europe and North America. The Soviet Union under Stalin had moved on from the radical experiment with history of the October Revolution and its immediate chaotic aftermath, through rapid industrialization and the forced collectivization of agriculture, and into something resembling a normal modern society and economy, albeit with distinctively Russian and heavily authoritarian characteristics. The CPSU and with it the Communist International had been purged of all but their most subservient activists and conformist intellectuals. Across Europe, extreme right-wing nationalism had overturned the norms of liberal democracy and installed paramilitary regimes, first in Gramsci's native Italy, then in Germany and eventually Spain. Everywhere the left, from the mildest social democracy to the furthest revolutionary communism, was in disarray and retreat. No wonder Gramsci considered himself out of action for most of those catastrophic ten years, and by the end dared to espouse little more than a cautious gradualism, while setting himself the historiographical task of explaining proletarian revolution's bitter defeat. And of course the final irony of his last decade, noted by more than one sympathetic observer and surely clear to him, was that imprisonment by Mussolini saved him from Stalin's purges, just as the wilful marginality and apparent obeisance of the little band of Italian communist exiles protected most of them.

Gramsci was excused the tawdry compromises required of those notionally free comrades for simple survival: for example, Palmiro Togliatti the always outwardly loyal Stalinist, or Gramsci's first political mentor and fellow *ordinovisto* from Turin Angelo Tasca, who ended up a government official in collaborationist Vichy and died soon after the war in sad disgrace. Furthermore, a major element in Gramsci's originality was his extraordinary feel for the attitudes and outlooks of ordinary people, their 'common sense' and the popular ideology, culture and folklore through which it was expressed, which a career of humdrum political organization would surely have blunted if not eliminated altogether. He may have been described by his friend Piero Gobetti (who died of bronchitis and heart failure in February 1926 in exile in Paris, aged just 24, after the Fascist beating he'd received the previous year) as a 'party man through and through' in the early 1920s, but by the end of his life he was anything but.[1] We have no clear indication from Gramsci himself how, in those very final years, he viewed his life's work. He had not been able to work systematically on his notebooks since at the latest 1935. Most of his original notes had been completed between 1929 and 1933, in just over three short years of lucid, concentrated research, which were also the years of deepest personal isolation and emotional torment. He managed, one way or another, to take the notebooks with him from prison in Turi to the Cusumano and Quisisana Clinics in his very last years of incapacity, but for much of that time most were kept in storage on the insistence of the prison authorities, who required him to make separate special applications to consult them. Towards the end he was in no physical or mental condition even to consult, let alone add to, adapt or re-order them.

When he died, Tatiana Schucht – his most constant companion and clearly the first person to appreciate their significance – managed to smuggle the notebooks out and deposit them in the vaults of the Banca Commerciale, whose Director Raffaele Mattioli was a sympathetic acquaintance (Tanya would leave for Russia in 1939 and die from tuberculosis in the hardest wartime year 1941; her sisters Evgenia and Julia would lead long lives, Soviet loyalists throughout, together raising Delio and Giuliano, who became respectively an engineer and a musician). A year later, the notebooks were taken to Moscow in the Soviet diplomatic bag under the personal supervision of Vincenzo Bianco, who had been Gramsci's primary contact with the exiled party leadership and his family in Russia. Initially there was no general interest in their contents. In the deathly atmosphere of late-1930s Russia and impending world war, the comrades had other concerns. If anything, given what they knew about Antonio's most recent views on inner-party controversy, a certain reticence would have been entirely understandable. While Togliatti, in a letter to Piero Sraffa asking after any instructions left by Gramsci, expressed a wish to preserve his old comrade's political and literary legacy, he was almost certainly thinking of articles and documents composed before the arrest in 1926.

What changed everything was the Second World War. Fascism and Nazism were militarily vanquished and, while never entirely eliminated from political discourse, morally and legally tarnished. The ensuing forty years of Cold War was in effect an uneasy settlement between the managed capitalism of the West and the state socialism of the East, which at least initially left plenty of space for local variants, especially in the immediate flush of anti-Fascist, 'democratic' victory. These included Italy, where a previously broken, outcast *PCI* emerged from the Resistance as the largest and most powerful mass Communist Party ever to operate in a liberal democracy, and by far the largest single party in the new state, led by an intact, experienced and highly capable central group under the 'wily old fox' Togliatti. While maintaining a facade of Stalinist conformism abroad, they had preserved an unusual degree of openness and pluralism amongst themselves which served them well in the new era.[2] Back in Italy after the war they had the good practical sense to steer a social democratic middle course based on social coalition, cultural engagement and political compromise, endorsed by Stalin for at least those few years when 'The Boss' was still enjoying the global prestige of victory in the Great Patriotic War and promoting similarly 'national popular' strategies across the whole Soviet sphere of influence. This averted the civil strife that overwhelmed the equally well-placed but harder-line Communist Party in Greece. In 1948 the *PCI*'s programme of economic reconstruction and democratic renewal would have propelled them into national government, and by their own lights towards a suitably 'western' proletarian hegemony, if the CIA had not interposed the largely contrived parliamentary formula of Christian Democracy. But the Italian communists exercised enormous political, cultural and institutional power for the next fifty years of their existence. The legacy and aura of Antonio Gramsci were key assets throughout the *PCI*'s ascendancy, dutifully tended by Togliatti and his successors.

*

Gramsci's prison notebooks were first published in Italian by Einaudi in six volumes between 1948 and 1951, selected, annotated and re-ordered in a fashion that aroused much subsequent controversy. It was felt by some that the post-war *PCI* were releasing only those materials which appeared to correspond to its own new strategy of a parliamentary road to socialism and a national culture. There were also suggestions that the party was creating a foundation myth that Gramsci himself would have loathed, not least because its popular iterations were often far from the historical reality. For G. A. Williams, this amounted to 'a species of Gramsci cult of quite remarkable scope and intensity'.[3] Gramsci became 'The Holy Ghost of Italian Communism', with streets and squares in almost every town and city named after him. A further, more selective but balanced anthology, edited by Mario Spinella and Carlo Salinari, was published by *Editori Riuniti* in 1963, as part of a corrective process Williams describes as 'virtually unique' amongst Communist Parties of 'opening its archives to sympathetic but independently minded historians … a magnificent historical enterprise which has successfully reconstructed the early history of the party but has thrown open the whole field to passionate, informed and principled controversy'. Finally in 1975, a complete, definitive edition of the prison notebooks was published in four volumes, edited by Valentino Gerratana.

The first Italian edition of 218 *Lettere del Carcere*, Gramsci's prison letters, was published by *Einaudi* in 1947. Again, they were selected and amended for political purposes, most blatantly to delete friendly references to Amadeo Bordiga, who as we have seen had preceded Gramsci as Secretary of the early *PCd'I* but was now regarded as an ultra-leftist by the post-war *PCI*. Nonetheless, it was a commercial and critical success, and won a major literary prize the following year. This partial edition was superseded in 1965 by a new, comprehensive and definitive edition of 428 letters annotated by Sergio Caprioglio and Elsa Fubini. The first substantial collection of writings from before Gramsci's arrest and imprisonment was selected and edited by Paolo Spriano, the foremost Italian communist historian, and published as *Scritti Politici* in 1967. A biography *Vita di Antonio Gramsci* by Giuseppe Fiori was published in 1966, beautifully written and subsequently translated into English by Tom Nairn, if arguably over-reverential towards its subject (in keeping with the *PCI* foundation myth), notably generous towards the Gramsci and Schucht families, and in some matters of detail incorrect, as well as plainly tied to the *PCI*'s political prerogatives (Fiori was himself an Italian Senator).

Since 1972 there have been over 20,000 works by or about Gramsci published in Italy, reflecting his status as an established historical figure, amenable to continuous re-evaluation and re-interpretation, rather than a set of ideas subject to passing intellectual fashion. In recent decades there has if anything been a second flowering of Italian Gramsciana, overseen by the venerable Gramsci Institute in Rome, with several further volumes of letters to a far wider circle of correspondents published from the 1990s to the present, and a new complete edition of the Prison Notebooks published in 2007. A massive Gramsci dictionary, with six hundred entries contributed by over sixty people, was published in 2009. Occasional controversies still blow up over whether a particular article in the early Italian socialist press should be attributed to Gramsci. Letters are newly discovered or re-attributed, and sometimes challenge our established accounts (most interestingly in recent years, on Gramsci's early relations with the Schucht sisters). However, the study of Gramsci is now largely confined to academia even in Italy, with the decline of the organized political left, the revival of the far right in modernized, populist form under Berlusconi and then Salvini, and what Paul Ginsborg has called the 'infantilization' of Italian popular culture.[4]

It has been argued that Gramsci in translation has had more impact on the British left than on any other political movement outside Italy itself. There have been two main sources of Gramsci in English, which have made very different claims on the Gramscian legacy. The first was associated with the *New Left Review*, mainly in its latter-day incarnation under the editorship of Perry Anderson. The first New Left, established in 1956 and loosely led by academic and cultural luminaries like E. P. Thompson, Raymond Williams and Stuart Hall, many of them disillusioned ex-communists, had also been interested in Gramsci, albeit in a less focused way than Anderson's second New Left, which assumed control of *New Left Review* in 1962 and took it in a more theoretical, and generally leftist, direction. In 1964 the playwright Trevor Griffiths began work on the play *Occupations*, focused on an imagined encounter between Gramsci and a Soviet trade emissary during the Turin factory occupations of 1919–20, which was eventually staged in 1971 by the Royal Shakespeare Company.

The second and later Gramscian centre was the Euro-communist wing of the Communist Party of Great Britain, whose intellectuals adopted Gramsci as their primary theorist in the 1970s. At events like the Communist University of London and in publications like *Marxism Today*, they sought to apply an array of Gramscian concepts to contemporary circumstances and events, in a spirit of mass politics and 'broad democratic alliance' untainted by the authoritarianism of Stalinism or the ultra-leftism of Trotskyism (though *Marxism Today* was surprisingly uninterested in Gramsci himself, carrying just one article on Gramsci in its 1980s heyday, Stuart Hall's 1987 'Gramsci and Us').[5] British Eurocommunism, with its Gramscian underpinnings, had its purest practical expression in the CPGB's revised *British Road to Socialism* formulated in 1977, but faltered and fell away under the impact of inner-party conflict and external Thatcherism.

There have been overlaps and collaborations, as well as divergences and conflicts, between these two 'centres' of British Gramscism, most obviously the magnificent *Selections from Prison Notebooks* (1971), edited by two NLR associates Quintin Hoare and Geoffrey Nowell-Smith but published by the CPGB's publisher Lawrence and Wishart. There have also been quite separate and subsidiary sources of Gramsci material such as Pluto Press, associated (at least in its earlier years) with the International Socialists/Socialist Workers Party. The IS/SWP were especially interested in Gramsci's factory council period, for *ouvrieriste* reasons of their own, and in 1975 published two exhaustive studies of the factory council movement by Gwyn A. Williams and Paolo Spriano. Pluto also published one of the very first Gramsci primers, a translation by Anne Showstack of a book originally written in Italian by A. Pozzolini in the heady days of 1968, and very much reflecting the excitable mood of the time. In 1976, Pluto published the rather more measured and generally well-regarded *Gramsci's Marxism* by the American Carl Boggs, whose argument that 'a definite thematic continuity underlies Gramsci's theoretical work from the early period to the Prison Notebooks' ran counter to other leftist conceptions of 'a radical break in Gramsci's thought pre/post 1926 brought about by the "Bolshevization" of the PCI'.[6] The Institute of Workers Control and its publishing arm Spokesman, both connected to the Bertrand Russell Foundation, also took an interest in Gramsci, especially the earlier political writings. *Socialist Register* and its publishing arm Merlin, a group of intellectuals in and around the Labour Party best known for their critique of parliamentary socialism and Labourism (most notably Ralph Miliband and John Saville), produced a number of articles on Gramsci and most significantly Alastair Davidson's book *Antonio Gramsci: Towards an Intellectual Biography*, which argues for a pre-Leninist, non-doctrinaire Marxist Gramsci. Davidson's account is strong on Gramsci's Crocean-idealist roots, but weak on the Prison Notebooks, and if its publication was intended by *Socialist Register*/Merlin to establish a third centre of British Gramscism, it plainly didn't come off.

So at this stage we have the 'revolutionary' Gramsci of the factory council years set against the 'reformist' Gramsci in prison (his final, somewhat tongue-in-cheek, summation of his own politics was actually 'gradualist'), broadly mirroring the controversies of the 1960s and 1970s in Italy itself, where they really did have an immediate bearing on political affairs. Elsewhere these matters of categorization and periodization were largely confined to the inner core of hardened ideologues and heresy-hunters. The more common take on Gramsci was enthusiasm and excitement, a sense of theoretical breakthrough and creative liberation, not always supported by textual understanding. At last, the stale atmosphere of both official and oppositional Marxism could be dispelled, and we could start thinking afresh about our cultures, histories and politics. In the 'post-everything' excitement of the late twentieth century, the real historical Gramsci rather tended to get left behind (most obviously in the magazine-format *Marxism Today*).

The reception and application of Gramsci elsewhere followed a similar pattern, with local variations depending on Communist Parties' orientation towards Eurocommunism, the applicability of Gramscian concepts to local histories and circumstances, or the level of interest in Gramsci taken in academic institutions. So in France Gramsci was filtered through the intellectual discourse of the *Parti Communiste Francaise*, and generally subordinate to the political prerogatives of the party. The *PCF*'s leading intellectual Louis Althusser took upon himself the role of sympathetic critic, setting Gramsci's originality against his alleged deviation from Marxist-Leninist orthodoxy. The *PCF* never wholeheartedly embraced Eurocommunism. With the collapse of the *Programme Commune* under the ascendant Socialist Party of Francois Mitterand, their own electoral prospects went into rapid decline, while the intellectual and cultural predominance of French Marxism was soon swamped by the iconoclasm of postmodernism and other passing fads. The Spanish Communist Party under Santiago Carillo was initially much more enthusiastic about Eurocommunism and its Gramscian roots, until Carillo came under challenge from young intellectuals and activists and reverted to rather more traditional 'administrative methods' of party management. In Greece, Gramsci was absorbed into the emergent post-dictatorship politics of the democratic left, which would eventually take shape in the avowedly Gramscian/ Eurocommunist current within the governing, post-crisis party Syriza very capably led by Alexis Tsipras.

In the United States, Gramsci was always more welcome in academia than in the wider polity, so while the definitive translations and some of the most incisive commentaries were undertaken by American academics, Gramscian concepts have had very little traction in political practice and popular discourse. In the Soviet bloc there was very little interest in Gramsci, beyond his symbolic value as a historical martyr of Fascism. Following the collapse of communism, there is even less, despite Gramsci's own time in the country and the family connections he accrued (including his Russian grandson and namesake, Antonio Gramsci Jr., author of a well-regarded family memoir). In those Communist Parties that remain in power (most notably China and Vietnam), study of Gramsci has generally been confined within the parameters of official Marxism-Leninism, and followed the twists and turns of government policy. According to Xin Liu (an American-based academic), their twenty-first-century hybrid models of managed capitalism and state socialism have provoked new interest in Gramsci, especially on the role of intellectuals in maintaining cultural hegemony, but I doubt there is much overlap with discussion of the same topics in Europe and America.[7]

In the developing world, the concept of subalternity has been used to illuminate the travails of postcolonial societies like India, but like all national liberation struggles the project has been largely confined to disaffected subgroups of the indigenous colonial-era elites. As a fellow Gramscian once pointed out to me, for all their focus on 'history from below' and 'subalterns as agents of political and social change', the members of the famous School of South Asian Subaltern Studies are notably 'Brahmin'. They represent one example of how in recent times Gramsci has been almost wholly absorbed into the routines and frameworks of academic institutions, staffed by what he called 'traditional intellectuals' ultimately beholden to their paymasters, in contrast to the 'organic intellectuals' which would emerge from within the subaltern classes to organize a new hegemony, and thereby neutralized as a political or cultural force in broader society.[8] In the West, this process of neutralization (or, Gramsci's own favoured term, *trasformismo*) mainly involved corralling Gramsci into the academic subject of cultural studies, which briefly flowered as a branch of sociology concerned with the burgeoning politics of identity before rather disappearing into its own self-referential jargon, processes and techniques, taking (for most people) Gramsci with it. My central aim in this book has been to restore him to politics and history, to apply Gramsci's guiding principle of 'absolute historicism' to his central concepts by explaining how they emerged from the lived experiences and relationships of a real human personality immersed in his times. I have attempted this through a careful, chronological reading of the letters and notebooks in their full American translations (plus Derek Boothman's masterly *A Great and Terrible World; The Pre-Prison Letters*), only recently readily available.

*

Being Gramscian in the twenty-first century can be deeply frustrating. On the one hand Gramsci's political insights, historical perspectives and master concepts of hegemony and subalternity make more sense than any other intellectual framework in the last hundred years of our often puzzling times and circumstances; in particular, how and why people submit to their own oppression and exploitation. This is what led US alt-right 'shock-jock' Rush Limbaugh to describe Gramsci as the left's secret weapon, and rejoice in its reluctance to use it. On the other hand, Gramsci is barely known outside a small coterie of devotees, nostalgic for that roughly ten-year period across the 1960s and '70s when the organized left seemed set to transcend its historical confines of social democracy and the twin dogmatisms of Stalinism and Trotskyism, but now mostly confined to academia and busy for much of the time with the kind of 'bloodless erudition' of which Gramsci himself was consistently scornful. Attempts at Gramscian analysis of contemporary themes, such as my own *The Politics of New Labour* (2011), remain forlornly marginal. All those Gramsci-related or -inspired MAs and PhDs, which is how my own book originated, are not what he had in mind when he proposed the new-style, post-Machiavellian revolutionary party of the Modern Prince. If people have heard of him, it's usually from some half-remembered reference in a university lecture, or a simplistic rendering of hegemony by political commentators out to impress. Even in his native Italy, where he is monumentalized as a serious historical figure, the study of Gramsci is largely a matter of preserving the legacy rather than its creative application, a form of institutionalization which keeps the flame aglow but prevents it catching fire. The dire state of Italian politics and society – captured most faithfully for me by the two best Italian movies of recent times, Matteo Garrone and Roberto Saviano's *Gomorrah* and Paolo Sorrentino's

La Grande Bellazza, and culminating in a majority party with openly Fascist trappings – is proof of that. There have been no significant political leaders on the Italian left since Enrico Berlinguer, the architect of the historic compromise which brought the *PCI* close to national government in the late 1970s, only to fall away again in the ensuing 'years of lead' under the combined onslaught of the deep state, remnants of fascism, organized crime, the CIA and the Red Brigades. When the self-appointed heirs to Gramsci gather around his urn of ashes in the Protestant Cemetery in Rome on the anniversaries of his death, not far from the family plot of his last landlords the Passarges, and declaim their readings and speeches like some obscure religious sub-sect, you have to wonder what he himself would have made of it. In his deep ambivalence towards his native country and (as Tom Nairn once argued) his abiding Sardism, Gramsci's fierce social moralism would find many ready targets in contemporary Italy.[9]

There are Gramscian traces all over our own politics and culture, from the little Caesars of Brexit to the rather larger Caesar who occupied the White House in 2016. More broadly, our epoch is defined by the lingering hegemony of Thatcherism, its carefully and constantly adjusted mix of coercion and consent, and the transformist adjustments to it of various, successive, similarly malleable Labourisms, all set against a background of the deepening subalternity of capitalism's lower orders, the revived self-confidence of the transnational bourgeoisie and the historical bloc with which it protects, disguises and insulates itself. Our entire political economy is dominated by 'pensioners of economic history', the baby boomers who have derived so much corporate personal benefit from the top-down neo-liberal 'passive revolution' of the last forty years. Safely ensconced in their superannuated, health-insured, multi-propertied, extended retirement, they have set about pulling up the drawbridge on succeeding generations and anyone else deemed to be left behind. These 'active elderly' are our demographic equivalent to 'the monkey people' (or even more harshly 'scum of society') whom Gramsci identified as the backbone of Italian fascism. His sharp gaze would have been just as fixed on our debased popular culture. As a long-time professional theatre critic, Gramsci would have been enthused by the re-emergence of immersive drama as our most powerful topical art form, whether on television or in live theatre, but profoundly depressed by the domination of our mass entertainments by shallow celebrity and lazy, formulaic repetition.

So much of contemporary life lends itself to what Stuart Hall called 'thinking in a Gramscian way', the creative application of the philosophy of praxis, absolute historicism, and (less seriously, Gramsci's own self-deprecating description of his take on Marx) 'passionate sarcasm' of which his 'open Marxism' consisted.[10] The risk is that it leads to a rather desperate search for consolation in some kind of gradualism, where Gramsci himself joked his own politics had ended up in his despondent final years. Hall in his own old age told me that the best he hoped for was some form of social democracy. Many other former Euro-communists were finally and fully disillusioned by the initially promising New Labour project, which on occasions declared Gramscian inspirations. They have mostly lapsed into what David Purdy described to me as an uneasy quietism, which also happens to be a handy summation of Gramsci's final mood. But if Gramsci is, as Hall and others have suggested, our foremost philosopher of defeat, he can still help us explore the full character and consequences of the historic defeat of the organized communist and socialist left, turning on that sorry record the full force of his 'pessimism of the intellect' alongside an abiding 'optimism of the will'. This process of analysis and self-criticism, in my opinion, has never been fully undertaken. We can see all around us the consequences of further failure by my generation of left-wing activists and thinkers – we self-styled organic intellectuals of the 1960s and 1970s – to transmit the benefit of our generally dispiriting experience, what works and what doesn't, to the next one. I hope this book goes some small way to putting that right.

NOTES

Chapter 1

1   A. Gramsci, *Letters from Prison*, ed. and trans. L. Lawner (London 1979), pp. 277–81.
2   As far as is known, the bronze casts of Gramsci's face and hand were never made.
3   J. Buttigieg, Introduction to A. Gramsci, *Prison Notebooks Vol. 1* (New York 2007), p. 2.

Chapter 2

1   A. Davidson, *Antonio Gramsci: Towards an Intellectual Biography* (London 1977), p. 14.
2   Ibid., p. 15.
3   A. Gramsci, *Selections from Prison Notebooks* (London 1971), p. 134; *History, Philosophy and Culture in the Young Gramsci* (Saint Louis, 1975), p. 29.
4   R. J. B. Bosworth, *Mussolini's Italy* (London 2006), p. 81.
5   Davidson, *Antonio Gramsci: Towards an Intellectual Biography*, p. 15.
6   Ibid., pp. 19–20.
7   Ibid., p. 19.
8   A. Gramsci, *Letters from Prison* Volume 1, ed. and trans. F. Rosengarten and R. Rosenthal (New York 1994), p. 15.
9   G. Fiori, *Antonio Gramsci Life of a Revolutionary*, trans. T. Nairn (London 1970), pp. 11–12 (all subsequent references to Fiori are from this book).
10 G. Fiori, pp. 16–17.
11 Ibid., pp. 14–15.
12 Ibid., p. 17.
13 Gramsci, *Letters from Prison*, trans. L. Lawner, p. 74.
14 G. Fiori, p. 28.
15 Gramsci, *Letters from Prison*, trans. L. Lawner, p. 73.
16 Ibid., p. 92.
17 R. J. Bosworth, *Mussolini's Italy* (London 2005), p. 41.
18 G. Fiori, p. 45.
19 Gramsci, *Letters from Prison*, trans. L. Lawner, p. 124.
20 G. Fiori, pp. 29, 34.

Chapter 3

1   The prize-winning 1979 film by the Taviani brothers, *Padre Padrone*, provides a vivid mid-century snapshot of the daily lives of the families of smallholders in Sardinia, albeit fifty years of questionable 'progress' after 1900 (the title of a rather more tendentious film by Bernardo Bertolucci).

2 G. Fiori, p. 43.

3 Ibid., p. 50.

4 A. Gramsci, *A Great and Terrible World – The Pre-Prison Letters 1908–26*, ed. and trans. D. Boothman (London 2015), 'Introduction', p. 11.

5 Gramsci, *Letters from Prison*, trans. L. Lawner, p. 87.

6 Gramsci, *A Great and Terrible World – The Pre-Prison Letters*, trans. D. Boothman, p. 247.

7 A. Gramsci, *Selections from Political Writings 1910–1920*, trans. J. Matthews (London 1977), p. 3.

8 Gramsci, *A Great and Terrible World: The Pre-Prison Letters 1908–1926*, p. 67.

9 G. Fiori, p. 38.

10 Gramsci, *A Great and Terrible World: The Pre-Prison Letters 1908–1926*, p. 63.

11 A. Gramsci, 'The Light Which Went Out', *History, Philosophy and Culture in the Young Gramsci*, ed. P. Cavalcanti and P. Piccone (St. Louis, 1975), p. 26.

12 A. Gramsci, *Selections from Prison Notebooks*, ed. and trans. Q. Hoare and G. Nowell-Smith (London 1971), p. xix.

13 Davidson, *Antonio Gramsci – Towards an Intellectual Biography*, p. 49.

14 Ibid., p. 51.

15 Gramsci, *A Great and Terrible World: The Pre-Prison Letters 1908–1926*, p. 73.

16 G. Fiori, pp. 52–3.

17 Gramsci, *A Great and Terrible World: The Pre-Prison Letters 1908–1926*, p. 72.

18 Ibid., p. 72.

19 Ibid., p. 74.

Chapter 4

1 A. Gramsci, *Selections from Cultural Writings*, ed. D. Forgacs and G. Nowell-Smith (London 1985), p. 33.

2 G. A. Williams, *Proletarian Order: Antonio Gramsci, the Factory Councils and the Origins of Communism in Italy* (London 1975), pp. 13–14, 47.

3 A. Gramsci, 'The Turin Factory Councils Movement', in *Selections from Political Writings 1910–1920* (London 1977), ed. Q. Hoare, pp. 310–20.

4 Gramsci, *A Great and Terrible World: The Pre-Prison Letters 1908–1926*, p. 79.

5 G. Fiori, p. 71.

6 Gramsci, *A Great and Terrible World: The Pre-Prison Letters 1908–1926*, p. 83.

7 Ibid., p. 85.

8 D. Mack Smith, *Mussolini* (London 1993), p. 74.

9 P. Togliatti, *On Gramsci and Other Writings* (London 1979), p. 35.

10 Davidson, *Antonio Gramsci: Towards an Intellectual Biography*, p. 55.

11 P. Togliatti, *On Gramsci and Other Writings* (London 1979), p. 42.

12 Davidson, *Antonio Gramsci: Towards and Intellectual Biography*, p. 62.

13 Gramsci, *Letters from Prison*, trans. L. Lawner, p. 112.

14 Gramsci, *Selections from Cultural Writings*, p. 53.

15 G. Fiori, p. 88.

16 Gramsci, *A Great and Terrible World: The Pre-Prison Letters 1908–1926*, p. 89.

17 Ibid., p. 95.

18 Davidson, *Antonio Gramsci: Towards an Intellectual Biography*, p. 63.

19 G. Fiori, pp. 95–6.

20 Mack Smith, *Mussolini*, p. 16.
21 Williams, *Proletarian Order,* pp. 31, 42; Williams pointedly observes that Fiori's classic Gramsci biography 'does not mention the Mussolini project', p. 42, ft. 11.
22 Gramsci, 'Active and Operative Neutrality', *Selections from Political Writings 1910–1920,* pp. 6–9.
23 Williams, *Proletarian Order*, p. 50.
24 Gramsci, *A Great and Terrible World: The Pre-Prison Letters 1908–1926,* p. 95.
25 Davidson, *Antonio Gramsci: Towards an Intellectual Biography,* p. 76.
26 A. Gramsci, 'Schools of Labour', in *A Gramsci Reader,* ed. D. Forgacs (New York 2000), pp. 59–62.
27 A. Gramsci, 'General Introduction', in *A Great and Terrible World – The Pre-Prison Letters,* ed. Boothman, p. 15.
28 A. Gramsci (signed Alpha Gamma), *Il Grido del Popolo,* 29 January 1916.
29 Gramsci, *Selections from Prison Notebooks,* p. 37.
30 Gramsci, *A Great and Terrible World – The Pre-Prison Letters,* p. 96.

Chapter 5

1   Gramsci, *A Great and Terrible World – The Pre-Prison Letters,* p. 99.
2   A. Gramsci, *Selections from Cultural Writings,* ed. D. Forgacs and G. Nowell-Smith (London 1985), pp. 386–7. This volume contains the largest dedicated selection in English of Gramsci's notes on journalism, pp. 386–425.
3   Gramsci, *Selections from Cultural Writings,* p. 73.
4   G. Fiori, p. 112.
5   Ibid., p. 110.
6   I. Deutscher, *The Prophet Armed* (Oxford 1970), p. 54.
7   J. Reed, *Ten Days That Shook the World* (New York 1919), p. 78.
8   A. Gramsci, 'The Revolution against *Capital*', in *A Gramsci Reader* (New York 2000), pp. 32–6.
9   M. W. Martin, *Futurist Art and Theory* (Oxford 1968), p. 23, ft. 1.
10 A. Gramsci, *Selections from Political Writings 1910–1920,* pp. 34/37; V. I. Lenin, speech to Comintern Congress 1923.
11 *History, Philosophy and Culture in the Young Gramsci,* p. 21.
12 Ibid., p. 18.
13 A. Gramsci, 'Philanthropy, Good Will and Organisation', *Avanti!* 24 December 1917; 'Our Marx', *Il Grido del Popolo,* 4 May 1918.
14 *The Open Marxism of Antonio Gramsci,* ed. C. Manzoni (New York 1974), p. 7.
15 Gramsci, *A Great and Terrible World,* pp. 100–1 and ft. 10.
16 A. Gramsci, 'Men or Machines?' in *The Antonio Gramsci Reader,* pp. 62–4.
17 A. Gramsci, 'Class Intransigence and Italian History' in *The Antonio Gramsci Reader,* pp. 40–4.
18 A. Gramsci, 'Philanthropy, Good Will and Organisation', *Avanti!* 24 December 1918.
19 Gramsci, 'Literature', in *History, Philosophy and Culture in the Young Gramsci* (St. Louis 1975), pp. 23–6.
20 S. Parker, *Bertolt Brecht: A Literary Life* (London 2014), p. 1.
21 Bowie, *Interview Magazine,* 2002.
22 A. Gramsci, 'The Watchmaker', in *History, Philosophy and Culture in the Young Gramsci* (St. Louis 1975), pp. 36–7.

23   Forgacs, 'Introduction', *Selections from Cultural Writings*, p. 16.
24   J. Willett, *The New Sobriety: Art and Politics in the Weimar Period* (London 1978), p. 11.
25   M. W. Martin, *Futurist Art and Theory 1909–1915* (Oxford 1968), p. xxvii.
26   A. Gramsci, 'The Light Which Went Out', in *History, Philosophy and Culture in Young Gramsci* (St. Louis 1975), p. 28.
27   G. Fiori, p. 104.
28   Gramsci, *Selections from Cultural Writings*, pp. 77–86.
29   D. Forgacs, in A. Gramsci, *Selections from Cultural Writings*, p. 12.
30   Gramsci, *Letters from Prison Volume 1*, ed. F. Rosengarten, p. 84.
31   Gramsci, *Selections from Cultural Writings*, pp. 70–3.
32   Ibid., p. 75.
33   Ibid., pp. 56–67.
34   Ibid., p. 411.
35   G. Fiori, p. 114.

Chapter 6

1   Mack Smith, *Mussolini*, p. 91.
2   G. Fiori, p. 118.
3   A. Gramsci, *Prison Notebooks Vol. 1*, ed. J. Buttigieg, 'Chronology' p. 71.
4   G. Fiori, p. 118.
5   A. Gramsci and P. Togliatti, 'Workers Democracy', *Selections from Political Writings 1910–1920*, pp. 65–8.
6   Davidson, *Antonio Gramsci: Towards an Intellectual Biography*, p. 165.
7   G. Fiori, p. 121.
8   Williams, *Proletarian Order*, p. 175.
9   Fiori, *Life of a Revolutionary*, p. 124.
10   Gramsci, *Selections from Political Writings 1910–1920*, p. 318.
11   G. Fiori, pp. 126–7.
12   Gramsci, *Selections from Political Writings 1910–1920*, p. 190.
13   Gramsci, *A Great and Terrible World*, p. 102.
14   Gramsci, *A Great and Terrible World: The Pre-Prison Letters 1908–1926*, pp. 102–4.
15   G. Fiori, pp. 141–2.

Chapter 7

1   W. Laqueur, *Weimar – A Cultural History* (London 1974), p. 54.
2   Willett, *The New Sobriety*, p. 156.
3   Mack Smith, *Mussolini*, p. 41
4   A. Gramsci (published in the communist fraction's weekly *Il Comunista*, 6 December 1920), *A Great and Terrible World: The Pre-Prison Letters*, p. 105.
5   V. Degott, *Liberty in Illegality* (Moscow 1923)
6   Davidson, *Antonio Gramsci: Towards an Intellectual Biography*, p. 94.
7   A. Gramsci, 'The Conquest of the State' in *L'Ordine Nuovo* (July 1919), *Selections from Political Writings 1910–1920*, pp. 74–5.

8   A. Gramsci, 'The Return to Freedom' in *Avanti!* (June 1919), *Selections from Political Writings 1910–1920*, p. 71.

9   V. I. Lenin, *False Discourses on Freedom* (Moscow 1920).

10 G. Fiori, p. 144.

11 A. Gramsci, *Selections from Political Writings 1921–1926*, ed. and trans. Q. Hoare (London 1978), pp. 159–60 and ft. 83.

12 A. Gramsci, 'The Rome Congress', in *Selections from Political Writings 1921–1926* (London 1978), pp. 93–117.

13 G. Fiori, p. 150.

14 G. Fiori, p. 151.

15 Gramsci, *Letters from Prison Vol. 1*, ed. F. Rosengarten, p. 131.

16 Mack Smith, *Mussolini*, p. 45.

Chapter 8

1   Gramsci, *A Great and Terrible World*, p. 108.

2   Ibid., p. 113.

3   Gramsci, *Letters from Prison Vol.1*, ed. F. Rosengarten, p. 121.

4   S. Fitzpatrick and A. Rabinovitch, *Russia in the Era of NEP* (London 1991), pp. 78–9.

5   Gramsci, *Selections from Cultural Writings*, p. 49.

6   Ibid., p. 52.

7   A. Gramsci, *Selections from Cultural Writings*, 'Introduction', p. 19.

8   R. J. B. Bosworth, *Mussolini's Italy*, p. 14.

9   Williams, *Proletarian Order*, p. 183.

10 Gramsci, *A Great and Terrible World*, p. 21.

11 Ibid., p. 111.

12 Ibid., p. 114.

13 Ibid., p. 119.

14 I am especially grateful to Derek Boothman for unearthing and explaining this potentially crucial misunderstanding.

15 Serge, *Memoirs of a Revolutionary*, p. 165.

16 Gramsci, *Letters from Prison*, ed. L. Lawner, p. 103.

17 M. Lermontov, *A Hero of Our Time*, trans. N. Randall (London 2009).

18 Gramsci, *A Great and Terrible World*, p. 106.

19 Gramsci, *Letters from Prison*, ed. L. Lawner, p. 127.

20 Gramsci, *Selections from Political Writings 1921–26*, pp. 129–31.

21 Ibid., p. 130.

22 Gramsci, *Selections from Political Writings 1921–1926*, pp. 153, 136, 145.

23 G. Fiori, pp. 160–1.

Chapter 9

1   R. Von Mayerburg, *Hotel Lux* (Munich 1978).

2   Gramsci, *A Great and Terrible World: Pre-Prison Letters*, p. 112. A number of these affectionate notes have only recently been correctly identified as addressed to Evgenia, rather than (as before) Julia, which suggests that the transfer of Gramsci's attentions from one sister to another took rather longer than previously thought, and that along

the way his feelings remained somewhat unclear, if not downright ambivalent. I am grateful to Derek Boothman for these fresh attributions and insights.

3 Gramsci, *Letters from Prison*, ed. L. Lawner, p. 135.
4 Gramsci, *Selections from Political Writings 1921–1926*, p. 183 and ft. 104.
5 G. Fiori, p. 161.
6 Gramsci, *A Great and Terrible World*, p. 167.
7 Gramsci, *Letters from Prison*, ed. L. Lawner, p. 157.
8 S. Fitzpatrick, *Everyday Stalinism* (London 2000); there has been some debate in Italy, involving the Gramsci/Schucht family themselves, over whether this constituted a formal marriage at all.
9 Serge, *Memoirs of a Revolutionary*, p. 172.
10 Gramsci, *A Great and Terrible World*, p. 322.

Chapter 10

1 Gramsci, *A Great and Terrible World*, p. 206.
2 Serge, *Memoirs of a Revolutionary*, p. 178; Serge's own name was of course just one of several pseudonyms.
3 Gramsci, *Selections from Political Writings 1921–1926*, p. 191.
4 Mack Smith, *Mussolini*, pp. 11, 20.
5 Serge, *Memoirs of a Revolutionary*, pp. 133–4.
6 Ibid., pp. 186–7.
7 G. Fiori, p. 178.
8 Gramsci, *A Great and Terrible World*, p. 207.
9 Ibid., p. 210.
10 Gramsci, *Selections from Political Writings 1921–1926*, p. 194.
11 Ibid., pp. 209–12.
12 Ibid., pp. 213–17.
13 Gramsci, *Selections from Political Writings 1921–1926*, p. 193.
14 Ibid., p. 157.
15 Ibid., p. 188.
16 Ibid., p. 185.
17 Ibid., p. 188.
18 Ibid., pp. 174–5.
19 Ibid., pp. 178.
20 Ibid., pp. 199–200.
21 Ibid., p. 185.
22 G. Fiori, p. 169.
23 Mack Smith, *Mussolini*, p. 69.
24 Serge, *Memoirs of a Revolutionary*, pp. 186–7.
25 Gramsci, *A Great and Terrible World*, p. 278.

Chapter 11

1 Mack Smith, *Mussolini*, p. 63.
2 Ibid., p. 76.
3 Gramsci, *A Great and Terrible World*, p. 316.

4   Ibid., pp. 320–1.
5   Ibid., p. 322.
6   G. Fiori, p. 178.
7   Ibid., p. 182.
8   Ibid., p. 175.

Chapter 12

1   Mack Smith, *Mussolini,* p. 119.
2   G. Fiori, p. 185.

Chapter 13

1   Mack Smith, *Mussolini,* p. 104.
2   G. Fiori, p. 190.
3   Gramsci, *A Great and Terrible World,* p. 339.
4   G. Fiori, p.192.
5   Ibid., pp. 193–6.
6   Gramsci, *Selections from Political Writings 1921–1926,* p. 167.
7   Mack Smith, *Mussolini,* pp. 2–4, 9; the most striking of these similarities is contained in Smith's description of the young Mussolini as 'a hermit and a misanthrope' (p. 9).
8   G. Fiori, p. 197.

Chapter 14

1   Serge, *Memoirs of a Revolutionary,* p. 165.
2   Gramsci, *A Great and Terrible World: The Pre-Prison Letters,* plate 15.
3   G. Fiori, p. 202.
4   Gramsci, *A Great and Terrible World: The Pre-Prison Letters,* p. 317.
5   G. Fiori, p. 203.
6   Gramsci, *Selections from Political Writings 1921–1926,* pp. 426–32.
7   A. De Grand, *In Stalin's Shadow; Angelo Tasca and the Crisis of the Left in Italy and France 1910–1945* (Northern Illinois, 1986), p. 78.
8   G. Fiori, pp. 205–6.
9   Bosworth, *Mussolini's Italy,* p. 50.
10 Mack Smith, *Mussolini,* p. 147.

Chapter 15

1   Antonio Gramsci, *Letters from Prison Vol. 1,* ed. F. Rosengarten, p. 67.
2   Ibid., p. 58.

3   Sraffa, arguably Gramsci's most steadfast, loyal and helpful friend, was subsequently best known for his work on the classical economist David Ricardo, as well as his influence on Gramsci and Ludwig Wittgenstein amongst others.
4   Mack Smith, *Mussolini*, p. 101.

Chapter 16

1   A. Gramsci, *Letters from Prison Vol. 1*, ed. F. Rosengarten (New York 1994), pp. 70–1.
2   Mack Smith, *Mussolini*, p. 147.
3   Gramsci, *Letters from Prison Vol. 1*, ed. F. Rosengarten, pp. 118–19.
4   P. Spriano, *Antonio Gramsci and the Party: The Prison Years*, trans. J. Frazer (London 1979), p. 26.
5   Gramsci, *Letters from Prison Vol. 1*, ed. F. Rosengarten, p. 138.
6   Spriano, *Antonio Gramsci and the Party: The Prison Years*, pp. 40, 44, ft.10.
7   Ibid., pp. 33–48.
8   Gramsci, *Letters from Prison Vol. 1*, ed. F. Rosengarten, p. 83.
9   Ibid., p. 199.
10 G. Fiori, p. 230.

Chapter 17

1   Gramsci, *Letters from Prison Vol. 1*, ed. F. Rosengarten, p. 213.
2   Erysipelas is now easily treated with a course of antibiotics, and is usually healed within fourteen days. It is indeed milder than shingles, which the author endured during the preparation of this volume.
3   G. Fiori, p. 233.
4   Gramsci, *Prison Notebooks Vol. 1*, ed. J. Buttigieg, pp. 176–7. There is another citation of Jacques Riviere in Susan Sontag's introduction to G. Bataille, *Story of the Eye* (London 2001), where she approvingly applies to pornography his observation of the tendency of 'art to become a completely non-human activity, a supersensory function, a sort of creative astronomy' (p. 90), and loosely associates his writings with the beginnings of Dada and Surrealism.

Chapter 18

1   A. Gramsci, *Prison Letters*, trans. H. Henderson (London 1988), p. 87.
2   Ibid., p. 89.
3   Ibid.
4   Ibid., p. 95.
5   Ibid., pp. 95–6.
6   Ibid., p. 99.
7   Gramsci, *Letters from Prison Vol. 1*, ed. F. Rosengarten, p. 282.
8   M. Kennedy, *The Constant Nymph* (London 1924).

9   Gramsci, *Letters from Prison Vol. 1*, ed. F. Rosengarten, p. 304.
10   Fiori, *Life of a Revolutionary*, p. 103. This note itself, approvingly cited by Fiori and undoubtedly amusing, is rather odd; Togliatti must have known that Gramsci's correspondence was subject to several layers of surveillance.

Chapter 19

1   Gramsci, *Prison Notebooks Vol. 1*, trans. J. Buttigieg and A. Callari, pp. 495–6; Gramsci had been using the term 'monkey people' since at least early 1921, when he wrote an article under that name for *L'Ordine Nuovo* that began 'Fascism has been the latest "performance" offered by the urban petty bourgeoisie on the stage of national political life', Gramsci, *Selections from Political Writings 1910–1920*, pp. 372–4.
2   Gramsci, *Selections from Prison Notebooks*, pp. 281–4.
3   Mack Smith, *Mussolini*, p. 104.
4   Gramsci, *Prison Letters*, trans. H. Henderson, pp. 91–2.

Chapter 20

1   Gramsci, *Prison Notebooks Vol. 2*, p. 111.
2   Ibid., p. 112.
3   Ibid.
4   Gramsci, *Selections from Political Writings 1910–1920*, p. 41.
5   Gramsci, *Prison Notebooks Vol. 1*, p. 182.
6   Ibid., p. 242.
7   Ibid., p. 319.
8   Davidson, *Antonio Gramsci: Towards and Intellectual Biography*, p. 37.

Chapter 21

1   G. Fiori, p. 257.
2   Barth Urban, *Moscow and the Italian Communist Party*, p. 54.
3   Gramsci, *Letters from Prison Vol. 2*, ed. F. Rosengarten, p. 23.
4   Ibid., pp. 200–1.
5   Ibid., pp. 115–16.
6   Gramsci, *Selections from Prison Notebooks*, p. 302.
7   Gramsci, *Letters from Prison Vol. 1*, ed. F. Rosengarten, p. 356.
8   Gramsci, *Letters from Prison*, ed. L. Lawner, p. 220.
9   Gramsci, *Letters from Prison Vol. 1*, ed. F. Rosengarten, p. 359.
10   Gramsci, *Letters from Prison Vol. 2*, ed. F. Rosengarten, p. 9.
11   Ibid., p. 12.
12   Gramsci, *Prison Letters*, trans. H. Henderson, pp. 146–7.
13   Gramsci, *Letters from Prison*, ed. L. Lawner, p. 194.
14   Ibid., p. 196.
15   Ibid., pp. 199–201.

Chapter 22

1 Gramsci, *Letters from Prison Vol. 2*, ed. F. Rosengarten, p. 58.
2 Gramsci, *Prison Letters*, trans. H. Henderson, p. 158.
3 Dostoyevsky, *The Insulted and The Injured* (1861).
4 Gramsci, *Prison Notebooks Vol. 3*, pp. 143–4.
5 Ibid., p. 400.
6 Ibid., p. 288.
7 Gramsci, *Letters from Prison Vol. 2*, ed. F. Rosengarten, p. 54.
8 For Gramsci's partial absorption of Lenin's conception of hegemony, see Perry Anderson's 'The Antinomies of Antonio Gramsci', *New Left Review 100*, January/February 1976.
9 I use the term 'potentially hegemonic' advisedly, to indicate what Gramsci always saw as a predominantly constructive and creative revolutionary project. The term 'counter-hegemony', often attributed to Gramsci, never appeared in his writings. It was coined by Togliatti to support the *PCI's* post-war strategy of parliamentary participation and national reconstruction, in other words supposedly 'prefigurative struggle' within the established hegemony. For Gramsci, notwithstanding his own final 'gradualism' (and the historical reality of post-war American and Soviet super-power hegemony), this would have run the risk of any form of *sovversismo* or 'alternativism', of being absorbed within the ruling historical bloc under capitalism, which was of course the *PCI's* ultimate sorry fate.
10 Gramsci, *Prison Notebooks Vol. 1*, p. 335.
11 Gramsci, *Selections from Prison Notebooks*, p. 276; I recently came across a rather odd rendering of this commonly quoted sentence as 'The time of monsters', with reference to resurgent twenty-first-century Fascism.

Chapter 23

1 Mack Smith, *Mussolini*, pp. 171, 182.
2 Gramsci, *Prison Letters*, trans. H. Henderson, p. 169.
3 Gramsci, *Letters from Prison*, ed. L. Lawner, p. 249.
4 Gramsci, *Letters from Prison Vol. 2*, ed. F. Rosengarten, p. 238.
5 Gramsci, *Prison Letters*, trans. H. Henderson, p. 184.
6 Gramsci, *Letters from Prison Vol. 2*, ed. F. Rosengarten, p. 237.
7 Gramsci, *Prison Letters*, trans. H. Henderson, p. 203.
8 G. Fiori, pp. 276–7.
9 Gramsci, *Prison Notebooks Vol. 1*, 'Chronology', p. 92.
10 Gramsci, *Letters from Prison Vol. 2*, ed. F. Rosengarten, p. 306.
11 Gramsci, *Letters from Prison*, ed. L. Lawner, p. 265.
12 Gramsci, *Letters from Prison Vol. 2*, ed. F. Rosengarten, p. 383.
13 Ibid., p. 375.
14 Spriano, *Antonio Gramsci and the Party: The Prison Years*, p. 181.

Postscript

1 Gramsci, *Selections from Prison Notebooks*, p. 73 ft. 42.
2 J. Barth Urban, 'Introduction', *Moscow and the Italian Communist Party* (New York 1986), pp. 15–22.

3   Williams, *Proletarian Order*, pp. 305–6.

4   P. Ginsborg, *Italy and Its Discontents* (London 2006).

5   Pearmain, *The Politics of New Labour*, p. 139.

6   C. Boggs, *Gramsci's Marxism* (London 1976), pp. 15–16.

7   Xin Liu, 'Gramsci's Presence in China', *Carte Italiane* Vol. 7 (2011), pp. 69–80.

8   Gramsci, *Selections from Prison Notebooks*, p. 6.

9   T. Nairn, 'Antonu su Gobbu', in *Approaches to Gramsci*, ed. A. Showstack Sassoon (London 1982), pp. 159–79.

10   S. Hall, 'Gramsci and Us', *Marxism Today*, June 1987; Gramsci, *Prison Notebooks Vol. 1*, p. 118.

SELECT BIBLIOGRAPHY OF WORKS IN ENGLISH BY OR ABOUT GRAMSCI

Key Texts, all by A. Gramsci

The Antonio Gramsci Reader: Selected Writings 1916–1935, ed. David Forgacs (London 1988).

A Great and Terrible World: The Pre-Prison Letters 1908–1926, ed. and trans. Derek Boothman (London 2014).

History, Philosophy and Culture in the Young Gramsci, ed. Pedro Cavalcante and Paul Piccone (St. Louis 1975).

Letters from Prison, ed. and trans. Lynne Lawner (London 1973).

Letters from Prison, Vols. 1 and 2, ed. and trans. Frank Rosengarten and Raymond Rosenthal (New York 1994).

The Modern Prince and Other Writings, ed. Louis Marks (London 1957).

Prison Letters, ed. and trans. Hamish Henderson (London 1988).

Prison Notebooks Vols. 1, 2 and 3, ed. and trans. Joseph A. Buttigieg and Antonio Callari (New York 2007).

Selections from Cultural Writings, ed. and trans. David Forgacs, Geoffrey Nowell-Smith and William Boelhower (London 1985).

Selections from Political Writings 1910–1920, ed. and trans. Quintin Hoare and John Matthews (London 1977).

Selections from Political Writings 1921–1926, ed. and trans. Quintin Hoare (London 1978).

Selections from Prison Notebooks, ed. and trans. Quintin Hoare and Geoffrey Nowell Smith (London 1971).

Commentaries, Applications and Background

C. Boggs, *Gramsci's Marxism* (London 1976).

R. J. Bosworth, *Mussolini's Italy* (London 2005).

A. Davidson, *Antonio Gramsci: Towards and Intellectual Biography* (London 1977).

G. Fiori, *Antonio Gramsci: Life of a Revolutionary*, trans. Tom Nairn (London 1970).

J. Joll, *Gramsci* (London 1977).

D. Mack Smith, *Mussolini* (London 1994).

A. Pearmain, *The Politics of New Labour: A Gramscian Analysis* (London 2011).

A. Pearmain, *Gramsci in Love* (Winchester 2015).

V. Serge, *Memoirs of a Revolutionary*, trans. Peter Sedgwick (London 1963).

A. Showstack Sassoon (ed.), *Approaches to Gramsci* (London 1982).

D. Mack Smith, *Mussolini* (London 1994).

P. Spriano, *Antonio Gramsci and the Party: The Prison Years*, trans. John Fraser (London 1979).

J. B. Urban, *Moscow and the Italian Communist Party* (New York 1986).

J. Willett, *The New Sobriety: Art and Politics in the Weimar Period* (London 1978).

G. A. Williams, *Proletarian Order* (London 1975).

INDEX